STORYTELLER

Asheville-Buncombe
Technical Community College
Learning Resources Center
340 Victoria Rd.
Asheville, NC 28801

STORYTELLER

The Classic
that Heralded
America's
Storytelling Revival

Third Revised Edition

RAMON ROYAL ROSS

August House Publishers, Inc.
LITTLE ROCK

Printed in the United States of America

10 9 8 7 6 5 4 3 2 1   PB

LIBRARY OF CONGRESS CATALOGING-IN-PUBLICATION DATA
Ross, Ramon Royal.
Storyteller / Ramon Royal Ross : [text illustrations, Ramon Royal Ross;
photographs, Suzanne Kramer; index, Gloria Irene Ross].—3rd. ed.
p. cm.
Includes bibliographical references and index.
ISBN 0-87483-451-1 (pbk. : alk. paper)
1. Storytelling. I. Title
LB1042.R67   1996
808.543—dc20   96-17345

President and publisher: Ted Parkhurst
Executive editor: Liz Parkhurst
Project editor: Sarah Scott
Text illustrations: Ramon Royal Ross
Photographs: Suzanne Kramer
Cover design: Harvill Ross Studios Ltd.
Index: Gloria Irene Ross

The paper used in this publication meets the minimum requirements of
the American National Standard for Information Sciences—Permanence of
Paper for Printed Library Materials, ANSI Z39.48-1984.

AUGUST HOUSE, INC.   PUBLISHERS   LITTLE ROCK

Permissions and Acknowledgments

Chapter One

"The grass has not grown greener ... our respect and affection." From *Foxfire 2*, edited by Eliot Wiggington (Garden City, New York: Anchor Press, 1973). © 1970, 1971, 1972 by the Southern Highlands Literary Fund, Inc.

Chapter Three

"Wicked John and the Devil." From *Grandfather Tales*. © 1948, renewed 1976 by Richard Chase. Reprinted by permission of Houghton Mifflin Co. All rights reserved.

"In any memorable novel ... background for magical happenings." From *The Seed and the Vision* by Eleanor Cameron. © 1992 Eleanor Cameron. Used by permission of Dutton Children's Books, a division of Penguin Books USA Inc.

Chapter Four

"As he took on more length ... split fire wood, built pigpens ..." Excerpt from *Abe Lincoln Grows Up* by Carl Sandburg, © 1928, 1926 by Harcourt Brace & Company and renewed 1956, 1954 by Carl Sandburg, reprinted by permission of the publisher.

"I went to work ... conclusion that Art betters Nature." From *Seven Horizons* by Charles Finger. Reprinted by permission of Robert A. Leflar.

Chapter Six

"On the simplest cultural level ... at unobservably low intensities." From *Language, Thought and Reality: Selected Writings of Benjamin Lee Whorf*, edited by J.B. Carroll. Reprinted by permission of MIT Press.

"Trains." From *I Go a-Traveling* by James S. Tippett. © 1929 by Harper & Row Publishers, Inc. © 1957 by James S. Tippett. Reprinted by permission of HarperCollins Publishers.

"The Visitor" by Ian Serraillier. From *A Second Poetry Book,* edited by John Foster (Oxford University Press, 1980). Reprinted by permission of Anne Serraillier.

"Waiting for the Barbarians." From Cavafy, C.P., *Selected Poems,* translated by Edmund Keeley and Phillip Sherrard. © 1972. Revised edition 1992. Reprinted by permission of Princeton University Press.

"The Best Liar." From *Three Rolls and One Doughnut* by Mirra Ginsburg (New York: Dial Press, 1970). Reprinted by permission of the author.

"The Rabbits Who Caused All the Trouble." Copyright © 1940 by James Thurber. Copyright © 1968 by Rosemary A. Thurber. From *Fables For Our Time*, published by HarperCollins.

For Gloria

Contents

Preface to the Third Edition

When I was four, my sister Carol, a worldly six, would lead me out the back door of the big farmhouse into the cool September night. Across Spring Creek the orange twinkle of campfires beckoned, and we made our way through the wet pasture grass and over the plank bridge to where the prune pickers camped.

There waited Old Scotty and Whitey; the Moon family; the Cricket family; Red and Shorty. Oh, the stories they told, filling me with magical visions: of Georgia, where people spoke so slowly it was like watching molasses pour out of a jug, just hearing them talk. Of distant California, where palm trees grew so tall they held up the sky. Of gleaming cities and long dusty roads. Of tragedies—tents catching fire and children burning. Of heroic deeds: Red rushing in and saving the Cricket twins, nearly losing his life doing so. "Look! You can still see the scar, where Red's hair hasn't never grown back. Oh, he was brave, he was, my Red!"

Those fruit pickers were my first storytellers. They filled my head and heart with their pictures and their dreams.

Since then, I've met their brothers and sisters: puppeteers, dancers, toymakers, aspiring actors, musicians—all with stories to tell, and endless ways of telling them. I've watched my good friend King Povenmire take a thousand teachers on a Lion Hunt, transforming a hall into a safari. I've watched a penniless stutterer, on a bus in the middle of Oregon, at night, coax a petulant child into sleep with a nonsensical puppet play—the puppets themselves no more than bits of cloth, cleverly knotted. Around campfires, I've danced "Draw a Bucket of Water" until dizzy. And danced, with children and their teachers, that same dance in countless schoolrooms across the West.

That's what this book is about—all those joyous and magical human endeavors we call Story. In these pages I've described some of that storytelling for you—the excitement of choral speaking, when for a brief time we *are* a huge iron train, hurtling across the prairie; the swirling, dusky words and sounds, when we sing together that old song, "Red River Valley"; the wonderful shiver when "The Lady in White" gets told, and we know it really happened, right here in Walla Walla, or Sioux City, or Schenectady.

Why, one might be tempted to ask, should any of that matter? Why, at a time when computers build cars and answer telephones and describe the furthermost stars, should our longing for story persist?

I asked myself that question twenty-five years ago, when I wrote the first edition of *Storyteller*. The world, it seemed to me, was going to hell in a handbasket if we didn't do something about it. And what was it we were supposed to do? Build bigger arsenals against our enemies? Erect walls of steel around our cities? Punish the poor for their embarrassing and everlasting poverty?

Or talk. Talk to our neighbors. Tell stories to our children. To our parents. To ourselves.

And listen. Listen to the wind and the sea and the creek outside our window. Listen to the mockingbird singing its heart out in the camphor tree at four o'clock on an April morning. Listen to the roar of Interstate Eight an hour later on that same day. Listen to the wail of police sirens and the *thump-athump-athump* of rescue helicopters. Listen to the world, and all its real and imagined sounds.

And laugh. Laugh at our mistakes. Laugh at our frailties and vanities. Laugh at the picklements we've created and continue to create for ourselves and our worlds.

Recently I read a report by a learned scholar that children grow up smarter and better adjusted if their parents engage in "language play" with them during their first months of life. Who knows? Maybe one of these days a researcher will come to the world-shaking conclusion that all of us need stories to be better adjusted adults.

While waiting for that publication to arrive, I'd suggest we begin, on our own, a storytelling crusade. You'll find, I believe, help and encouragement for that crusade in the present edition of this book. I've rewritten every page, proposing new materials, weeding out everything I or my students haven't tried and had success with. I've added bibliographic entries where appropriate, without abandoning old and admired friends. I've clarified instructions to the point where even I understand them.

Storytelling, at its best, is a way for people to come to know themselves. To come to know others. That's the magic I'm after. That's the magic I hope you'll share.

—*Ramon Royal Ross*

1. The Harvest of Language

The story was the bushman's most sacred possession. These people knew what we do not; that without a story you have not got a nation, or culture, or civilization. Without a story of your own to live, you haven't got a life of your own.

—Laurens Van Der Post

Michelle, aged five, squirmed with delight on my knee, for Uncle Dick, the man with the Monkey, had come to dinner again. He'd sat in the living room while the children gathered 'round on the rug in front of the fire, his old gnarled hands fashioning a mouse from his handkerchief—a clever mouse that leaped away from him and scurried across the worn tiled floor. Now we big folks had drunk our glass of wine, the roast and the mashed potatoes and gravy had disappeared, and the pink cake and the brown ice cream had threaded their delicious cold smooth path, and her daddy smelled of coffee, and she'd just piped, "Uncle Dick, did you bring the Monkey?"

Yes, he had. And that worn and tattered bit of a hand puppet with a sad, wise face and two bright brown glass eyes peeped out of the blue denim bag where he slept when there weren't any children around.

Oh, the tricks he did! He flirted with Susan and tried to kiss Michelle. Tim's red hair got all mussed by the Monkey's inquisitive little hands, and the Monkey even blew Uncle Dick's nose for him.

At last it was time for the Monkey to say good night. He waved to everyone, and then, with Uncle Dick helping him, made a bed for himself in the old denim bag, and snuggled deep in a little blanket of soft cloth.

Later—five minutes, maybe—we heard a snore.

That evening was just one of many when songs and stories and puppets and general foolishness brought joy to my family and friends. I've tried to puzzle out for myself what it was about those evenings that made them such joyous occasions. I've decided it was the words that did it; the words we spoke and listened to during those hours together. The words caused us to draw closer together, sharing thoughts and ideas.

Sharing feelings. Creating for ourselves a community. Embracing one another in fellowship and love.

While all animals possess the power to communicate, their communications have little in common with those of humans. Animals express threat or fear, hunger or pleasure. Humans formulate and express ideas; things visible and invisible, the event of yesterday and the plan for tomorrow, the dream of the dreamer, or the embodiment of the heart and mind of a tiny monkey into a fragment of fuzzy brown cloth.

The riddle of human destiny may absorb our waking hours and cause us to sleep fitfully at night. But the story and the song help us, young and old, live with that riddle. They lighten our hearts even while they're providing commentary on the ancient questions: Who am I? Where am I headed?

Many of the songs and stories written down here are "as old as the hills." Others were minted yesterday. But all of them share one thing in common: they are the voices of people telling us about themselves—telling us about their dreams, their yearnings for love, their sly tricks, their banquets and crusts, their prayers for peace, their confrontations with death and birth. Telling us about them. Telling us about us.

How can we convert those written words into speech? That's the challenge. For it's not with the inert world of print—those "little dried herbals," as Jean-Paul Sartre called them—that we're concerned. Rather, we're after the pulsing, throbbing stream of speech. And not just spoken language. Hands, eyes, feet—all are called into service as we share with children and adults the gifts of the storyteller.

Not every one of us can be an Uncle Dick, for his was a rare gift compounded of talent and study and place of birth and love. But all of us can learn to give and receive pleasure from the various acts of storytelling; from passing along old and new tales, from singing, and dancing, and playing games. From creating and using puppets. From improvisations and readers' theater.

Storytelling is organic; part of the behavior specific to being human. Building on this inherent tendency to tell—to be a storyteller—is what we're setting out to do here. Who has not sung "Down in the Valley," or played "London Bridge is Falling Down," or told or listened to "The Three Little Pigs"?

Happily, the time is right for the storyteller. Recently I visited with a batch of sixth graders, showing them toys I'd made out of sticks and fragments of cloth and fur, string and leather. I showed them a spinning top, a flipper-dinger carved from cane that grows wild along the Sweetwater River, an idiot stick, a moon spinner, a bull roarer. We sang old songs and did a silly clapping game. We went on a Lion Hunt and did some impromptu theater with an old song—"Billy Boy"—they costuming themselves using bits of clothing I'd brought along in an old satchel. I showed them how to make some simple puppets, and told them Richard Chase's "Wicked John and the Devil."

Here we were, these children and their teachers and me, in that drab pale-walled California classroom on a fog-bound morning, caught up in the wonder and mystery of these simple games and stories and toys. Eleven-year-olds, sated on a diet of mini-bikes and computer games and plastic dolls that drink and wet and cry, touching those hand-made toys as if they were alive. The spirit with which they engaged in the choral reading, chants, and clapping games, and the attentiveness with which they listened to the rascally adventures of Wicked John would have flattered any storyteller.

And it wasn't only the children who were caught in that web of storytelling. We adults, teachers and parents, were ensnared in the mesh of wonder. We were drawn into the realization, for a brief time, that we were still available to experience newness and delight in these antique doings.

A day later, I was with eighth graders, a dozen at a time, all day long, talking about the Oregon Trail. We sang cowboy songs and read excerpts from Lewis's and Clark's diaries. We sharpened turkey feathers into quill pens and they wrote lonely letters home, spattering and scratching their way through thoughts, bending over their penmanship like sixth century monks, sealing their letters with hot wax. (We ran out of matches and one eighth-grade girl loaned us a lighter! Ah innocence!)

But it's not just in classrooms where one sees various forms of storytelling taking place. Parents and children making their way into the kitchen, experimenting with old recipes for sour-dough bread, bottling home-brewed root beer, preparing foods they've grown or gathered themselves—dandelion greens, watercress, wild pecans, Jerusalem artichokes. Churches celebrating folk masses. Aspiring musicians rummaging through closets and basements and garages for old instruments, polishing them, tuning them, and giving them another chance for making music. Neighbors gathering together at Christmas time to sing carols and collect food and clothing for the less fortunate. Not too long ago, our local newspaper carried an article about architects designing new train stations for our community. One station was a quonset hut—to complement some historical old tin sheds—leftovers from World War II—which are still in use in the neighborhood.

All of these, I would submit, are a kind of storytelling.

We look deep into these fragile human endeavors, and the deeper we look the more enchanting and joyous they become. We are on the trail of something we do not fully understand; some tendency on our part to come together around the fire and share human comradeship as our ancestors did, shutting out for a few minutes the loneliness and the night.

Marshall McLuhan was right. The medium does alter the message. Attending a concert in the park is not the same as listening to a recording of that concert. Reassembling *King Lear* from tens of thousands of tiny points of light is not the same as sitting in a hushed theater, seeing the play unfold. And that, in turn, differs from sitting with friends at home, reading *King Lear* aloud. A sense of personal contact is lost, somehow, when we view on film even the most talented entertainer. It's just not the same as when we're clasping hands with others in a simple country dance, or sitting at the elbow of a performer who responds to us, catches our thoughts with his, warms to our laughter and heeds our flagging interest.

I've been rereading *Foxfire 2,* reading about Maude Shope as written by Barbara Taylor and Sheila Vinson, two high school students who interviewed her. Though seventy-six years old, Maude still rides her mule, Frank—a mere child of thirty-two. In the mountains of North Carolina where she has lived all her life, Maude has participated in corn shuckings and log rollings. She's raised twelve children, acted as a midwife, spun wool from her own sheep, and then made clothing from the cloth she produced. In their numerous interviews with Maude, the students learned to appreciate and respect her ways. As they put it:

> *The grass has not grown greener up at Maude's and she has never won any world titles or medals, but if there were ever one to be recognized for just plain, simple, old-fashioned ways, Maude would surely be a prime candidate. She lives rough, but she has pride, dignity, warmth, joy and enthusiasm for life that is boundless. She has our respect and affection.*[1]

"Pride, dignity, warmth, joy, and enthusiasm for life ..." Not a bad list. And how do we start bringing into our own lives some of those traits? I would propose, for starters, that we begin with storytelling—play party games and dances, folk sayings and folk language, puppetry, old tales, ballads, songs, quilt making and toy making, studying family albums, recollecting medicinal remedies and handed-down recipes for dandelion wine, spouting jump-rope rhymes like:

> *I had a little brother*
> *His name was Tiny Tim.*
> *I put him in the bathtub*
> *To see if he could swim.*
> *He drank up all the water*
> *He ate up all the soap.*
> *He died last evening*
> *With a bubble in his throat.*

The why of this is apparent. There's a humanism inherent in sharing language, sharing stories, dancing and singing in the old ways. These are kindly approaches to learning about yourself and those around you. At a time when a good-size segment of the population whirls through life without humor, at breakneck speed, a strong and vital strain of tenderness, love, and slippery feeling stuff needs to be introduced and tended.

And that's where the storyteller comes in. It's not unrealistic to hold to the belief that the simple pleasures of folk participation can alter a person's view of himself and reawaken him to the miracles that happen when people touch one another with hands and eyes and words. For storytelling, in my view, is anchored in language at its gentlest and best.

Thus far we've looked briefly at the harvest to be gathered from storytelling; a harvest of closeness, of community, of people enjoying one another. Like all harvests, this one takes work. In the next couple of pages we'll be discussing that work; what we'll be doing and won't be doing in the chapters remaining to us.

Ruth Sawyer tells of her Irish nurse, Johanna, who not only had the gift for storytelling but also the good sense to refrain from turning a tale into a sermon:

> *I can see her face, fairy-ridden. I can hear the soft Irish burr on her tongue which made the words join hands and dance, making the fairy ring that completely encircled me. I can hear her begin the tale of "Wee Meg Barnileg," knowing it already well myself, and feeling the stinging mortification of Meg's own behavior, which might well have been mine. But Johanna pointed no moral and drew no application. There was the tale—I could take it or leave it; and always I took it.*[2]

Like Miss Sawyer, I think it's burdensome for the storyteller to say, at the end of the tale, "And the moral of this story is ..." or, "And now, boys and girls, what do you think this story is trying to teach us?" Any teacher worth his salt knows that the wisdom that precedes moral behavior is not transmitted by words, particularly not by those words that are only bloodless paraphrases of the story's richness. Better to tell the story and let the listener decide for herself if she can use what that story has to say to her in her own life.

Don't misunderstand me. Part of the fun of a story or an activity lies in talking it over. "What about that little teen-age devil? I wonder how he felt when Wicked John tried to trick him like that? What would you have done if you'd been the Devil? What if you'd been John?"

But that's different than searching for a "lesson." Morals are, after all, better caught than taught.

Nor will you find in these chapters hard and fast rules to follow. Rules are fine, but they never quite work like one would hope—and never, somehow, bring one nearer to the understanding of folk dancing, or ballad singing, or tale telling. For that, practice is what's needed—comfortable practice with a variety of materials.

Finally, these pages will not attempt to sketch, even briefly, the history of storytelling. For those who might wish to delve further into that history, I've suggested some readings at the end of this chapter.

So much for the Will Nots. What about the Wills? We will, in the following chapters, discuss as fully as possible those language arts we engage in and share with others. Stories, poems, games, and dances will be our store of materials. Suggestions for storytelling with your own family stories and the stories of others, choral reading, puppetry, flannel board stories, folk dances and games will be included, so that you may plan a story hour, prepare it, and share it with a group.

We are, as I said earlier, already storytellers. All of us. But we can grow in that art. Clearly, we all want to make the best possible use of the talents we own. Who knows? Perhaps one of us is an undiscovered Homer. For if not one of us, then who?

To help us develop our own talents as storytellers, we'll look at stories together and see what we can do to enhance our tellings.

We'll look at the story hour, and consider what makes that event a success, taking into account such aspects as physical setting, a balance of activities, audience participation, and pacing.

Because oral language plays such an important part in the life of the child, we'll relate much of what we do here to children. While this is not a methods book, I would propose that a language arts curriculum that is both useful and aesthetically satisfying could be built around the activities associated with storytelling.

To further that storyteller's curriculum, I have placed suggestions at the end of each chapter which relate to the language arts portion of an elementary or middle school classroom. Used appropriately, these will add zest to school life. Examples of materials within each of the areas discussed will be included, together with bibliographies for additional readings.

Teachers, parents, recreation directors, pastors, volunteer workers, park rangers—all practice the participating arts. They may tell stories before bedtime, or gather the young of the congregation for a story as part of the church's or synagogue's service, join hands with others in a clearing under the pines to celebrate the gift of life and movement with an old dance, or speak across languages with the droll farce of Punch and Judy. But no matter what their professions, all use language in one or more of its forms to instruct and give pleasure to others.

Would that we all performed that art well! I have watched preschoolers wriggle and shift on a church basement floor while a preacher belabored them with the story of the prodigal son, trying, unsuccessfully, to teach them about the nature of generosity and forgiveness. Listening to him, I thought back to my own boyhood, seated on an apple box out in the orchard, while Scotty, an unschooled fruit-picker, spun stories of his boyhood in Scotland to me that lifted me out of myself. The thick burr and tongue-wrestled words were no barrier to understanding, for he knew what that minister had yet to learn—the way to tell a story so that the listener is taken out of himself and permitted to enter another realm.

Laurens Van Der Post, the great South African storyteller, tells of seeking out the elusive Bushmen of the Kalahari. These shy people, when he came to know them, shared with him everything they possessed—everything, that is, but their stories.

These they kept hidden—secret. Van Der Post eventually realized why. It was because the story was the bushman's most sacred possession. These people knew what we sometimes forget; that without story you cannot have a nation, or a culture, or a civilization. Without a story of your own to live, you haven't got a life worth living.[3]

A story of our own. A life of our own. But a story and a life to share. That's what we're after. For all who would reach out for that magic—parents or teachers, park rangers or preachers—this book is written.

NOTES

1. Eliot Wiggington, ed., *Foxfire 2* (Garden City, New York: Anchor Press, 1973), p. 18. Copyright 1970, 1971, 1972 by the Southern Highlands Literary Fund, Inc.
2. Ruth Sawyer, *The Way of the Storyteller* (New York: Viking Press, 1962), pp. 17-18.
3. See Laurens Van Der Post, *Lost World of the Kalahari* (New York: Morrow, 1958).

ACTIVITIES

Listed below are some questions to start you thinking about the stories you already carry around with you. First answer these questions about yourself, then interview a member of your family or a friend, asking them the same questions or others which might naturally follow.

1. Where were you born?
2. What other events happened on that day? (My students and I use the University newspaper archives for this purpose.)
3. Why did your family name you what they did?
4. What is the history of your family name? Has it changed over the years?
5. What is the earliest memory you have?
6. What is the earliest dream you can recall?
7. What are some of your recurring dreams?
8. What were three of the most memorable events of your school years?
9. What was the happiest day of your life? What made it the happiest?
10. What is the most frightened you've ever been?
11. Have you ever witnessed or been a part of an inexplicable event?
12. What is your favorite precious or semi-precious gem?
13. What is your favorite metal?
14. What tree do you like best?
15. Are there numbers which seem special to you?
16. What is your "totem" animal?
17. What is your biggest fear?
18. Is there a place in the world which feels most like where you belong?
19. Who was your favorite teacher?

20. Who is your "hero/heroine"?

21. What is your favorite color?

22. What holidays does your family celebrate?

23. What stories do you remember from your own childhood?

24. Who is the most interesting person in your personal world?

25. If you could do anything you wanted for a day, what would it be?

BIBLIOGRAPHY

The following books have been of interest to me and are good reading for anyone wishing to know more about the history of folk literature.

Chase, Richard. *American Folk Tales and Songs*. New York: Dover, 1971. The tales, songs and ballads in this book were collected from the Appalachian Mountain folk, and are rich in detail and in what Chase—Uncle Dick—refers to as "original fibers"—that sense of belonging to a certain group and sharing in the richness of that group. An amateur's guide to tale collecting, included in the book, will interest readers, providing, as it does, "... opportunities to rediscover for yourself certain basic human values—traditions that lead us all to a better realization of lasting things in a changing world."

Clarke, Kenneth and Mary. *Introducing Folklore*. New York: Holt, Rinehart & Winston, 1963. In writing this book, the Clarkes aimed for a text that contained elementary concepts which most folklorists would agree upon. There are chapters on folklore as prose narrative; song, music, and dance; various superstitions, remedies, and magic; lore of special groups; and collecting.

Emrich, Duncan. *Folklore on the American Land*. Boston: Little, Brown, 1972. This book was undertaken, according to Emrich, to give the general reader some idea of the breadth of folklore in America. It is a beautiful work, amply illustrated with photographs, touching on American names, street cries, legends and tales, folk songs and ballads, children's folklore, as well as superstitions and folk beliefs.

Opie, Iona and Peter, eds. *The Oxford Dictionary of Nursery Rhymes*. Oxford: Clarendon Press, 1951. This monumental work contains a rich store of detail concerning nursery rhymes and games. Notes on origins, uses, first appearances, and related sources are given for more than 500 rhymes. An excellent introduction (pp. 1-45) elaborates on the many interesting aspects of the rhymes: quality, sources, age, equivalents throughout the world, classifications, and present day universality. Indexes of notable figures and first lines are given, together with many illustrations in black and white taken from original sources. (A charming companion to *The Oxford Dictionary* is *I Saw Esau,* also edited by the Opies with illustrations by Maurice Sendak. Cambridge, Massachusetts: Candlewick Press, 1992.)

Sawyer, Ruth. *The Way of the Storyteller*. New York: Dryden Press, 1946. While the entire book would be of interest to the student of storytelling, the three chapters entitled "Storytelling—a Folk-Art," "The Antiquity of It," and "Pattern for the Past" are of special interest, treating the character of storytelling as it has come down to us from the past. Many personal anecdotes enliven Miss Sawyer's narrative.

Thompson, Stith. *The Folktale*. New York: Dryden Press, 1946. The author discusses the nature and significance of folktales, their history, and their spread throughout the world. He traces folktales through both civilized and primitive cultures, and develops his index of motifs, in which the basic characteristics in each of the stories are identified.

Wells, Evelyn K. *The Ballad Tree: A Study of British and American Ballads, Their Folklore, Verse, and Music, Together with Sixty Traditional Ballads and Their Tunes*. New York: Ronald Press, 1950. In this book Miss Wells introduces the reader to ballad study, using in her first chapter the Robin Hood cycle as an example. Frances James Child and Cecil Sharp, American students of balladry, are studied, together with their European counterparts and predecessors. The traditions and history of balladry are related to our present day revival of interest in folk songs and folk singing.

2. People to People

And when we have come to the place that's right
We shall be in the garden of love and delight ...

—QUAKER HYMN

I have been in lonely places—the high mountains of northern Idaho, the desert coastline of Baja California—but the loneliness in those places is a natural one. It is a loneliness we intrude on for a day or a week, pushing the emptiness back a few feet from the campsite with fire, food, songs, and children's voices. At the end of that time, we pack up our trappings and take to the road. The loneliness, crouched just outside camp, steals back in as if we'd never been there at all.

I have been lonely, as have all of us. But the loneliness seems to be most acute when I'm alone in a place where I've been with others, and now they're gone. Once, when I was a teenager, my parents left me to care for the farm while they and my sisters went off on vacation. I looked forward to being my own boss for a few days.

But as their car drove out the lane, jouncing up and down under the weight of their vacation gear, the loneliness settled down on me like a gray presence. The big barn, always a warm and golden place, smelling of animals and the sweet odors of alfalfa hay, was filled with loneliness. I walked out to the orchard, with its dark-foliaged rows of trees. Loneliness studied me from every branch.

The house was the worst of all. A hush prevailed where there should have been a hundred human sounds. So lonely was the house, in fact, that I packed a bedroll and spent the nights sleeping in the barn, where at least there was the comfort of the animals: pigeons uttering their throaty night calls in the loft overhead, cows rummaging for wisps of hay in the bins below.

I have been lonely, on occasion, since that week. There are times when I, like others, seek out loneliness. This is when I take off—for the desert, the lake, a bike ride on the brush-covered hills behind Mt. Miguel. Being alone is cherished then, for it is a self-imposed loneliness from which I may return, and in a place that has not been created by people. But to be alone in a theater, or a school room, or on a playground—alone in those places where there should be others—brings on a heaviness of spirit that is hard to overcome.

Not by Bread Alone …

"Man does not live by bread alone" is more than a worn phrase. It is a singular truth. Consider the ways in which we reach out to others: kissing, strolling arm-in-arm, back scratching, love making, holding hands, hugging—these are but a few of the ways in which affection and love are revealed. They come to us so naturally that we cannot imagine life without them.

Yet accounts of children raised in isolation from others, never knowing a caress or a kiss, unaccustomed to the generous strength of a hand given to help, are unvarying in their dismal evidence. Without the touch and feel of others of our kind, we grow up less than what we might have been.

Even the idioms of our language reflect an awareness of the importance of touching one another. "I've got you under my skin"—the old song says. "Let's get together sometime," and "Keep in touch"—are conventional farewell remarks. And then there are idioms that recognize the fact that not all our contacts with others are pleasant ones. "She's a pain in the neck." "He makes me sick."

The folk arts give us one lively source of positive experiences in touching and holding, beginning with the little ones—children aged three months to two or three years—for which there are the so-called infant amusements, such as "Put Your Finger in Foxy's Hole," which perhaps you have played:

> *Put your finger in Foxy's hole*
> *Foxy's not at home;*
> *Foxy's at the back door*
> *Picking at a bone.*

In this ancient game the thumb and forefinger are brought together to form Foxy, who lurks in his cave, created by cupping the fingers of the other hand and pressing the forefinger and thumb together. Little Jonathan or Susan or Lauren is encouraged to put a finger in Foxy's hole—"Go on, just put your finger in there, Lauren, Foxy's not home!"—and receives a sharp nip from the thumbnail underneath, for Foxy, alas, has returned home, hungry for good fat meat.[1]

Or what about "This Little Piggy Went to Market," or "Patty Cake"? All these, and their kin, make use of poking, tickling, pinching, slapping, and other acts of touching and feeling. Still others, like "Ride a Cock Horse to Banbury Cross," require the teller to hold the young one astraddle a crossed leg and jog her up and down in rhythm with the song. Not surprisingly, these rhymes have flourished through the centuries and throughout the world. Take "This Little Piggy," for example:

This little piggy went to market.
This little piggy stayed home,
This little piggy had roast beef.
This little piggy had none.
And this little piggy cried
Week, week, week,
All the way home.

How many fond mothers and fathers have pinched the toes of their little ones while reciting that old rhyme? A good many, for this verse, or variants of it, can be traced in printed form back to 1760, and it is conjectured that it was transmitted orally for generations before anyone took the trouble to write it down.[2]

Nor are rhyming games, with their accompanying pinching, slapping, and jogging confined to the western world. Here is a similar rhyme found in China:

This one's old
This one's young
This one has no meat.
This one's gone
To buy some hay,
And this one's gone to the village.[3]

Games involving touching and holding, then, are common among people all over the world. And, without knowingly searching for a reason for so doing, all of us—parents, uncles and aunts, older brothers and sisters, have intuitively used these games as far back into the past as we can tell. For the infant's pleasure, of course. But also for our own.

And it's not just with the infant and the young child that we play at touching and holding. For the grownups there are circle and square dances, with their dizzying clasping, holding, and releasing of twenty different hands in less than a half-minute—hands as rough and dry as freshly dug potatoes, or as warm and steamy as sausages. Hands so finely boned and slender one fears to break them with a touch. These games hold a natural charm for us, for they yield opportunities to make physical contact with other humans.

I remember playing Pass the Ring at Uncle Dale's house, long ago. What sensations burst through our hands, wriggling and burrowing like tiny animals, as we passed to those around the circle my Aunt Mabel's fragile wedding band, while "It," observing us, tried to decide where the ring was being held.

Tag, Hide and Go Seek, Sardines, Red Rover, Statues—these are some of the outdoor games that involve holding another person. Do you remember those games? Do you remember the warm summer nights, the mysterious darkness, the smell of fresh-cut grass, the touch of others?

To See and Be Seen ...

Touching and holding aren't the only important things for people. The sight of other humans gives us perhaps one of our greatest pleasures. Think of the hours spent at cafés and ball games, in libraries and waiting rooms and camp grounds, watching people. In lonely desert stretches of the United States, motorists typically celebrate the sight of other motorists by honking their horns and waving. To be alone is good, but only if the loneliness is one from which we can return to the sight of others.

Solitary confinement—what melancholy the words summon! There is something terribly imprisoning and fearsome in the thought that any creature, and particularly a human being, might be consigned to a life away from his fellows. Those who have read *Robinson Crusoe* or *Island of the Blue Dolphins* can recollect the ache one felt at the abnormal conditions in which Crusoe and Karana were forced by circumstances to live, and can remember, with Crusoe, that mixture of joy and fear when a footprint, other than his own, was spied in the sand.

Over the centuries, sight has brought to mankind unrivaled pleasures. And that pleasure begins early. The youngest child is fascinated by the sight of others. "Bo-Peep," which Samuel Johnson defined as "The act of looking out and then drawing back as if frightened, or with the purpose to frighten some other," has been in written existence for over 600 years! The Opies tell of a certain Alice Causton who, in 1634, had to "play bo-pepe thorouwe a pillory" for failing to give a customer a full measure of ale.[4]

> *Bo-Peep, Bo-Peep, Little Bo-Peep,*
> *Now's the time for hide and seek.*

Poor Alice notwithstanding, those who have played this simple game with a young child know the delight it can give. Why does it yield such delight? Is it the movement, the sudden disappearance and reappearance, the nonsensical words? Whatever the cause, the results are unvarying: laughter, astonishment, anticipation, and a clenching and unclenching of tiny fingers in excitement as the child, like children of past centuries, takes part in his first organized game.

This same pleasure in seeing others and in being with them continues throughout our lives. Children clustered around a storyteller or ballad singer derive much of their pleasure from seeing the performer, watching her hold the dulcimer or guitar, watching her fingers move in quest of new chords, watching her coax a bit of fabric and a couple of buttons into independent life as a puppet, watching as her arms measure out the strides taken by the Giant in search of Jack.

Sight is not as crucial for generous human development as are touching and feeling. One may, like Helen Keller, grow full and complete without ever having had the power to see.

But not to see others—that would be hard to take.

To Speak and Be Spoken to ...

Sasha, the Russian Blue, just stretched and yawned at her favorite sun-warmed spot on the old Persian rug, then weaved her way over to ask me to scratch behind her ears. Cats are not the only creatures that send messages without words. Humans, too, communicate much this way. The ways we touch others, the clothes we wear, the cars we drive, the way we walk, all speak messages from us to others about the values we hold, the causes we back, the friends we count.

When we communicate, we are transmitting meanings. Those meanings do not require signals agreed on in advance by the communicants. A man may communicate love for a woman by ardent glances. He may do it by showing off. The person telling a story uses much unspoken communication. She may touch a listener's shoulders to show how the emperor's tailors measured him for his fine new clothes. Or she may cup her hands to demonstrate the space required for Thumbelina to take her nap. The pantomimist and the dancer send meanings without the benefit of words.

But though we may communicate much without words, spoken language is by far the most important medium through which we build ideas and tell others of them. And for spoken language to take place, we rely on the voice.

The voice, like a violin, comes in various shapes and sizes and is capable of playing both high and low tones. Like violin strings, two small bands of tissue—the vocal chords—stretch across the larynx or voice box. When we breathe, those bands are relaxed and idle. The air passes through with little or no effort. But when we speak, we tighten those strings of tissue by pulling them with the muscles attached to them. Then, as we move air from our lungs across those strings, that air vibrates them and causes sound to be produced. How tightly we draw the strings determines how high or low the sounds will be. Simultaneously, the voice box with its two strings helps determine how loud the sounds will be, and what resonance and quality they will possess. The sounds thus produced are still not intelligible speech; tongue, lips, and teeth are needed to help shape them. Muscular adjustments of the palate, jaw, lungs, and nasal passages bring resonance and color to the voice.

All of this, going on at the same time, suggests that the dexterity required to speak would tax the most linguistically talented creature. And yet we do speak, for the most part, rather easily in our native tongue. We only find out how important it is to begin use of the speech mechanisms at an early age when we try to imprint new patterns of speech or a new language into our neural system after we have grown older. Then we begin to appreciate how really busy we are when we talk.

What we speak is *language*. Sasha, the cat, was communicating with me when she swished her tail around my trouser leg and rubbed her cheek against my shoe. *Communication*, such as Sasha was engaged in, refers to the entire spectrum of ways in which we send our feelings and thoughts to others. *Language*, on the other hand, is a limiting term and refers to the use of a specific system of symbolic activities through which we transmit thoughts and feelings to others. Symbols are the primary tools in a world of meaning. Speech sounds are symbols which we and others in our community have agreed will represent particular meanings.

Language competency is irretrievably bound up with group activities and group behavior. The community in which we live, consisting of those people whom we know and love, and who provide satisfaction of our wants, determines what our language will be. Studies of the development of language among young children have found that a period critical in the development of oral language occurs early in the child's life—probably before the age of seven. If that period is passed by without satisfactory language development, permanent damage results.[5]

For the storyteller, language is an instrument to be played with all the skill that falls within her grasp. She may choose to use that language to play with words, as in the nonsense rhyme:

> *Barber, barber, shave a pig,*
> *How many hairs will make a wig?*
> *Four and twenty, that's enough.*
> *Give the barber a pinch of snuff.*

Or she may use it for telling an old story from Europe such as "Mrs. Vinegar," or from Africa, such as "The Goat Well." In telling such stories, we link ourselves into the long chain of tellers who have shared these two adventures with others over the centuries.

Or it may be that the teller uses language to recall a personal adventure. Perhaps it is an account of a shrimp-gathering expedition far out in the waters of the Sea of Cortez, or the recollecting of a Halloween prank years ago, and the following morning, when the sheriff came to the house for a "visit."

Perhaps language is used to teach a song: "Careless Love" or "Fox Went Out on a Chilly Night" or "Gypsy Davey."

Whatever the use, the words are there—to be selected out of the thousands we know, to be shaped and sorted, to be strung together to make meanings clear, and to be given in all their magic to the listener.

To Love and Be Loved ...

Up to this point we have talked about the needs we have to be with others, to touch them, to see them, to communicate with them through gesture and speech. We have seen how the folk arts have intuitively utilized these fundamental necessities for living useful and happy lives. The child playing "London Bridge," or dancing "Skip to My Lou," or listening to "Wicked John and the Devil" is learning about the shapes, the textures, the sounds of other human beings. She's also learning, although she doesn't know it, how to be human.

Important though they are, however, these acts of touching and feeling, hearing and seeing others are, in themselves, not enough. Unless these actions are made in love, they will account for little. Sigmund Freud defined mental health as the ability to work and the ability to love. If we hope for rich and satisfying lives for ourselves and for others, we will accomplish our goal by participating in these acts with love.

What is love? Greeting card manufacturers print identical verses in a million valentines. Preachers spend as much of their sermon time extolling love as they spend lambasting sin. The husband asks his wife if she loves him: "Do you really love me? ... No, I mean *really*."

There are different meanings to the word, but the love we are concerned with here is that kind in which you let someone else know that you are "all for" her. Being "all for" another person means that you will stand behind her, that you will back her up, that you will support her, that you will actively participate to help her.[6]

It seems to me that here is the heart of the storyteller's role, and the character and quality that sets her apart both as an artist and as a person. Her performance—the act of communicating with others, whether it be with puppets, songs, or dances—is not an "act" that she can start and stop at will, but is as truly as she can make it an expression of herself. Nor is her performance patronizing—a gift of the great to the small. The very power of folk art lies in its concern with equality.

Only when the performer becomes part of the group, sensing its needs, tuned to its vibrations, willing to let her own self be revealed as openly and truly as possible, letting the stories she tells and the songs she sings be a statement of who she is and what she believes, only when she feels a genuine sense of being all for those within the group will she be successful in her art.

Being generous with oneself is not easy. Self-esteem often demands that we put on a mask to hide ourselves from those around us. Actions we have engaged in from birth onward have resulted in reactions from people. The approval or disapproval they convey shapes us, and causes us to close off bits and pieces of ourselves from sight.

One result of this is that our behavior is shaped into acceptable patterns for the society in which we live.

But the other result is that we learn that we have a good side and a bad side, and we begin to think that the bad side—the side that quarrels, that speaks openly and honestly with others, that lets emotion have an equal voice with reason—must always be hidden if we are to remain lovable.

This pretense that we are something other than what we really are causes us to behave in cautious ritualized ways, since we have learned that this is one way to protect ourselves from criticism. However, self-exposure is necessary if we are to grow as people and as storytellers. And exposure is difficult, for what we fear may happen might really happen. We might be laughed at. We might be involved in fierce arguments that we lose. We might make fools of ourselves. We might—worst of all—lose the store of love and respect that others feel for us and that we have so carefully tried to foster over the years.

It is not likely that these things will happen, because our self-regard is generally too low, rather than too high. The assumptions we have made about what we consider to be our bad traits are the left-overs from childhood and no longer apply. A child is generally chastized for independence; in an adult, that same behavior is cherished.

To See Ourselves ...

It is unfortunate that in our general notions of love we ordinarily do not include the obligation to talk straight to those we care for. Maslow points out the irony that exists when, by not criticizing, we allow someone we value to make the same mistake over and over again.[7] While we appear to do this out of kindness, in reality it may be that we do not criticize because of the fear of being struck back.

To fully realize ourselves, and make ourselves capable of giving generously as storytellers, will only be possible as we learn that there is no need to hide a part of ourselves, to be rigid and stereotyped, and to wear a mask that we think will be acceptable to others.

Rather, we will strive for an unself-conscious freedom to be ourselves. By so doing we will come to that point where we forget our weaknesses and limitations and convey our own sense of delight and our desire to share that delight with our audience.

Within our society it has generally not been acceptable to criticize others, particularly face-to-face. For this reason, we must alert ourselves to two kinds of reactions from those around us, one direct and open, the other indirect. The smile, the gesture, the crinkle of skin around the eyes, or the looking away, the quiet restlessness of boredom are all indirect responses from others upon which one may base self-reappraisal.

These indirect communications are being sent to us all the time from those around us. While they may be useful in helping us revise our storytelling behaviors, they have limitations. They do not give the communicant an opportunity to explain what it was we did that made him respond as he did. Sensitivity on our part tells us when we are receiving positive and negative reactions to our telling, but we aren't sure what caused them.

For this reason, direct, descriptive information pertaining to our performance is most helpful to us in our task of becoming storytellers. Getting this information is not easy. Enlisting the help of friends is one source. Unfortunately, they may only report what they see that goes well. "Don't say anything if you can't say something nice," is an oft-quoted bit of conventional wisdom that becomes ingrained in much of our behavior.

Even if the response we get from those around us is direct and honest, we may not tend to accept it in the same terms under which it was offered. If, for example, criticisms are leveled at us for our performance, we tend to look at the evaluative aspects of the comments, rather than at the instructive and descriptive aspects. In scanning the critical remarks, we often see first those that deal somewhat directly with our feelings of self-worth. Thus, even though someone has given us descriptive data about our telling of a story, describing to us gestures, voice quality, and delivery techniques she would like to see modified, we may incorrectly interpret these remarks to mean that she is seeing something wrong with us rather than with our gestures or delivery. If we have those incorrect perceptions, attempts at helping us are sabotaged.

One solution to this problem of feedback is the tape recorder. My students and I often use this device at home when we're rehearsing, telling our stories into it, and then listening to the playback. The recorder provides us with a reliable and accurate version of what we said, and permits us, in private, to cull out extra words and phrases, sharpen dialogue and dialect, correct rate and volume, and develop characterization. Occasionally I ask my students to turn in brief recordings of a portion of a story to me, and I record my remarks on the same tape and return it to them.

Useful as the recorder is, however, it cannot substitute for the live audience and its reactions. I know that I, certainly, tell a story differently when I'm sitting alone with a tape recorder than when I'm with a live audience. For this reason I would suggest that in a storytelling class students be given plenty of opportunities to share reactions with one another.

At one time, we experimented with a check-list which we would complete after a person had told her story. We'd consider aspects of the storytelling, such as facial expressions, eye contact, use of dialogue, appropriateness of the story to the audience, and mark those with a numerical rating from 1 (high) to 5 (needs improvement).

At the end of the check-list, more or less as an afterthought, I put a little space for what I called *General Reactions to Story and Storyteller.*

For several weeks, we laboriously paused after each story and filled out the check list. And came to the conclusion that the only part of the check list any of us paid any real attention to were the *General Reactions.*

So, we threw the whole thing out and adopted new and less rigid procedures. I asked students to bring their own audio tapes to class, and we assigned a person to operate a tape recorder at every class meeting. Thus, every student took home a tape of her story—and the discussion that followed, if she chose to have that taped.

At the conclusion of a student's performance, I'd ask her what sort of evaluation she'd like. She might want me, as the instructor, to give her some coaching on a particular aspect of the story—her use of dialogue, various gestures and movements, facial expressions, and the like. Or she might, on her own, select a mentor from the class—another student whose style and technique she admired—and ask that student to give her some coaching. She might want to talk to us about her own reactions to her telling—what she thought she did right and wrong, and ask us if we'd had any of the same responses. Or she might not want any evaluation at all; for some students, simply managing to get up and tell a story—without notes—was in itself a sort of victory. Or, and this was rather common, a student might ask the rest of us to write a few sentences—a paragraph or so—touching on specific or general aspects of her telling.

Over the years, we've found that procedure works out pretty well. As the teacher, I generally try to limit my suggestions for change to no more than one or two items, not wishing to weigh a student down with what might be perceived as negative remarks.

And now, thinking about it, I wonder if my students don't do the same thing to each other and to me—trying to balance candor and generosity.

At Night All Cats Are Gray ...

Most of us tend to make rapid decisions about people, classifying them immediately upon seeing them. Rather than studying specific traits and then fitting them together to form a general impression, we instead obtain an almost instantaneous impression, often from one tiny bit of data.

A number of years ago, when instant coffee was just coming into common use, Mason Haire, a psychologist, prepared two grocery lists. The lists were identical except that one specified instant coffee and the other, drip ground coffee. Haire gave the alternate lists to subjects in his experiment, with none of them aware that an alternate list existed. They were then asked to characterize the person who had prepared the shopping list. The following main characteristics appeared when the descriptions were studied:

- Forty-eight percent of the people described the person buying instant coffee as lazy; four percent described the person who bought drip ground as lazy.

- Forty-eight percent of the people described the person who bought instant as failing to plan household purchases and schedules well; twelve percent described the drip ground person that way.

In their descriptions, people saw the person using instant coffee as haphazard in her planning, shiftess and lazy, living alone or only recently married, while the person using drip ground was seen as being frugal, careful in her planning, thoughtful with respect to her family, and so on. Bear in mind that the *only* different item in the two lists was the coffee. All other items remained identical, and yet persons reading the two lists made detailed characterizations from what they read.[8]

In another early study, primary children were shown sketches of boys and girls in classroom situations. In these sketches, the children were fighting over books, not working, showing reluctance in participating through singing or drawing pictures, and the like. Children in the study were asked what they thought the teacher would do with the children in each of the pictures. Their answers showed that many children saw their teachers as threatening, punitive persons; boys felt more harried by teachers than did girls; and—the good news—first-graders were more frightened of their teachers than were more experienced second-graders.[9]

What meanings do findings like these hold for us as storytellers? First of all, they make us aware that first impressions tend to be stereotyped.

I recall vividly my first sight of a famous storyteller. He was already an old man, bent and gnarled as an apple twig, leaning on a cane as crooked as himself—a rough maple stick burnished by much use. His stories were from the Southeastern hill country. That walking stick of his was consistent with the view he had of himself—a view he wanted others to share—warm, earth-bound, unpretentious.

Clowns make use of costumes as instant sources of identification. So do policemen. Horn-rimmed spectacles and a tweed jacket cause us to react to a person differently than a Stetson hat and cowboy boots, or denims and a tee shirt. If a storyteller wishes to create an audience "set," toward her, the costume she chooses is a good place to start.

Not only do we stereotype the storyteller; we tend, also, to generalize about the persons in an audience in much the same way that teachers sometimes generalize about children in a classroom. "They're all bright," or "You have to watch them all the time."

The handicap of such remarks is obvious. It keeps us from seeing individuals and reacting to individuals. Just as Haire pointed out earlier that we form impressions of individuals from tiny bits of data, so do we form impressions of classes from scraps and shreds of evidence.[10]

Fortunately, with time, stereotypes can be made to disappear. In the study of classroom behavior mentioned earlier, second-grade children saw their teachers as less punitive than did first-grade children. During World War II, white American bomber pilots lost many of their prejudices toward black Americans after participating in bombing missions during which they were protected by black fighter escorts.

The Place That's Right ...

The human needs—to communicate, to touch, to feel, and to love can be met through the art and the craft of the storyteller. Once the storyteller and her audience have enjoyed a story or dance together, have sung "Tom Dooley," or laughed together over the antics of a puppet, they begin to see each other as articulate and unique persons.

The storyteller is, in a sense, an orchestra leader. Beginning with the formalized structure of an existing composition—a tale, a song, a game—she and the audience—her musicians—create a new work. The gift of the storyteller is to draw people together through a range of experiences: stories and songs, puppetry and folk games, dances and choral verse.

The next chapters will speak of that range, and give examples and suggestions for development of the art and the craft of the teller.

NOTES

1. Iona and Peter Opie, eds. *The Oxford Dictionary of Nursery Rhymes* (Oxford: Clarendon Press, 1951), p. 175.

2. Ibid., pp. 348-50.

3. Ibid.

4. Ibid., p. 93.

5. Paul Bloom, ed. *Language Acquisition: Core Readings* (Cambridge, Massachusetts: The MIT Press, 1994). This collection reviews the literature related to language development, word meaning, syntax and semantics, morphology, and acquisition of language under special circumstances. Bloom, in summarizing the findings, states unequivocally that without early language stimulation by parents and others, a child's language will never develop to its full extent.

6. Ashley Montagu, *The Direction of Human Development* (New York: Harper, 1955). Montagu treats extensively the basic and acquired needs of man in chapters 6, 7, and 8 of this classic work. While he does not offer a definition of love, he does describe love as "the process of communicating to another that you are 'all for' them, that you will support them, not merely that you will accept them, but that you are actively for them."

Other writers cited by Montagu also stress the responsible aspects of love, including relationships which are most conducive to optimal development; making something or someone grow; working for the growth and development of another's powers; creating a state of responsiveness with others.

7. A.H. Maslow, "Summer Notes on Social Psychology of Industry and Management at Non-Linear Systems, Inc." (Del Mar, California: 1962).

8. Mason Haire, "Projective Techniques in Marketing Research," *Journal of Marketing,* 14 (1950), pp. 649-56.

9. Sandra R. Cohen, reported in "Roundup of Current Research," *Transaction Magazine,* 6 (1969), p. 6. Miss Cohen concludes her remarks with the citation of a ditty popular among elementary children:

> *Glory, Glory hallelujah*
> *Teacher hit me with a ruler.*

10. S.E. Asch, "Forming Impressions of Personality," *Journal of Abnormal Social Psychology,* 41 (1946), pp. 258-60. In this study Asch read lists of traits to two groups of college students and then asked the two groups to write imaginative sketches of the kind of person who would have such a combination of traits. The two lists are as follows:

> List A: Intelligent, skillful, industrious, cold, determined, practical, cautious.
> List B: Intelligent, skillful, industrious, warm, determined, practical, cautious.

Notice that the *only* trait that differs in the two lists is warm/cold. And yet this one trait made great difference in the ways in which other traits were viewed. The following are two typical sketches:

> From a person reading List A: "This is a very ambitious and talented person who would not let anyone or anything stand in the way of achieving his goal. Wants his own way, he is determined not to give in, no matter what happens."

> From a person reading List B: "This person believes certain things to be right, wants others to see his point, would be sincere in an argument, and would like to see his point won."

Asch's two groups were also given a list of additional traits and asked to check those they thought fitted with their general impression of the person they described. The warm person was generally seen as generous, wise, happy, sociable, popular, and humorous. The cold person was more often perceived as shrewd, irritable, ruthless, and self-centered. Asch's conclusions were that the characteristics we see in a person enter into a dynamic interaction. Some of these characteristics assume central roles around which the other characteristics cluster. Until we have found the central part—the major or dominant characteristic of a person—we do not fully understand that person.

ACTIVITIES

The activities suggested here and in the following chapters are intended to stimulate your abilities as a storyteller. If you are a teacher, however, you may find them equally useful as language development activities among your students.

1. Try to recall a lonely time in your own life. What caused that time? What were some of your feelings? Tell these to a friend or fellow storyteller.

2. How many persons did you touch today? How many persons did you talk with? Meet visually? How many of these contacts were more than a chance brushing against strangers or the ritualistic conversations of greeting, requesting, and the like?

3. In a group, attempt to stop communicating with others. Do not speak. Do not use eyes or gestures. Do not respond to any communication efforts by others. What feelings come over you as a result of this activity? How do you account for these feelings?

4. Sit facing someone, looking directly into that person's eyes. Try not to look away. Maintain eye contact for as long as you can—at least three minutes. Try to "talk" to the person with your eyes. Afterwards, share feelings with your partner.

5. Write a description of a person, using the following adjectives as a source of information: *intelligent, industrious, determined, cautious, skillful, cold, practical.* When you have finished, read note 10 for this chapter.

6. Describe a person who told stories to you. What qualities do you remember about that person?

7. In this chapter we have seen ways in which the folk arts relate to the basic needs to communicate, to touch, and to love. Are there other basic needs that are related to the storyteller and her art? If so, what are they?

8. Write a description of a person you know well. Make the description one that would cause others to view that person with favor. Write a second description of the same person, this time making the description one that would invoke disfavor. Now analyze your two descriptions. What words and phrases made the difference to you?

3. Your First Story

For lo, the storyteller comes,
Let fall the trumpet, hush the drums ...

—Anonymous

Since ancient times, storytelling has included the arts of song, story, dance and mime. Perhaps the storyteller was the shaman performing his wizardry in the recesses of a smoky cave. Or a grandmother singing a lullaby in the chaparral forest. He was the wandering gleeman of medieval days, linking people to people as he shared his bagful of tales, songs, and gossip. Or a troubadour—a welcomed guest in the halls of lords and kings, recounting epics of great deeds—bringing mirth, magic, and wonder to his listeners.

It is with this tradition that we now join ourselves. Our first step will be the learning of "Wicked John and the Devil," a tale from the Appalachian Mountains— one I first heard from the great American storyteller, Richard Chase, more than thirty years ago.[1]

Since Richard told me the tale, I have shared it many times. Thinking back to all those tellings, I have written a marginal commentary in which I share my own reactions to the story; the way in which I interpreted those characters, observations about dialogue, dialect, phrases and words that struck me as particularly felicitous or unusual and that I wanted to maintain in my own telling, comments on the harmonious blending of various plot elements, and my responses to overall tone and quality of the story. In short, a more or less guided tour through the tale as I myself prepared it for telling.

I would suggest that you cover these margin notes as you read the story through for the first time. Then, when you've finished the first reading, think of how you might tell the story. Say a phrase or two to yourself. See what mental pictures you have formed of Wicked John, or Saint Peter, or the Devil. Recollect the thread of narration that holds the story together. Then reread the tale, this time with my notes available. Compare your reactions with mine.

But now I want you to imagine yourself seated with friends and family on a braided rug. Firelight flickers and casts shadows on rudely planed log walls. An old man is seated in a straight backed kitchen chair, his weathered features and gnarled and arthritic hands illuminated by yellow lamp light. He has been showing us some simple toys country folks enjoy; a moon spinner, a smoke-grinder, an idiot stick. But now he settles back to tell a story.

"Ah, let's see now," he muses in his rich, broadly accented country voice. "What's a story I can tell that won't put the lot of ye to sleep." He pauses for a few seconds, seeming to shuffle through the stories in his mind for exactly the right one. "I've just the tale," he tells us. And, saying that, he begins "Wicked John and the Devil."

One time there was an old black-smith named John. He was so mean they called him Wicked John. Mean? Aa-aa Lord! He didn't wait till Saturday night for *his* dram. He'd just as soon start in drinkin' of a Sunday ... Monday... Tuesday. It didn't differ. He stayed lit up all week anyhow. Talked mean. Acted mean. Independent minded. He wasn't afraid of nothin' nor nobody.

Notice how quickly the storyteller moves into the tale. By the end of the first sentence we've a good picture of Wicked John.

"Lit up ..." My father used to say, when telling about someone who had had a little too much to drink, "He's really lit up tonight..."

What other colorful and regional language can you find in these first few paragraphs? Include them in your own telling.

One thing about him though; he always did treat a stranger right. And one mornin' Wicked John was workin' there in his shop when an old beggar came to the door, crippled up with rheumatism, all bent over and walkin' on two sticks. Looked right tired and hungry-like. Stood there till fin'lly Old John hollered at him, says, "Well come in! Confound! Come on in and sit down! Rest yourself."

Here's our second character, "... crippled up" with rheumatism, all bent over. Can you feel "crippled up" when you describe him?

Note the use of first person dialect. "Well, come in!" What's John's voice like when he says that? Gruff? Hearty?

The old beggar heaved over the sill, stumbled to where there was a nail keg turned up, sat down. John kept right on workin', talkin' big; but seemed like the old man was so give-out he couldn't talk much. So directly Old John threw his hammer down and headed for the house. "You wait now. Just sit right there."

Now, a quick shift—you're the beggerman. Look around for a place to sit ... (But keep your feet planted where you are.)

Came back with a plate full of vittles: boiled sweet tater, big chunk of ham-meat, beans, greens, slice of cake—

Note the specificity of detail here: "...vittles, boiled sweet tater, big chunk of ham-meat, beans, greens ... pitcher of sweet milk ..." Be specific as you tell the story.

and he'd even gone to the spring-house and fetched a pitcher of sweet milk. "Here, old man! Try these rations. I hope you can find something here you can eat."

"Thank ye. Thank ye."

"Oh hit ain't much. If I can eat it three times a day every day, you can stomach it once I reckon."

Wicked John he went on back to work a'hammerin' and a'poundin'. Watched the old beggar out of the corner of his eye: saw him lay the plate and glass to one side directly and start to get up. He let his two walkin' sticks fall to the ground.

Commenced straightenin' up, straightenin' up, all the kinks comin' out of him. There was a flash of light all at once. And the next thing old John knew—there, r'ared up in the door, was a fine stout-like old man; had a white beard and white hair, long white robe right down to his feet, and a big gold key swingin' in his hand.

Old John stood there with his jaw hangin', and his eyes popped open.

"Well John, I don't reckon you know me, do ye?"

"Why, now, what happened to that old beggar? And where-in-the-nation did you come from—where folks dress like that?"

"I don't see you've got any way of knowin' me, John, since you never been inside a church-house in your whole life. I'm Saint Peter."

"Aw-w-w, now! You expect me to believe that?"

"It don't differ whether you believe it or not. I'll just tell you how come I'm down here. Once a year I walk the earth

Here's fine understated humor. Wicked John brings out all this scrumptious food, and then acts as if it's barely fit to eat. Use these lines, or ones close to them, in your own telling.

"Straightenin' up" ... As you tell this portion of the story, imagine yourself being transformed from an old beggar to St. Peter, strong and tall and noble. What body movement shows that?

Minimal shift of stance, so that you're no longer the old beggarman, but John ...

"Where folks dress like that ..." I often add, "wearing nightgowns around all day and such ..."

Don't you like the idea of a hill country Saint Peter who says things like "... it don't differ you whether" and "... wish for anything you've a mind to"?

to see can I find any decent folks left on it. And the first man I run across that treats me right I always give him three wishes. So you go ahead, John. Wish for anything you've got a mind to, and hit'll be that'a'way. Take your three wishes, and be careful now."

Well, Old John he was grinnin' at Saint Peter like he didn't believe none of it. He was already pretty high that mornin', so he looked around; started wishin' on the first thing would pop into his head.

"Three wishes, huh? Well now—see that old high-back rockin' chair yonder? I keep it there so I can sit and rest everwhen I get done with ar' job-of-work. But—don't you know!—these dad'blame loafers that hang around in here of an evenin'!

"Nearly every time I go to sit down, there sits one of them lazy no-'count fellers a'wearin' out the seat of his britches in my rocker. Hit makes me mad! And I just wish that anybody sits there will stick to the chair-bottom and that old rocker rock 'em till they holler! Hold 'em stuck fast–till I let 'em go."

Saint Peter was writin' it down with a gold pencil in a little gold note-book. "That's one, John."

"Aa-aa Lord! Lemme see now. Well, take my big sledgehammer there. Every day after school these blame school kids come by and borrow it. I have to hunt it up where them boys have dropped it in the weeds. Well! I wish that anybody teches that hammer will stick to the handle and hit'll pound right on! Shake the daylights out of 'em, till I let 'em go."

Saint Peter was scowlin' and shakin' his head like he thought old John was

John's his old, cantankerous self again. Look around, as if you're John, sizing up the smithy, trying to think up something to wish for ...

... And sees the old high-back rocking chair ... How will he look when his eyes focus on it?

"... a'wearin' out the seat of his britches ..." another example of vivid regional speech. You may want to make a list of these so that you are sure of including them in your telling.

Switch roles ... You're Saint Peter now, writing in your notebook ...

There's something not quite right here, and it amuses us. The storyteller makes a point of John's "meanness"—and yet, this is the same man who hands out food to a stranger and whose shop is apparently a favorite stopping place for all the neighborhood. Would kids borrow a sledgehammer from someone who terrified them? Or neighbors stop by to sit and talk?

Another quick shift. You're Saint Peter, scowling ... disappointed ...

A ten-pound Sledge Hammer

wastin' his wishes pretty bad.

But John was mean, like I said. *He* didn't care! Looked at Saint Peter mischievous-like, grinned sort of devilish, says, "One more wish, huh, Peter? All right. Now. There's that big firebush just outside the door. Gets full of all them red blooms real early in the spring-of-the-year. I like my old thornbush but hit's been mommicked up right bad here lately; folks backin' their wagons over it, horses tromplin' it—and these here high-falutin' folks comin' over the mountain a'fox-huntin' on horseback—their little red coats flappin' out behind. Looks like they got to stop and break ridin' switches off that bush every time they pass here. I wish that anybody teches that firebush, it will grab 'em and pull 'em headforemost right down in the middle where them stickers are the thickest–hold 'em there till I let 'em out."

Saint Peter quit writin', shut his little book, put it and the gold pencil back inside his white robe, says, "Mighty sorry wishes, John. Looks like you might have made one wish for the good of your soul. You've sure wasted your chance. But that's what you've wished for and hit'll be that'a'way just like I said. Well, I got to go now."

"Oh, just stay the night, Peter."

"Can't stay."

And Saint Peter stepped over the doorsill and he was gone from there, and Wicked John couldn't tell which-a-way he went nor nothin'.

Well, you'd a'thought old John might have done a little better one way or another after havin' a saint right there in his shop, but it didn't have no effect on

---

"... Looked at Saint Peter ..." Here, as in other place, the pronoun at the beginning of the sentence is omitted ... characteristic of this regional speech you'll want to incorporate in your telling ...

"Mommicked up"—there's one of those words that never quite makes it into a dictionary, but we are nontheless, absolutely certain as to its use and meaning.

Mime shutting the book, putting it in your breast pocket ...

How would Saint Peter deliver this speech? Perhaps shaking his head sorrowfully ...

"Oh, just stay the night ..." a characteristic farewell remark—with no expectation that the guest will accept the invitation..

Take a good long pause here, to let your audience know there's a shift in the story, comparable to a scene change in the theater.

him. Aa-aa Lord! He got meaner than ever. Somebody'd come and John would tell 'em, "Sit down." He'd trick a man into helpin' hammer somethin' with that big sledge—and let it shake 'em awhile 'fore he'd make it turn loose.

So, one way or another, Wicked John turned so cussed he got to be the meanest man in the world. And the Devil—he keeps pretty good track of what's going on up here, you know—he got worried.

Decided that wouldn't do; havin' anybody out-do him in meanness. So he sent for old John. Wouldn't wait for him to die. Sent one of the little devils to fetch him right now.

Old John looked up one mornin' and there, standin' in the door, was a little horned devil—about a fifth-grade-size devil—little horns just startin' to bump up on his forehead.

"Come on, old man. Daddy sent me to get ye. Said for me to bring ye right on back."

Old John had his hammer raised up, starin' at that little devil—started in hammerin' again. Says, "All right, son. I'll be ready to go with ye in just a few more licks. Got to finish this one horseshoe. Come on in. Hit won't take me but a minute."

"No. Daddy said not to wait."

"All right! All right! Come on in. I'll be as quick as I can."

The little devil he came on inside, frettin'. Watched old John pound a few licks. Looked around inside the shop—and made for that old rockin' chair. Eased down in it, r'ared back and started rockin'. Says, "You hurry up now. Daddy'll sure get mad if we take too long."

Note how quickly events are summarized at this point—a good storytelling technique for moving through information that's necessary for the story but which doesn't merit the dialogue and detail we've supplied earlier.

"The meanest man in the world ..." an important phrase, for it gives us a reason to introduce the Devil into the narrative.

Richard Chase always made the first devil a fifth-grader. I usually introduce him as a kindergartner—dress him in red underwear—the kind with the feet sewed on, and use a hand gesture to show how tall he is.

And, of course, a nice, high, sassy kindergartner's voice ...

Can't you just imagine Wicked John already scheming how to trick the little devil. "... Huh! Oh, sure, I'm gonna drop everthing! Sure I am! You bet!"

Maybe John even hinting the little devil might want to have a seat ... casting a glance off that way ...

"... made for that old rockin' chair." You're going to have fun with that line, and so is your audience. Pause after you've said it, to let them savor what's going to happen next.

John finished that shoe, soused it in the coolin' tub, threwed it on the ground. The little devil started to get up. Heaved a time or two. And directly that poor little devil's head was goin' *whammity-bang!* against the chairback.

"Oh, mister, I'm stuck!"

"Now! Hain't that too bad!"

"Ow! Please mister! Let me up!"

"I'll let you go if you get out of here and not bother me no more."

"Yes, sir! I'll leave right now! And I'll not *never* come back!"

"All right. Away with ye!"

And the rockin' chair throwed him out on the ground and—*rippity-tuck!*—out the door, and down the road!

John went on with his work, and in a few minutes there was another'n—a little devil about high-school-size, little horns spikin' up. Stood there in the door actin' biggity. Says, "You come on here, old man."

"Why, hello, son. Come on in." John kept right on workin'.

"You stop that poundin' and come with me. Ye hear?"

"Why, I can't stop now. This thing's red-hot and I'm bound to finish it 'fore we leave."

"No, now! You quit right where you're at. Daddy said if I didn't fetch you back in five minutes he'd roast me good."

John kept right on—*bam! bam! bam!*

"Huh? Can't hear ye. I can't talk till I get done with this wagon tire."

Well, that little devil saw old John was havin' it kind of awkward the way he had to hold up that big iron wagon tire and beat it one-handed. So he lumbered right on inside the shop.

"Stand back then, old man. You hold

Practice this until you get the contrast you want between the little devil's high-pitched voice and Wicked John's low, gruff tones ... back and forth between the two, very fast ...

... and here comes another devil—I make him junior-high sized—with a squeaky, just-beginning-to-change voice ...
What about reaching up to the top of your own head to show those little horns "spikin' up"?

Another quick dialogue—high-pitched voice for the junior high devil, low and gruff for John, your own for the storyteller ...

... Here's John, so innocent and friendly—but after all, he's a working man and can't leave a job half done ...

"He'd roast me for good!" Interesting how this common phrase takes on new meaning here.

Mime this, to show how difficult it all is for poor, overworked John ...

that thing and let me pound it. We got to hurry."

Leaned over and picked up the big sledgehammer, started swingin' it. Wicked John, he held the tire up and turned it this-a-way and that-a-way. Pulled it out from under the hammer directly, cooled it in the big tub, and leaned it against the wall.

"Much obliged. Hit's finished. What ye poundin' so hard for?"

And old John went to laughin'. Well, the way that hammer was swingin' that little devil around, jerkin' him up and down with his legs a'flyin' ever' which-a-way—hit was a sight-in-this-world!

"Ow! My hands is stuck! Oh please, mister! Make this thing turn me loose!"

"You promise to leave here?

"Shore I promise!"

"And not come back?"

"Yes, sir! No, sir! You won't never catch me here again!"

"Then away with ye!"

When the hammer let go, it slung that little devil up in the rafters. He hit the ground, and when he got his legs untangled, he streaked out the door and went dustin' down the road.

Then it wasn't hardly no time at all 'til Wicked John looked up, and there, standin' in the door—with his old goat horns roached back over his head, and his forked tail a'swishin', and that big cow's foot of his'n propped up on the sill—was the Old Boy. His eyes were just a'blazin'. Old John kept right on with his work.

"Howdy-do! Come on in."

"You come on here, old man! And I ain't goin' to take no foolishness off ye

Be sure to keep the order of events straight: Kindergarten Devil—chair; Junior High Devil—the sledgehammer ...

Mime this quickly—turning the tire around and then pulling it away ...

Does John *really* need an answer to that question?

John's having a good time! How about a good, gruff laugh ...

Can you suggest the little devil's dilemma with a bit of mime? (Remember, if you're miming holding a hammer—leave room for the handle.)

Note the absence of speech tags (e.g., "John said" ... "the Devil said" ... Eliminate those in your tellings as much as you can, here and in other stories—let vocal changes tell your audience who's talking.

A brief pause, signalling a new scene ...

Wicked John watches a devil disappear down the road.

... And the story continues.

We can pretty much predict who it's going to be this time. After all, this is the third visitor ... and some fine description ... "old goat horns roached back" ... "forked tail" ... "big cow's foot of his'n ..."
I generally say the line "... was the Old Boy himself" with a substantial feeling of awe. After all, he is the Devil!
... But John's not awed. Not a bit!

What—or who—will the Devil sound like?

neither!"

"All right, sir. Just as soon as I get done. Promised a man I'd sharpen this mattick head 'fore twelve. Hit won't take but a few more licks. Come on in, confound it, and sit down!"

"No! I'll not sit in no chair of you'rn!"

"Suit yourself. But we'll be ready to go quicker if you'll hit this mattick a lick or two while I hold it with the tongs here. Just grab the big sledge leanin' there on the door jamb and ..."

"No! I ain't goin' to tech no sledge-hammer neither! You done made me mad enough already, old man, the way you done my boys. And I'm takin' you off from here right now!"

Old John r'ared up, says, "You and who else? Jest tech me! I dare ye!"

The Devil made for him and old John let him have it. And such a punchin', knockin', beatin' you never did see! Poundin', scratchin', kickin', buttin', like two horses fightin'. Wicked John was mean, like I said. He wasn't goin' to take nothin' off nobody, not even the Devil himself. They had a round or two there by the door, and fin'lly The Devil grabbed old John by the seat of his britches and heaved him outside.

John twisted around some way or other and got hold of the Devil's tail —kinked it up, you know, like tryin' to make an unruly cow go in the barn —yanked right hard. Well, that really made the Devil mad.

"Blast ye, old man! I'm goin' to lick the hide off you right now. Just see if I don't. Where'll I get me a switch?"

And the Devil reached to break him a switch off that firebush. Time he touched

Someone you know? Mine always sounds a little like my Irish grandfather ...

And John's response ... The nerve of him—trotting out the same old trick a third time!

The Devil seems to have had the same English teacher Saint Peter had ...

What's a mattick? When you're getting a story ready for telling, be sure you know the meanings of all the words ...

John's selling, but the Devil's not buying ... in fact, he's getting more and more irritated ... you'll want to practice this dialogue over and over. A slight shift of position helps tell the audience when John is speaking, and when it's the Devil ...

... and now John's been bedeviled enough ...

Sometimes I augment this list ... tickling, pulling hair ...

Another place for one of those all-important pauses, to let the audience relish that it knows what the Devil doesn't know ...

it, hit wropped all around him and jerked him headforemost right down in the middle of all them long stickers.

The old Devil he tried to get loose, but the more he thrashed around in there the more he got scratched, till fin'lly he had to give up; his legs hangin' limp out the top of the bush and his head 'way down in there.

"Mister?"

Old John was laughin' so hard he had to lean against the shop.

"What ye want now?"

"Please, sir. Let me out."

"Who was that you was goin' to whip? Huh?"

"Nobody—Now will you let me out of here?"

"I'll let you out of there on one condition: you, nor none of your boys, don't ye never—none of ye—ever come back up here botherin' me no more. You promise me that and I might let ye go."

"Hell, yes, I promise. Now please will you make this bush turn loose of me?"

The bush let go, and when the old Devil crawled out he had leaves and trash caught on his horns, and his old, long black coat torn to rags. He turned around and when he got his legs to workin', such a kickin' up dust you never did see! They tell me that when the Old Boy left there he wasn't moseyin'!"

❖ ❖ ❖

So Wicked John never was bothered by any more devils after that. Just kept on blacksmithin' there in his shop. Lived on 'til he was an old man. Stayed mean, too—just as mean as ever right up to the day he died. And when he fin'lly did die, he didn't do a thing but go straight up to the Pearly Gates.

The Devil
Deep down
in stickers

"Mister?" ... An interesting choice of word ... What's the Devil been calling John up to this point? ... How will the Devil say that word? Boldly? Timidly?

"Please, sir ..." More pleading on the part of the Devil ...

... And John, of course, savoring every moment ... knowing exactly what terms he's going to demand ...

Children love hearing the storyteller say "Hell." They turn to each other. "Did you hear that ...?"

"... he wasn't moseyin' ..." another fine understatement ...
And, of course, another pause, suggesting time passage.

Bam! Bam! Bam!

Saint Peter cracked the door, and when he saw who it was, he backed off a little, says, "Uh—oh! Er—hello, John. Just what did *you* want?"

"Well, Peter—seein' as you knowed me, I thought that maybe ..."

"Why, John, you can't come in here."

"Oh, I know I can't *stay*, but I'd sort of like to take me one look around, see them golden streets, hear me a little harp music, and then I'll go."

"Can't do it, John. Can't do it. You wait a minute. I'm just going to show you your accounts here on the record. Hand out the book, one of ye."

Saint Peter reached and took the big book, licked his thumb and turned the pages.

"Here you are—Now, here's your two pages in the ledger, John. Look there on the good-deed side. All the ninety-two years you've lived, three entries, way up at the top of the page. But over here on the *other* side—Why!—hit's black, clean to the bottom line. And all the meanness you've done the past twelve years, you can see for yourself, it had to be writ in sideways."

Saint Peter shut the book and took off his spectacles, says, "I'm sorry, John, but you can't put one foot inside here. So if you'll excuse me now—" And Saint Peter backed through the gates and reached and shut 'em to.

Well, old John he just shuffled around and headed back down the stairsteps.

❖   ❖   ❖

That day, several devils was there in front of the gate to Hell, playin' catch

Saint Peter ... puzzled, bewildered ... It's been a long time, and why in heaven's name would this old man he barely remembers be coming up here ...?

And John, slightly abashed. Now that he thinks of it, this is Heaven! A nice place to visit, but he wouldn't want to *live* there! And yet, there *are* all those stories ... golden streets ... harp music ... angels taking flying lessons ...

But Saint Peter's not to be fooled with ...

Saint Peter calls back over his shoulder. Turn your head slightly at this point in his speech ... lick your thumb and mime page turning ...

... mime pointing to the page ... Patient, tolerant Saint Peter, trying to show John the record as it really is ...

... a way of doubling the amount of space available for writing ...

... mime taking off your glasses ...

Have you ever tried to get rid of a door-to-door salesman? ... Remember that time as you say these lines ...

And John, speechless for the first time since we've known him ...

A brief pause, and the story continues ...

with a ball of fire. And one of 'em happened to be that first 'un was sent to
fetch Wicked John. He chanced to look
off down the road directly.

His eyes popped open and he
missed his catch. Turned and ran through
the gates just a'squallin', "Daddy! Oh
Daddy! Run here quick!"

The old Devil came and looked
out. And there, headed right that way,
with his hands in his pockets, a'whistlin',
and just a'weavin' down the road, was
Wicked John. The Devil turned around,
says, "Bar the door, boys! Bar the door!"

So when old John got there, there
was the gates to Hell shut and padlocked; the little devils peepin' out from
behind the mine-props and coal piles
scared to death, and the old Devil
standin' 'way back, says "Uh-unh! You
ain't comin' in here. Don't ye come no
closeter. You just turn around here where
you're at and put off! I done had enough
of you. Now git!"

Old John stood there scratchin' his
head. Says, "Confound!"

Turned to the Devil, says, "Looky
here. I got no place to go. I went up yonder and Saint Peter told me I couldn't get
in up there, and now you've gone and
locked me out down here. Why! I don't
know where to go to, now."

The Devil studied a minute,
grabbed up some tongs, reached in one of
his furnaces and got hold of a hot coal.
Edged over 'side the gate and handed the
tong-handles out the bars.

Says, "Here, old man. You just take
this chunk of fire and go off somewhere
else—and start you a Hell of your own."

❖　❖　❖

I so admire the language here—"playing
catch with a ball of fire"—such an innocent
pleasure ...

Another opportunity to use your Little Devil's
voice ...

"Bar the door, boys! Bar the door!" Is that
panic we're hearing in the Devil's voice?

"... Shut and padlocked ..." Not exactly a
friendly welcome ...
"... little devils peepin' out from behind the
mine-props and coal piles" ... Good storytelling details ...

"... closeter" ... The spelling of this regional
variant of *closer* tells you how it should be
said ...

And Wicked John, completely befuddled.
Turned down everywhere ...

How will John seem in this scene? Has he
lost a little of his own bluster?

Mime the Devil reaching for coals, handing
them out to John ...

As gruffly as Wicked John might have said it.

"A Hell of your own ..." the climactic line.

Followed by a pause ...

And right to this day, they say that in The Great Dismal Swamps—somewhere over yonder between Virginia and Carolina—you can look out on a night and see a little bob of light movin' around out there.

One old time name for it is the Will-o'-the-wisp, and some old folks call it the Jacky-my-lantern. Now some people that don't know any better—these schoolteachers and college professors —they'll try to tell you it's nothin' but some kind of marsh gas a'lightin' up out in the swamps.

But you'uns know better now, don't ye?

Intimately ... after all, this is just between you and the audience ... No one else is to know.

A Little Devil spies Wicked John heading his way....

A pitch knot hisses and bursts into flame, casting orange light across the room. We look about—persons awaking from a trance. The storyteller has worked his magic, taking us into another land and another time.

How did he do it?

Answering that question is like trying to map the arcs and swoops of a butterfly. In spite of our efforts, our first stories may seem, when compared with Uncle Dick's magic, mechanical and contrived. Time, temperament, talent—these must be factored in. It's like comparing the playing of a Chopin Polonaise by a gifted pianist and that of an earnest student—the notes are the same, the time and rhythm are the same, but the first is art; the second, aspiration towards art.

And so, a caution: analyzing how one gets a story ready for telling doesn't guarantee that it will come to life.

But at least you'll have something to hold on to during your first tellings.

There! Having said that, let's get started.

Find the Story You Want to Tell

It's not always easy to find the right story—one's own story. At first, that's surprising. One would think that a quick trip to the library would do the trick. Grab a collection or two of stories off the shelf—any one of them will do.

But somehow it doesn't work that way. At least not for me. I leaf through this book of stories, and that, and still don't come across the tale that's exactly right. After all, this is a story I'm going to live with for some time—at the least, a few hours—more likely days—months—even, as in the case of "Wicked John"—years.

What is it one looks for—longs for—in a story? Often, the response springs from our unconscious; we may not be able to state what it is in a story that makes us like it so much, but we'll know when we find it. The story may be a sad one, or charming and witty. It may be full of rich language, or heroic in proportion. But most of all, it's a story we like and want to share with others.

When you find such a story, you'll feel its power stir inside you. You'll have the feeling that you've been in this territory before; the story will speak of conditions, convictions, aspirations, and fears that you have known in your own life.

Often, I suggest to my students that they choose for their first story one from their own cultural or ethnic heritage. Part of the reasoning behind this assignment is pedagogical; given the diversity of a University classroom, such an assignment gives my students and me exposure to stories from around the world.

But more importantly, that assignments puts my students in touch with those stories that form their own mythic past; the stories their parents and grandparents and great-grandparents heard as children. These stories are often the complete and natural expression of the inner self. Somehow, they embody in their depths an unexpected fidelity to real experience.

When I first heard "Wicked John," I felt that kind of resonance. I remembered Harley Boyer's blacksmith shop out on Winesap Road, near my Grandmother's house. Apple orchards framed the old unpainted wooden building. In the distance were the foothills of the Blue Mountains, with their great fields of wheat, serrated by ravines where pines competed with poison oak and wild sumac for a place in the sun.

The shop was a pleasant place, with its acrid smells of metal, the bright coals of the hearth blazing in the dim light, the ringing sounds of steel striking iron. A worn kitchen chair or two stood outside the shop on sunny days. Inside, next to the door, was a grimy soft drink cooler, where Harley kept a plentiful supply of beer and various soda drinks. A battered can stood open nearby. Put in a little change, and help yourself to a bottle of pop drawn from the watery depths of the cooler.

Harley was a taciturn old man who reminded me of some mythological creature. Rivulets of tobacco juice furrowed their way through the stubble on his chin. He lunged about in his greasy overalls, shaping iron and bronze into knives, shovels, wagon tires. When the red coals gleamed and stirred blue and white, it furnished me with my first imaginings of what Hell must be like. If he'd plucked up a live coal from the forge and swallowed it, I'd not have been surprised.

Farmers brought Harley their horses for shoeing, and discs, harrows, plows, and mowing machines for repairs. Later, he got a welding outfit. He wore a helmet that fitted over his head, and seemed even more like someone from another world.

And so "Wicked John" was no stranger to me. Indeed, the language and rough sly humor in that story were the sort I knew from those childhood days. (Although I'm no longer absolutely sure how much of what I remember is true, and how much is a rearrangment of truth. But that's neither here nor there.) In short, "Wicked John" pleased me. It seemed real. Authentic.

By authentic, I do not exclude the fanciful and imagined. Perhaps you, like I, have been caught up at one time or another in your life with Hans Christian Andersen's stories: "The Tin Soldier," "The Darning Needle," "The Little Match Girl," or "The Ugly Duckling." Few characters in literature are more real to me than Andersen's. And that is, I think, because the emotions and feelings they express are ones I feel. An anonymous poet, writing nearly a century ago, said, "Fairy tales ... are more than knowledge and poetry in bottles. They are our dream and intuition, the hem of our garment of immortality." In my dreams, my intuitions, I knew the delicious sadness of the little Match Girl, left alone with her last few matches, and the pride and smug self-satisfaction of the darning needle, who fancied herself so fine.

So much for one set of reactions–my own. The second concern the storyteller has is, "How will my audience respond to the story?" Will it fit their mood, their level of sophistication, their character? Recently, I told a bloody English fairy tale, "Mr. Fox," to an assembly of third, fourth, and fifth graders. Do you remember the story? In it, a young noblewoman, Mary, steals into the castle of her betrothed and finds, hidden, in his closet, the "bodies and bones" of dozens of young women he's murdered.

I think the choice of stories was a bad one. "Mr. Fox" strikes too close to home—too close to the latent terrors some of these children feel when the morning paper carries account after account of senseless murder. Looking back, I think our time together would have been better spent with, say, Richard Kennedy's "Porcelain Man," or the Japanese fairy tale, "The Old Man and His Wen."

Nor would I tell "Wicked John" to a group of primary children. There's a bit too much subtle adult humor in the story, it seems to me. They'd probably prefer "Talk," or "The Little Girl Who Wasn't Afraid of Anything."

By necessity, selecting the right story requires extensive reading and listening on your part. Whether to tell one of Kipling's *Just So Stories,* or a Norse Myth such as "The Making of the Hammer," or take the listener to Pakistan with "The Farmer's Old Horse," or to Africa with "Talk," is a decision which cannot be made unless one knows these stories well and can judge their appropriateness for a particular audience.

Prepare the Story for Telling

Some traditionalists advocate exact memorization of a story so that the original telling of the tale is not lost. I have heard stories told in this way, and have myself, on occasion, committed stories to memory. There are advantages to exact memorization: if a story is learned in this fashion the teller need not fear that the style and manner of word and phrase choice of the original version will be lost. Rudyard Kipling's "Elephant's Child" draws much of its charm from the rhythm of the words he uses:

In the High and Far-Off Times the Elephant, O Best Beloved, had no trunk. He had only a blackish, bulgy nose, as big as a boot, that he could wiggle about from side to side; but he couldn't pick up things with it.

But there was one Elephant—a new Elephant—an Elephant's Child—who was full of 'satiable curiosity, and that means he asked ever so many questions. And he lived in Africa, and he filled all Africa with his 'satiable curiosity ...[2]

Tampering with such a story will not improve it. Better to learn the story "by heart," as schoolmistresses once put it.

Memorization has another advantage: if a story is memorized, the teller is free to interpret orally, without needing to recall where the story is going next.

These advantages notwithstanding, I do not recommend memorization for most stories. Several years ago my family and I visited a cavern in Wisconsin. As we trooped through chamber after chamber, lighted with tiny clear glass bulbs, our young guide recited geological and historical lore. One tourist interrupted to ask her a question. It was an unfortunate thing to do. She lost her place in her recitation, and had to begin again. After that, none of us dared interrupt, for fear we'd be in the caves longer than we cared to stay.

Memorization need not result in mechanical recitation, as it did for that young guide. But even the accomplished storyteller may automate his telling if the story is memorized. Somehow, there's no room left for the unusual and the unpredictable; the interruption of an eager child during the telling, the need to cut short a story because of time limitations or audience disinterest, the need to change and modify a story to suit an older or a younger group—these are difficult to accomplish if one relies on memorization. Donald Davis, comparing the storyteller to the museum curator, puts it this way: "Every time I take a group through a story, I'm going to take them differently, skipping some pictures, stopping a long time at others. If you recorded the way I tell that story ten times, it's going to be a different thing every time."[3]

I would recommend that one learns a story so that it remains faithful in character to the original. But once it's learned, follow Davis's advice, and tell it so the story fits the audience. The following guidelines are suggested:

1. Read aloud the story you want to learn several times through. As you read, listen to its rhythm and style. In "Wicked John," for example, the first paragraph sets an informal conversational tone which persists throughout; "Mean? Aa-aa Lord! He didn't wait till Saturday night for his dram ..."

2. Think of the major "bits" of the story, trying to find where one bit ends and another begins. A *bit* refers to a scene or piece of action. These bits give you an outline you can follow in telling the story. In "Wicked John," they might be as follows:

- Introduction to Wicked John; establishing the setting (a black-smith shop back in the hills); John's orneriness; the fact that he *did* always treat strangers right.

- Visit from Saint Peter; granting the three wishes; John's choices; Saint Peter's disappointment and departure.

- Increasing orneriness of Wicked John; visit by the Kindergarten Devil; the rocking chair episode.

- Visit by the Junior High Devil; sledgehammer incident.

- Arrival of Old Scratch; the fight and the fire bush; the promise to stay away from John.

- John's death and stroll up to Heaven; conversation with Saint Peter; rejection.

- Journey to Hell; consternation of the Devil and his young ones; Devil sends John away with a chunk of hell fire.

- John wandering around alone; the light in swamps; relating that light to the *ignis fatuus* (fool's fire); conclusion.

The bits I've outlined above may be different than those you'd pick. But the point is that thinking through the story and outlining it in your head will help you keep the story in mind so that it moves along in an orderly fashion.

3. Develop a sense of the characters in the story. Form a picture in your mind of the characters, the clothes they wear, the shape and size of them, unusual features, personality traits, their way of speaking, mannerisms, and the like. For example, here's how I see Wicked John:

> *Burly ... shuffling ... hands the size of baseball mitts ... greasy overalls with a blue bandana handkerchief sticking out from his back pocket ... chews tobacco (just like Harley) ... deep, slow voice with lots of glottal stops and starts ... smarter than he lets on, and not afraid of anyone or anything, as demonstrated in his unabashed behavior with Saint Peter, and in the wit and pluck with which he dispatches Old Scratch and his boys ...*

If you were asked, how would you describe Saint Peter? Or Old Scratch? Jot down words and phrases that come to you as you think about them. While you won't use these phrases in your telling, they help you get acquainted with your characters ... you know what they look like, how they dress, the way they talk. That knowledge informs your telling, giving it a sense of authenticity. If you don't have a clear picture of the characters in a story you're telling, neither will your listeners.

For both storyteller and audience, one especially important aspect of character is voice. What was Old Scratch's voice like? High pitched? Plaintive? Oily and unctuous? What about Saint Peter's voice? Or that of the little devil? Read dialogue for the various characters, matching voice and person so that there's a consistency between how a character appears to you and how he sounds. On your own, make up other speeches those characters might have said.

It may be that your view of the characters in a story will differ. They'll look different. They'll have different voices and behaviors. That's the way it should be. After all, once you've decided to learn a story, you own it. It's yours to interpret as you will. What matters, however, is that when you tell the story you're telling about people you know, and not just parroting what you've heard or read.

4. *Think through the setting of the story.* "In any memorable novel," Eleanor Cameron writes, "one has the sense of place interpenetrating all: a deep, wide, firm awareness emanating from the tale that makes us know—whether the place be actual or imagined—that it is intimately and vividly real to the writer's five senses and not simply cooked up or sketched in here and there to provide some sort of background for magical happenings."[4]

The same holds true for the storyteller. If someone were to ask you, would you be able to draw a map showing where "Wicked John" took place? What was the lay of the land? Hilly or flat? Forest, cultivated land, or desert? What direction did the smithy face? Were there other buildings around it? Where did the farmers live who brought work to John? Was there a village nearby? What trees and bushes grew in the neighborhood? Did the story take place last week or "once upon a time"? Where were Heaven and Hell and the swamp John wandered around in?

Such a map helps the storyteller move easily from place to place in a story, because it's familiar terrain to him. Richard Chase once told a group of us, "When you're telling a story, it's just like you're watching it take place, and telling people what you see happening." A map helps you see where the story is happening. I've sketched a rough one for "Wicked John" (at right). Looking at it, I notice that it looks a lot like Harley's shop on Winesap Road.

5. *Find phrases in the story you wish to use in your own telling.* As you tell a story, retain particularly apt words and phrases from the original. These words and phrases help preserve the character and flavor of the story, as well as passing on language patterns that have lived on through time. In "Wicked John" we are introduced to rural Southeastern Mountain dialect. The language is clear, colorful, and concise, full of wry humor and wit. Consider, for example, the following phrases:

*"an old beggarman came to the door; crippled up with
rheumatism, all bent over and walkin' on two sticks ..."*

*"Came back with a plate full of vittles: boiled sweet tater, big
chunk of ham-meat, beans, greens ..."*

*"There, r'ared up in the door, was a fine stout-like old man:
had a white beard and white hair, long white robe right down
to his feet ..."*

Phrases like these light up a story. The storyteller avoids the pitfall of "Once there
was a very very old man who lived in a very very very old house ..." and instead gives
listeners specific detail from which images can be constructed.

Read through the story again. What phrases and language patterns would you
like to use as you tell the story? Jot these down and practice saying them until they
slip easily from your tongue.

6. *Begin telling parts of the story aloud to yourself, testing out different ways of
uttering the same words.* For instance, how would John say:

*"Why, now, what happened to that old beggar? And where- in-
the-nation did you come from—where folks dress like that?"*

Is he surprised? Is he challenging the newcomer? Is he frightened? Or is he feeling a whole array of emotions? How are you going to show what John is feeling? In the first sentence, will you pause longer between *why* and *now,* or between *now* and *what?* Will you accent *happened,* or *old,* or *beggar?* How do these different pauses and stresses change the meaning of the story?

Experiment with other parts of the story, reading or telling them to yourself and stressing first one part of a sentence and then another; pitching your voice higher and lower, speaking slowly and then rapidly. Which patterns seem best to capture the mood and intent of the story?

7. "Block" the story, including postures, actions and gestures you wish to include. Blocking clarifies who the various characters in a story are. For instance, when John and Old Scratch are talking, very slight body shifts can be used to show change of character, with, say, Old Scratch facing slightly to the right as he speaks, and John facing slightly to the left. Old Scratch may be standing straight and stiff—John bent over, hulking.

Gestures help the audience visualize a character or an action. As a rule of thumb, however, it's better to understate gestures and actions in a story than to overdo them. A slight upper body movement is appropriate when one tells the lines "Commenced straightenin' up, straightenin' up ..." So is a slight head gesture when John says, "See that old high-back rockin' chair yonder ..." I generally show how tall the little devils are. And when telling how the littlest devil gets stuck to the chair, I move my own head back and forth ever so slightly to give a sense of the action I'm describing.

An action or gesture can help convey a feeling of region or country. A much-used Spanish phrase, *"así, así,"* corresponds to our "so, so," as in:

"How are you doing?"
"So, so."

However, the phrase *"así, así"* is *never* said without an accompanying hand gesture—palm down, rocking of the hand back and forth to complete the communication. In the same manner, we often shrug our shoulders when we respond, "So, so." If one were telling the Spanish tale, "The General's Horse," relating the modest indifference with which Padre Porko accepts the other animals' tribute, *"así, así"* would add color and authenticity to the telling, but if one used that phrase, a gesture would also be required.

Once you've made some tentative decisions regarding postures and gestures, practice them in front of a mirror to see how they'll appear to your audience.

8. *Prepare an introduction and conclusion.* "One time there was an old black-smith named John ..." is probably a bit too abrupt for most listeners. They need a settling down period. When Richard first told us that story, he began by sharing mountain toys with us, telling us a bit about mountain ways, recollecting for himself when he first heard the tale. Sometimes when telling "Wicked John" I ask if anyone in the audience knows what *ignis fatuus*—"fool's fire"—is. There exists, of course, a scientific explanation for this phenomenon that can be observed in swampy lands on dark nights. We talk about that bit of lore, and about Will-o'-the-wisp, and Jack-o-my-lanterns, and other strange mysterious lights that are seen occasionally, and that provides a nice lead-in to Wicked John and the coals the Devil gives him so that he can start his own kingdom.

I recommend that you have the conclusion for your telling well fixed in your mind. The story may provide you with all that needs to be said. "Wicked John" ends like this:

> *One old-time name for it is the Will-o'-the-wisp, and some old folks call it the Jack-o-my-lantern. Now some people that don't know any better—school teachers and college professors—they'll try to tell you it's nothin' but some kind of marsh gas a-lightin' up out in the swamps.*
> *But you'uns know better now, don't ye?*

What happens next depends, to some extent, on the setting. There'll be applause, hopefully. In a small group, you'll want to leave some time for audience comments. Young children, especially, like to share some of their own experiences after hearing a story. Certainly, within a school room where language development is stressed, there's justification for all manner of follow-up activities; from talking about the story to writing a new ending to inviting in a local blacksmith for a demonstration.

But I would avoid reviewing the story. After all, we aren't required to sing or hum melodies after attending a concert to verify the fact that we were listening. Generally, the same should be true of the storyteller. He gives the gift of the story, and there the matter rests.

9. *Finally, practice the entire story.* To this point, practice has been with frag-ments of the telling: gestures, phrasing and stress, vocal and postural effects, colorful phrases, sequencing, and the like. Now all of these must be smoothly put together into one whole, so that bit follows bit in simple and natural fashion. Since you will probably wish to practice the story several times, you may want to consider the fol-lowing during your practice:

Time the story for each practice telling. Does the story require fifteen or eighteen minutes to tell? If you take fifteen minutes during one telling, and twenty-five minutes during a second telling, have you improved the story, or simply weighted it down with needless detail? Try to pare a story down so that it takes no more than ten to fifteen minutes.

Tape record your story. Play back the telling, and listen for voice qualities you wish to cultivate and others you want to discard. This is a good time to catch nonfluencies and speech crutches, the *ah*s and *umm*s, the *you know*s and *like*s. Play back is also a good time to listen for parts of the story that seem slow and boring. If they bore you, you can be sure they'll bore your audience. Can you cut them or summarize them and improve the flow of the story?

Videotape your performance, or, if that's not available, tell your story in front of a mirror. Study the tape, noting dysfluencies, mannerisms, gestures, and vocal patterns. What things do you particularly like? Are there aspects of the telling you want to change?

Sharing the Story

In a way, discussion of seating arrangements and scheduling seem out of place at this point. We've learned a story and are eager to tell it, and instead talk of physical arrangements of time and space. And yet, these arrangements are critical to the success of the story-hour, for both the teller and his audience.

Ideally, stories should be told in a quiet place, free of distractions—a pleasant carpeted room or a shady lawn under a tree. But such accommodations are not always available. Much more often stories get told at the far end of a school gymnasium, or in a stuffy classroom with too many chairs and too little open space.

And so, one must work to what's available. Rearrange seating so that order and tranquility and intimacy become part of the story-hour. An audience too separated from the teller, or an environment filled with intruding sights and noises, detracts from the feeling of community you want to build.

Some storytellers engage in traditional rituals to change an environment into a private place for storytelling. Lighting a candle signals the time for a story to begin, and when the hour is ended, the candle is extinguished. I often show folk toys I've made—a gee-haw whimmydiddle, a bull roarer, a moon-spinner, a flipper dinger ...

You may wish to develop your own rituals for the hour. Sharing an object related to the story—perhaps an old horseshoe of the sort Wicked John made—would help create a mood or setting for that story.

Whether or not you develop a simple ceremony to set the stage for listening, I would suggest the following as general principles:

- Sit or stand where there are as few distracting elements behind you as possible. A dark curtain or blank wall is best, making it easier to focus on the story.

- Invite the audience to move in as close as comfortable, so everyone can see you and hear the story.

- Sit, rather than stand, if you're working with a small group, as it places you at eye level with your audience.

- If there's any question about whether the audience will have difficulty hearing you, use a microphone and amplifier. Familiarize yourself with the sound system well before the story-hour begins. Enlist someone to stand at various locations in the room while you run through a few practice lines.

Just as space, properly used, contributes to the success of the story, so does the arrangement and use of time. Perhaps the worst error a storyteller can make is to extend the story hour for too long. Almost as bad is to rush through a story in ten minutes when one needs fifteen to tell it well. Much better for audience and teller alike not to begin a story than to have insufficient time to enjoy it fully.

Generally, when I'm telling stories, I plan for several different activities, tying them together with a theme, and considering how much time I have. I'd recommend for most school-age audiences a story-hour not longer than 35 minutes for primary children, and between 45 and 50 minutes for middle and upper graders.

A suggested schedule might look like this:

- Show a folk toy or two(see also the bibliography at end of chapter for help with this)   **7-10 min.**

- Tell "Wicked John and the Devil"   **15 min.**

- Sing "Coming Around the Mountain," substituting phrases from "Wicked John," e.g:

  "Old Saint Peter came to see John one fine day ..."
  "John made wishes wicked as can be ..."
  "Kindergarten Devil tried out John's rockin' chair ..."
                 7 min.

- Teach a simple folk song and dance (e.g., "Draw a Bucket of Water," as in Chapter 9). Demonstrate with members of the audience. (In a classroom, it's fun to mix teachers and children for this activity.)   **10 min.**

Using such a schedule helps the storyteller pace activities to provide variety and audience participation, including singing, listening, suggesting new lines for the song, and the like, rather than spending the entire thirty minutes locked in on a single activities.

Summary

There! We've got one story ready for telling—a traditional, linear, regional tale—an American story—full of humor and old-fashioned charm. Not all stories are like that. In future chapters we'll be studying nonlinear stories; stories where everything happens at one and the same time, where our intent is to build a mood—a feeling. We'll be considering ghost tales and urban belief tales and scientific accounts. We'll look at puppets, flannel board stories, readers' theater, and choral reading. We'll create our own stories.

But throughout, much of what has been said here applies: the tales we tell are just as good as the respect we show them. There's much to do if one wishes to learn a story and present it successfully. No matter what form our storytelling takes, practice, care, and thoughtful work lie at the heart of a successful performance.

And yet, when one awakens the imagination and creative responses of an audience through his art, those efforts are repaid in full.

NOTES

1. "Wicked John and the Devil" is from Richard Chase's *Grandfather Tales* (New York: Houghton Mifflin, 1948, 1976). Mr. Chase collected the tale from Mrs. Jenning L. Yowell of Charlottesville, Virginia.

2. Rudyard Kipling, "The Elephant's Child," from *Just So Stories* (Garden City, New York: Doubleday and Company), p.63.

3. Donald Davis, cited in "Donald Davis: Every Story Tells a Picture," by Judith O'Malley, p. 52, *Wilson Library Bulletin* (The Bronx, New York: H.W. Wilson Co.), October, 1992.

4. Eleanor Cameron, *The Seed and the Vision* (New York: Dutton, 1993), p. 173.

ACTIVITIES

1. List all the old folktales you can recall. How many can you summarize? Five? Twenty-five? Fifty? No doubt you're surprised at the number you know.

2. Divide into bits one of the folktales you've listed above. Compare your divisions with those of another person working with you. Do you agree as to the important bits of the story?

3. Tell the story "Jack and the Beanstalk" from what you remember, having heard it in your own past. Read Richard Chase's "Jack and the Bean Tree" in his book, *The Jack Tales*. Then read Joseph Jacob's "Jack and the Beanstalk" in *English Fairy Tales*. How does reading these two versions of the tale affect your telling? What word pictures do you particularly like in each version? Which one is easier and more natural for you to tell?

4. Invent ten descriptive phrases that will add color and dramatic appeal to the story "Little Red Riding Hood." Think of phrases that give the story a rural twist. Now think of contemporary urban phrases. Compare your list with those of persons working with you.

5. Facial expressions, gestures, dramatic pauses, voice changes—all of these, used judiciously, contribute to the richness and color of a story. Select sentences from the story you are now learning, or use the sentences given below, for practice. Compare your interpretation with that of a friend.

- "Someone's coming," he whispered. "Get ready!"

- "Forty, forty-five, fifty ... There's but fifty ducats here! Tell me, lad, just kindly tell me, where do you suppose that money's gone and taken itself?"

- "In a far-off wood there lived three brown mice, and their names were Peter, John, and Henry. Peter was the oldest. Henry the smartest. John was—well—John was John."

6. Which of the phrases given below would you use in telling "Jack and the Beanstalk" to four-year-olds? Which phrases would be more appropriate for eight- to ten-year-olds?

- "eyes as big as saucers ... and a nose as long as your arm!"

- "He required little urging, and the swap was soon accomplished."

- "Oh, what a bean tree it was, with its gray trunk as thick as a fence post, and those lovely green branches that swayed in the sunlight—just right for a boy to climb, they were—and reaching clear to the heavens."

- "'You fool!'" shrieked his mother. "'You addlepated, curdle-brained nincompoop! Trading our beautiful Buttercup for a fistful of beans!' And, saying that, she flung the lot of them out the window."

7. Look again at the phrases you wrote for item 4 above. How might you change those phrases for a younger audience? An older one?

8. Use the suggestions from chapter 2 to help others improve their telling of a story. Ask for their help with yours.

9. Write descriptions for the characters in a story you plan to tell. Are there phrases you'll want to incorporate into your telling?

STORY SOURCES

Even the smallest city library carries collections of folk and fairy tales. My own university, San Diego State, lists more than five hundred entries under the single topic TALES—collections of stories from every cultural and ethnic group in the world.

Do not be put off by older copyright dates. My favorite edition of Andersen's *Fairy Tales and Stories,* edited by Signe Toksvig and Illustrated by Eric Pape, with hand-cut silhouettes by H.C. Andersen, was published by Macmillan in 1921.

While books will probably be your primary access to stories, you can gain first hand acquaintance with stories and their telling at storytelling festivals. Storytelling records and tapes are becoming increasingly prevalent. A catalog of some of the finest tapes and cassettes being made today is available from August House Publishers, P.O. Box 3223, Little Rock, Arkansas 72203.

Always remember, when using the work of another storyteller as a basis for your own telling, to give credit to the originator of the tale. And remember, too, your best tellings will be your own—don't imitate. Seek out various retellings, searching for those with the freshest and richest language. Pick and choose from the several versions of a story those bits which best suit you, and build your story from those.

Here are a few books to start you off:

Arbuthnot, May Hill. *The Arbuthnot Anthology of Children's Literature.* Illustrated by Arthur Paul and others. Glenview, Illinois: Scott, Foresman, 1952. Contains folktales, fables, myths, and fairy tales in addition to many other excellent stories suitable for telling.

Arbuthnot, May Hill and Mark Taylor. *Time for New Magic.* Illustrated by John Averill, Rainey Bennett, Wade Ray, Seymour Rosofsky, and Debi Sussmann. Glenview, Illinois & London: Scott, Foresman, 1971. This book, completed after May Hill Arbuthnot's death in 1969, is a representative collection of modern fanciful tales for children and young adults. Brief sketches of many fairy tale authors are given, along with special introductions, introductions to the stories themselves, and suggestions for their use.

Arbuthnot, May Hill and Mark Taylor. *Time for Old Magic.* Illustrated by John Averill, Wade Ray, Seymour Rosofsky, Debi Sussman, and Rainey Bennett. Glenview, Illinois & London: Scott, Foresman, 1970. This is a rich and varied collection of folktales, myths, and legends suitable for the storyteller and for listeners of all ages, though particularly ages four to fourteen.

Baker, Augusta. *The Talking Tree and Other Stories: Fifteen Tales from Fifteen Lands.* Illustrated by Johannes Troyer. Philadelphia and New York: J.B. Lippincott, 1955. Miss Baker retells fifteen delightful stories from various countries around the world.

Berger, Terry. *Black Fairy Tales*. Illustrated by David Omar White. New York: Atheneum, 1970. Handsome black and white illustrations complement these pithy tales and form an interesting contrast to similar tales from the Anglo-European experience.

Birch, Cyril. *Stories from a Ming Collection: The Art of the Chinese Storyteller*. New York: Grove Press, Inc., 1958. Here are eight stories translated by Mr. Birch from short stories first published in Soochow in 1620. Stories like these provide a window through which one can view Chinese culture of several hundred years ago.

Bryan, Ashley. *Beat the Story-Drum, Pum-Pum*. Illustrated by the author. New York: Macmillan, 1980. Wonderful woodcuts in black, orange, and red illustrate this charming collection of African tales, retold by Ashley Bryan. "Frog and Hen once met. They walked along together. Hen strut two steps, pecked at a bug. Frog bopped three hops, flicked his tongue at a fly ..."—it's not difficult to imagine the fun a storyteller would have, getting that story ready for telling.

Carey, Bonnie. *Baba Yaga's Geese and Other Russian Stories*. Translated and adapted by the author. Illustrated by Guy Fleming. Bloomington: Indiana University Press, 1973. Witty and sardonic stories.

Chase, Richard, ed. *Grandfather Tales: American-English Folk Tales*. Illustrated by Berkeley Williams, Jr. Boston: Houghton Mifflin, 1948. Wonderful retellings of traditional English tales marvelously transmogrified in the hill country of North Carolina.

Clarkson, Atelia and Gilbert B. Cross. *World Folktales*. New York: Charles Scribner's Sons, 1980. The authors have carefully chosen tales representative of the major geographical, ethnic and cultural regions of the world, along with an introduction to the study of the folktale and suggestions for further reading.

Courlander, Harold and George Herzog. *The Cow Tail Switch and Other West African Stories*. Illustrated by Madye Lee Chastain. New York: Holt, Rinehart & Winston, 1947. Amusing stories featuring traditional West African characters, collected by the authors from villages and towns throughout West Africa.

David, Alfred, and Mary Elizabeth Meek. *The Twelve Dancing Princesses and Other Fairy Tales*. Bloomington: Indiana University Press, 1974. An unusual collection of fairy tales, ranging from Grimm and Perrault to Oscar Wilde and James Thurber, with a fine introduction and new translations, many by David and Mary Meek.

Fillmore, Parker. *Mighty Mikko: a Book of Finnish Fairy Tales and Folk Tales*. Illustrated by Jay Van Everen. New York: Harcourt, Brace, 1922. Versions of Finnish stories, among which is "Terrible Olli," featured in the first edition of this book.

Fowke, Edith. *Folklore of Canda*. Toronto: McClelland and Stewart Limited, 1976. This collection of folktales and folklore includes regional stories, songs, and sayings collected throughout Canada. A sample: "Strong Wind," told by Alex R. McTavish. "... The wind at Macleod ... it blew so strong it blew a cow up against the barn. She starved to death before she could get down."

Grimm, Jakob Ludwig and Karl. *Grimms Fairy Tales, by The Brothers Grimm*. Translated and edited by Ralph Manheim. Garden City, NY: Doubleday, 1977. This translation is generally accepted as the premier collection of these strange and haunting stories which sprang out of the folk experience of Germany hundreds of years ago.

Hutchinson, Veronica S. *Chimney Corner Fairy Tales*. Illustrated by Lois Lenski. New York: Minton, Balch, 1926. This charming old book, the joint effort of two talented storytellers, has many tales just right for the younger child. Miss Lenski's illustrations are, as usual, delightful.

Jacobs, Joseph. *English Fairy Tales*. Third Edition. Illustrated by J. D. Batten. New York: G. P. Putnam, 1892. Classic collection of traditional English fairy tales, in which the humor and dramatic power is preserved by Jacobs. Includes "Mr. Fox," one of the most macabre of folktales.

Jordon, Philip D. *The Burro Benedicto and Other Folk Tales and Legends of Mexico*. Illustrated by R. M. Powers. New York: David McKay, 1960. Fresh and charming stories of Old Mexico, showing the influence both of the ancient Indian mythology and the coming of the Spanish.

Joseph, Joan. *Folk Toys Around the World and How to Make Them*. Illustrated by Mel Furukawa, with working drawings and instructions by Glenn Wagner. New York: Parents' Magazine Press, in Cooperation with UNICEF, 1972. Spear-the-fish, flip balls, prisoner's locks, thumb pianos, bull roarers—these and fifteen other toys are discussed, together with illustrations and working drawings. Should you wish to begin a collection of your own hand-made toys, this book, together with Dick Schnacke's (also included in this list) make a good starting point.

Kennedy, Richard. *Collected Stories*. Illustrated by Marcia Sewell. New York: Harper & Row, 1987. When Richard Kennedy published his first picture book, *The Parrot and the Thief* (reprinted in this collection) one reviewer wrote, "Kennedy's first sentence is assurance enough that the storytelling tradition is in good hands." Since that first story, Kennedy has demonstrated again and again a remarkable ear for language, and a rich blend of the miraculous and the ordinary.

Lang, Andrew, ed. *The Green Fairy Book*. Illustrated by H.J. Ford. London: Longmans, Green and Co., 1906. There are eleven other volumes, equally well done, with stories from all over the world, in this classic series.

Pyle, Howard. *The Wonder Clock*. New York: Harper, 1887, 1915. Another fine collection of stories, told and illustrated with inimitable Pyle wit and delicacy.

Philip, Neil. *Fairy Tales of Eastern Europe*. Illustrated by Larry Wilkes. New York: Clarion Books, 1991. "One of the best and most precious things we have on earth is the treasure trove of stories taken down by folklorists from the lips of narrators whose artistry would never otherwise have been known …" So concludes Philip in the introduction to this handsome collection of stories from the countries of eastern Europe.

Schnacke, Dick. *American Folk Toys: How to Make Them*. New York: Penguin Books, 1977. Dick Schnacke helped organize the Mountain States Art and Craft Fair for the West Virginia Centennial in 1963. This book springs from Schnacke's experiences as a toy maker. Excellent directions and helpful drawings will encourage even the most inexperienced wood-worker.

Sherlock, Philip. *West Indian Folk Tales*. Illustrated by Joan Kiddel-Monroe. New York: Henry Z. Walck, 1966. Vigorously told tales, these form a part of the myths and legends series, including books of stories from fifteen different cultures.

Sherlock, Philip. *Anansi, the Spider Man*. Illustrated by Marcia Brown. New York: Thomas Y. Crowell, 1954. Jamaican folktales, rooted in Africa.

Singer, Isaac Bashevis. *Stories for Children*. New York: Farrar, Straus & Giroux, 1985. In the introduction to this lively collection of his original tales, originally told in Yiddish, Mr. Singer says, "the power of the word is the best medium to inform and entertain the minds of our youngsters ..." Reading the stories, one is grateful there are no illustrations—they'd only be in the way.

Stoutenburg, Adrien. *American Tall Tale Animals*. Illustrated by Glen Rounds. New York: Viking, 1968. Another collection—remember *The Hurricane's Children?*— for those times when you feel like stretching the truth a little.

United Nations Women's Guild. *Ride with the Sun!* Edited by Harold Courlander for the United Nations Women's Guild. Illustrated by Roger Duvoison. New York: McGraw-Hill, 1955. An anthology of old tales collected from all countries within the United Nations, well written and well illustrated.

Yeats, William Butler. *Irish Folk Stories and Fairy Tales*. New York: Grosset & Dunlap, 1972. Ireland's great modern poet retells Irish stories and tales. Yeats has, as he puts it, "... tried to make [the book] representative, as far as so few pages would allow, of every kind of Irish folk-faith."

4. The Experience Story

Yet things happen. People live, love, struggle, vanquish, or are
vanquished, and they tell about it. They tell about their own
experience and the experience of others, and sometimes the
telling is interrupted with "That's not the way I heard it!"

—KENNETH AND MARY CLARKE[1]

Guess who called today!" my wife says.

I try. "Eleanor?"

"No, farther back than Eleanor."

I dig deeper. "Janie? Bev?"—The names of girls she lived with in college.

"No." And then she tells me. "John!"

"John? Really?"

And I'm back at Grove Elementary, where John and I taught school
together—our children riding the bus down out of the narrow Walla Walla River valley where their families raised apples and prunes on farms tucked between the river
and the steep canyon walls. I remember the town of LaGrande, high in the mountains, sweet with the August incense of pine resin, and John losing his wallet, with all
his honeymoon money in it, two hours before his wedding to Louise, and not blink-
ing an eye over its loss. (As best man I recommended he call off the marriage—I read
the loss as an omen.) I remember Portland, Oregon, sitting with John and Louise in
the dark, varnished clutter of Dan and Louie's Oyster Bar, happily coaxing shimmer-
ing oysters from their halfshells, steins of beer and bottles of tabasco and lemon
slices and black pepper at our elbow.

And now here's John, calling us from Washington, D. C., clear across the continent, on a rain-threatened December morning just to say hello and to let us know
that Louise and he and Heidi and Susan are well and thinking of us.

It's better than finding gold. It's finding a story, a stirring of memories—it's
finding my old and dear friend again.

When we think of the storyteller and his stock in trade, we tend to think of
folktales and fairy tales. But that's too narrow a view. All life experiences, whether
they come from reading, listening, doing, or imagining are the sources for stories.

After all, what is a story? To the historian the founding of a new country is a dramatic tale. A biologist might see in the 1938 appearance of the first living species of the coelacanth the fascinating stuff of a story. An investor, reading stock reports, sees a story in the rise and fall of the market. And Bartholomew Cubbins narrates events that happen only in his imagination in Dr. Seuss's *And to Think That I Saw It on Mulberry Street!* Plot, characters, setting, meaning—all lie in the stream of experiences in which we live.

And the range is endless. The story may be set in Finland, or African waters, or Baja California, or within the confines of a tea cup. It can happen "Years ago, when the world was young," or yesterday, or Sunday come next. It can be peopled with tyrants, humpbacked fish, or ourselves, and can range all the way from the ritualized formula of a fairy tale to the anecdotal impressions of a phone call.

Generally, though, the homemade stories that catch and hold our listeners in the tightest grip are accounts of happenings in our own lives—events that stirred our emotions at the time of their happening, and imprinted themselves on our memories. Perhaps it was the day a fierce rooster from the neighboring house came over and made friends with two little girls, letting itself be carried around in their arms as if it were a complacent cat. Or that lonely evening in a hospital, with the melancholy hum of machinery in the air, when the young patient misunderstood his nurse's instructions and agonized over the appropriate use of a bedpan. Perhaps it was that sticky gray morning at the train station in Shanghai when the American tourists realized they'd been abandoned by their young Chinese guide. Or that fine spring day when Paul and I sailed out into the Gulf of California in my sailboat to buy shrimp for supper.

In themselves, of course, memories are not sufficient to make good stories. Memories are just the starter. Take the incident in Baja California. What kind of story might one tell about that? It depends, of course, on who's telling it. Here's my recollection.

Camarones, Camarones

Shrimp. Wrapped in bacon, roasting over coals. Or ice cold, pink and orange, drizzled with lime juice and salt. We'd dreamed of shrimp all winter. And now, we were going to get our wish. Tomorrow, for sure.

We'd driven down into Baja California to camp for a few days during the Easter Holidays. We spent the first night in San Felipe—a fishing village on the Gulf of California, arriving at sunset—the sea golden with evening light, gulls wheeling overhead, the high barren mountains behind us, sand and dust everywhere. Main street swarmed with sad-eyed dogs and college kids boozing it up on cheap beer. Peddlers hawked clams, tortillas, fire-crackers, and enchiladas, fish tacos, coconuts and mangoes—everything but shrimp—from their tricycle stands. Half naked children sucked on huge bottles of Pepsi-Cola. Battered pickups and four-wheel-drive trucks lumbered through town on their way into or out of the back country.

It was in San Felipe, the next morning, that we first tried to buy *los camarones gigantes*—giant shrimp—for which these waters are famous. We went to the Chinese grocery store, a squat blue stucco building open in the front—reputed to sell everything—but the clerk shook his head. *"No camarones hoy,"* he said, his pigtail swinging from side to side under his black silk cap. *"Mañana."* He pointed down the street. There was a restaurant, he'd heard, where one might buy uncooked shrimp by the kilo. But when we asked the proprietor, a fat man wearing a dirty apron, he shook his head. *"Mañana,"* he said. *"Camarones mañana."*

We tried all over town, but everywhere the answer was the same.

"Mañana."

But we couldn't wait until tomorrow. Our vacation was too short as it was, and we were headed for Persebú, a good two hours away if we were lucky and didn't get stuck in the sand. Maybe next year, we told ourselves. Shrimp next year, for sure.

So we headed out. The road south was terrible; rocks the size of cantaloupe, bottomless sand where there wasn't any rock. We got stuck three times. But finally we inched past the last range of mountains and swung east toward the sea. We pitched our tents in a line along the top of the high white sand dunes and looked out at the warm clear waters, empty as far as we could see.

We'd brought with us three tiny sailboats—Sunfish, if you know the make. All that day we sailed them. When night came, after supper, we gathered around the camp fire and sang songs, "Where Have All the Flowers Gone?" and "Careless Love," "Never Get to Heaven," and "Gypsy Davey." The guitars and banjos jangled and twanged, and white stars glittered in the desert sky.

Later, after we had turned in for the night, I woke, puzzled. I could hear, in the distance, a throbbing sound, like a deisel engine makes. But before I could ponder its meaning, I was asleep again.

In the morning, though, there it was, plain as day—a boat—far out in the gulf. With its dark hull and strange projections on either side it looked like a giant bird resting on the water.

"It's a shrimp boat," Roy said. "It's got to be."

We stood looking at it.

"Why don't we sail out and see if we can buy some shrimp?" Paul suggested.

We talked it over. What if it wasn't a shrimp boat? What if, when we were halfway there, the boat decided to leave? What if we got there, and the people didn't like gringos?

We drank a beer, and swam, and watched the tide change.

"Tomorrow," someone said. "If it's still there tomorrow, we'll go."

"I vote for going this afternoon," Paul said, "And if nobody wants to come along, I'll go by myself."

That settled it. If one of us went, we were all going. So after lunch we stashed three one-dollar bills in our swimming trunks and set out. Perfect weather. A light breeze was blowing, and soon we were skipping over the water. Unfortunately, the wind was blowing from the southeast, exactly where the boat lay. And in that clear air distances were hard to judge. We sailed and sailed, tacking back and forth. The longer we sailed, the farther away it seemed.

Two of the boats turned back, but Paul and I sailed on. And then, just like that, the breeze shifted. Soon we were close enough to read the boat's name painted in white on her stern. *María de la Noche.*

We'd be aboard in five minutes, we told ourselves. We looked at the other boats, nearly out of sight. They'd be sorry now they'd turned back.

But then the breeze faded away into nothing and the afternoon tide began to bore in.

So close, but with no wind and the tide against us, we simply could not draw nearer. I pulled the dagger board up and began to paddle. Paul steered. Bit by bit we closed the distance.

Then I heard a shout. Paul had fallen in. I reached for him—and fell in myself. I managed to grab a line as our sailboat drifted past, and soon we were back on board again.

"They must think we're a couple of idiots," I said.

Paul laughed. "They're right."

We were close enough now to begin making out details on the *María*. She was a large, handsome ship, perhaps sixty feet in length, her lower half painted dull red; her top half a tarry black. The two wings we'd observed from shore were great arms reaching out from either side to catch and hold nets. A wooden platform, large enough for two men to stand on, hung at the end of each arm.

Two figures stood on deck, gazing down at us, unsmiling.

It occurred to me, just about then, that we were a very long way from shore. The air took on a sudden chill.

I shivered. "What'd you think?"

"About what?"

"What if they don't like gringos?"

Paul shrugged. "We've come this far, we're not turning back."

We were in shadow now, nearly alongside. Gazing up, the shrimp boat seemed big. Very big.

"*¡Camarones!*" I called. "*¿Tienen camarones?*"

Gold teeth flashed. A smile.

"*¡Si! Camarones!*"

They threw us a line. and dropped down a rope ladder. Brown hands lashed the Sunfish fast, and we scrambled up the tarry hull.

There were three fishermen—a middle aged man—the one with the flashing gold teeth—apparently the captain of the vessel; a boy, surely no more than twelve years of age, with a tangle of black hair—barefooted and wiry; and an old man—his toes creeping out from an ancient pair of cowboy boots—who hobbled out of sight as soon as we came on board.

The captain observed my shivering beneath my wet shirt and swimming trunks. "*¿Café?*" he asked, with as much dignity as if we were at a formal dinner.

I wish I could tell you how we sat there on that sun-filled deck, drinking steaming black coffee sweetened with condensed milk, holding the thick china mugs cupped between our hands. But that did not happen. All we could think of was the shrimp we had come so far to get, and the long, long way back to shore. And whether the cups would be clean. We shook our heads. *"No, grácias."*

The captain sat down on the canvas-covered hatch, motioning us to join him. It was apparent that his knowledge of English was as limited as was our facility with Spanish. But the meaning was clear. What did we have to trade? *¿Manzanas? ¿Naranjas? ¿Cerveza?* He tipped his head back and his adam's apple bobbed up and down in a pantomime of drinking.

I wished from my heart that we had apples and oranges and a case of beer to give to them. But all we had were the three bits of paper money, still soggy but intact. *"No tengamos naranjas o cerveza,"* I said in my halting Spanish, *"pero tengamos dinero."* I fished out the sodden wad of green paper.

He shrugged his shoulders and described an arc with his arm as if to ask where in that broad expanse he would spend it. *"No queremos dinero,"* he said. *"Queremos naranjas, cerveza, manzanas ..."*

He sat and gazed off into the distance, indicating a willingness to wait patiently until we conjured up what he wanted.

Paul and I looked at one another. What should we do? Get on our boat and sail back to camp? Why hadn't we thought to bring fruit and beer, instead of money?

Suddenly the captain got up from the hatch. He shouted something to the boy, who scooted forward to the cabin. We waited, not knowing whether we had been dismissed or not. The boy returned, a large, battered bucket in his hand.

The captain motioned for us to get up. He lifted the bleached canvas cover from the hatch and raised the wooden boards. The smell of fish and diesel fumes and wet burlap and manila hemp and the sea wafted up from the dark hold. He climbed down a rough wooden ladder with the bucket. Berth after berth was filled with crushed ice and shrimp—gigantic shrimp—some of them more than eight inches long.

He tossed one up to us. *"Camarones muy grandes,"* he said, pride in his voice. The bucket was full now. He threw on a few more for good measure and climbed back up the ladder, handing the bucket to us with more flashing of gold teeth.

We carried the pail over to the side and dumped its contents into the cockpit of the sailboat. I sought for some way to show our thanks. I pulled the money from my pocket and handed it to him. He shook his head. No. *"Es para el niño."* I said, thrusting the money into his hand, nodding at the boy.

I scrambled over the side and into our little boat. *"Grácias, grácias,"* we shouted as we sailed away. *"Adiós."*

Five minutes later, we looked back. We'd come a good distance, but could see, clearly, the three of them standing on deck, waving.

The trip back to camp was remarkably brief. Well before the sun had dropped out of sight we were beaching our craft on the sand, while children and grownups clustered around, admiring our haul.

That night we sat by the campfire and roasted shrimp wrapped in bacon and dipped in salsa picante—a fiery pepper sauce. In the distance we could hear the drum, drum, drumming of deisel engines. We could see the shrimp boat's dim lights. We talked of tomorrow. In the morning, first thing, we told ourselves, we'd sail out to them with regalos—presents—fresh fruit and beer. We'd take candy for the boy, and a pair of sandals for the old man.

Morning came. Beautiful, as usual. A slow breakfast. A walk in the desert. *Cerveza*. Lunch. A little nap. We talked about the fishermen. Somehow, the day was getting away from us. Tomorrow, for sure, we'd head out with our gifts. Today, we needed to rest up.

We ate iced shrimp drizzled with lime juice that evening while sipping our margueritas. We sauteed shrimp in garlic sauce for supper.

Late that night, something woke me. It was the sound of diesel engines, echoing across the water. The same, but different, though I couldn't say how. Before I could figure it out, I was asleep again.

The next morning, though, when I stumbled from my tent, the sea was empty.

The first time I told "Camarones" was to a group of teachers in Michigan. It was a cold, gray spring day, the whole landscape still crushed from the weight of winter. My family had been in Baja just weeks before, and the expedition out to the shrimp boat was bright in my mind, further sharpened by the contrast with this late winter storm far to the north.

A throng of details swarmed in my memory of that entire camping expedition: morning sunrises, hikes across the desert, the texture of a jellyfish, the velvety darkness of a desert sky.

Clearly, all that had happened could not and should not be included in that telling. But what to omit? To answer that question, I asked myself another: what framed that experience?

It seemed to me that the answer lay in the contrast between the Mexican fishermen and us—their lack of material things contrasted with our affluence; their dignity and our brash assertiveness.

In preparing the story for telling, then, details were selected that would call attention to that contrast, first in San Felipe, where beat-up trucks mingled with expensive four-wheel-drive vehicles, and carefree tourists bargained with ragged peddlers, and again on the shrimp boat, where our hurried and thoughtless manners were set against the deliberate and hospitable actions of the fishermen. Details were chosen to point out this contrast: our failure to greet them except to ask if they had shrimp, our hesitancy to sit down and drink a cup of coffee with them, our rush to depart, our half-hearted good intentions—all of these in sharp opposition to their obvious good will and generous sharing.

One reason for the appeal of "Camarones" is that it's clearly a story that carries meanings for the teller. It's more than an amusing adventure or a minor escapade; it's an account of contact between people and of the joy and sober reflection brought about by that contact.

Some other teller, living that same experience, might have found a different meaning in those events—his perceptions drawing him down another pathway from mine. It would be his story. No other story in the world could ever be quite like it.

A second reason that "Camarones"—and, for that matter, any experience story—holds such interest for the listener lies in the personal involvement we listeners feel with the teller. He was there; he drove the sand ruts of Baja, he scuffed his feet in the streets of San Felipe. He sailed those blue gulf waters, he climbed aboard the shrimp boat. All those details, and a hundred others, are immediately available to the teller. They're what makes the story fascinating. To the teller. And to his audience, as well.

You will not want to tell "Camarones." It's not your story. But there are many of your own experiences that make good stories. Think back to your own past. The weddings and funerals and wartime heart-breaks and fourth of July celebrations. The lost children. The accidents. The quarrel with a brother or sister or close friend.

Remember your father, uncle, or grandmother telling stories of events that stuck fast in their memories—strawing the road during the dusty summer days? Or that springtime morning when a band of Umatilla Indians, riding through, carried a child off for a quick gallop across the big front hayfield and back? Or when the family bought its first motion picture camera or video recorder? Or that warm August night when you should have been home in bed, and instead slipped out the window and off the porch and down the lane, dazzled by moonlight, looking for adventure?

What was it about those stories that made them memorable, both to the teller and to you?

"Strawing the Road" was told to me by my Aunt Winnie, when she was almost ninety. Seven miles of dirt road ran from the Oregon State Line to Walla Walla, and folks living along the road had gotten together and decided to "lay down" the dust. She was one of the girls who carried water to the men as they labored.

As she told the story I caught glimpses in her face of the girl who flirted with those young men as she ladled out dippers of water for them. "Goodness!" she mused, "Has it really been that long ago?"

What events in your life have that same clarity and vividness? Make a list, choosing from the thousands of happenings in your life the fifteen or twenty that stick in your consciousness.

Once you have these happenings listed, take a second look at them. Is there a common thread running through them; some quality or characteristic that resonates like the beat of a drum? It is, I believe, through this search for meaning that the storyteller begins to recall the nuances of an event that give it color and emotion. These stories—the ones that pack the biggest emotional wallop, are the ones you'll want to prepare.

Give the Story a Time and a Place

"Once upon a time and in a far-off place ..." is the beginning of many folk and fairy tales. In experience stories we create our own distant time and special place. Baja California is, for me, a wild and exotic landscape, and it is satisfying to share its lonely grandeur with listeners who have not been there. But the setting need not be exotic. The right words can make any place special. After all, *The Tale of Peter Rabbit,* one of the best loved of all stories, occurred in a vegetable garden.

What can you remember about the place where your own story took place? Was it outside, or in a house? If in a house, what was the house made of? Stone? Wood? Adobe? What time of day was it? What was the light like? What odors do you remember? What colors? What sounds and feelings?

Ask yourself these questions and others to stir up those memories you have stored away about that time and place. Then select the words that will help your listeners see and feel and touch that room, that field, that path in the same way you did. And remember, the setting of the story doesn't quit after you've named it in those beginning sentences. Rather, words and phrases chosen throughout the telling help the listener maintain a sense of being in the place described.

Choosing Details that Bring Characters to Life

We probably err, as storytellers, in pausing in our narration to describe characters. A better way, although it is more difficult, is to let the characters describe themselves by their actions. Here is a part of Carl Sandburg's word picture of Abraham Lincoln:

> *As he took on more length, they said he was shooting up into the air like green corn in the summer of a good corn year. So he grew. When he reached seventeen years of age, and they measured him, he was six feet, nearly four inches high, from the bottoms of his moccasins to the top of his skull.*
>
> *These were years he was handling the ax. Except in spring plowing time and the fall fodder pulling, he was handling the ax nearly all the time. He cleared openings in the timber, cut logs and puncheons, split fire wood, built pigpens ...*[2]

In this description, much more than physical characteristics are being told. Sandburg's choice of phrases—"Like green corn in the summer of a good corn year," "cleared openings in the timber," "built pigpens"—help with the setting of the story, as well as describing Lincoln's growth. "He was handling the ax nearly all the time" tells us he was tough and hard, but it also gives us insight into the life he led and into the willingness he displayed to participate in that life.

Think of the characters in the story you are planning to tell. What are salient aspects—mannerisms, demeanor, clothing, speech, behaviors—that you wish to share with your listeners? Jot down phrases and sentences that seem to carry the impressions you wish to convey. Try these out, saying them aloud. Are they comfortable phrases, natural and easy, or are they "literary"? Remember, you want your story to sound like you, talking. Avoid fancy language.

Cutting and Shaping the Original Incident

There is something inside most of us that quakes at the idea of altering the facts when we tell a story. Does it originate in our early teachings—"Thou Shalt Not Lie"? Will some omnipotent force reach out its righteous arm and strike dead the deceitful storyteller?

And yet, we all recognize that stories need pruning, cutting, shaping, and polishing. Early one spring, long ago, a couple of drifters—Jorge and Tex—showed up at the ranch, looking for work. My father set them to cutting asparagus. Tex wanted a guitar. He could talk of nothing else, and after the first pay check, he asked my father to drive him to town where he toured the pawnshops. He found the guitar he wanted and brought it home. That was Saturday.

Sunday afternoon my father walked over to the bunk house to visit for a few minutes. He asked Tex to play for him. Tex refused. He couldn't. The guitar was gone, he said. Vanished.

Father came back to the house, puzzled. "Funny thing," he told Mother. "I believe Tex did something to that guitar."

He was right. Later, when Tex wasn't around, Jorge told him what had happened. Tex hadn't been able to produce the sounds he'd hoped for from the guitar. Convinced that some evil spirit lurked inside, he'd smashed it up and thrown it in the stove.

There is, in that brief account, the yeast for a story. But it needs work. We can understand Tex's urge to destroy the guitar—if for no other reason than to battle forces beyond his power to control. Here, for me, is the heart of the story and its central truth. Rearranging and illuminating details can strengthen that truth.

Describing how Tex earned the price of the guitar—the tedious hours bent over, stooping and cutting asparagus from daylight until dusk, helping the listener see, perhaps for the first time, a field during harvest, when the casual glance says there's nothing there but an empty brown expanse, and only on closer inspection does one begin to see slender stalks breaking apart the heavy soil; pondering the bond that held Jorge, quick-witted and rational, to his slow-minded and ghost-haunted companion; reconstructing the incident so that the listener gains insight into Tex's character, perhaps by inserting clues and hints earlier in the story—these are a few of the aspects of the story that one might select for amplification and change.

In his lively autobiography, *Seven Horizons*, Newbery Award winner Charles

Finger tells of adventures that took him from his proper Victorian English home and carried him to Patagonia and Tierra Del Fuego. At one point in his account, Mr. Finger says:

> *I went to work with an odd company, bossing the loading of the Bootle, (a barkentine that carried wool, and hides, and tallow) and, with the money thus earned, I bought a couple of horses and gear. So the way lay open for limitless adventure, and much of that adventure I have told in my books, with a certain amount of imaginative trimmings. I have elaborated and transmuted because I could not help doing so; and I could not help doing so because, almost unconsciously, some particle in my brain insisted that to foreshorten here, and to color there, here to add and there to diminish, would make for a sort of completeness. If you drag something from its context you must need trim edges, satisfying yourself with the comforting and uplifting conclusion that Art Betters Nature.*[3]

There! If Charles Finger doesn't object to "elaborating and transmuting," neither should you nor I.

Recording the Story

One of the finest storytellers I ever knew could scarcely write his own name, and he surely never worked his way through a tangle of steps in preparing a story for telling.

I last visited him as he lay in the hospital, out of his mind with old age and so feeble that he could not raise himself up to look at me. He rambled on about wild horses, and boys that had never been thrown, and hinted vaguely of a treasure that lay in the bunk house cellar that they'd never find. As I was leaving, he said, with a hint of the old strut and fire, "Damned good thing you didn't come tomorry. You'd not find me here."

"Why, where will you be going tomorrow, Shorty?" I asked, as ready to believe as when I was a boy of five.

"Why, we're agoin' to work in the spuds tomorry," he said querulously, as if any fool ought to have known that. "Elmer and Red and me. We got the whole Baker place to dig before the frost gits' 'em. Yes, sir, by grab, we'll be out there a workin' long before *you've* tumbled out of bed ..."

And I believed him! Autumn smoke and muddy lanes under a silvering of frost, blackened potato vines and white potato flesh inside a warty hide—all this and more was carried along on Shorty's words. I could see him tomorrow morning, good as ever, bib overalls fringed at the cuff with wear, a sweaty Stetson hat slouched down over his forehead, digging spuds while I slept my way through private dreams.

Shorty needn't record his stories. But for those of us who possess less of the gift than he, pencil and paper or a tape recorder can be a powerful aid. We've been, most of us, pretty much brought up on the printed word. That I wrote these lines and that you're reading them is one evidence of our difference from Shorty. For us, recording our story in one way or another helps organize our material. Talk through the story into a tape or cassette recorder. Jot down notes and make an outline. Write out a draft of the story and edit it by reading it aloud and testing to see whether it sounds like talk written down.

Engaging in part or all of these activities encourages us to be both pungent and concise in what we say. Furthermore, recording the story helps us know how long the account promises to be, and gives us a chance to "trim edges," as Charles Finger puts it. Most importantly, though, this written or spoken record reveals to us if we've made clear to others the meanings we intended to bring to the story.

Practicing the Story

All that we talked about in the preceding chapter is true here as well: organizing the story into bits for telling; getting fluent with the beginning and conclusion; planning an introduction that will arouse the listener's interest and give him time to get ready for the story; selecting a vocabulary that is appropriate both for the story and to the persons in the audience; developing phrases and words that draw clear and vivid pictures for your listeners; experimenting with various inflectional patterns—all of these considerations separate mediocre stories from good ones.

Experience stories can be as dull as last week's newspaper. Who hasn't sat, bored beyond belief, while an acquaintance launches into one personal recollection after another? "To make a long story short" frequently accompanies such tales. Despite our invariable hopes, the teller never does.

On the other hand, personal experiences can be among the deepest and truest of the stories you tell. They represent an effort on your part to share yourself, taking a happening in your life and shining a light on it for others to see.

And If You Are a Teacher ...

While our concern in these pages has been with the person who wants to become a storyteller, much of what we've been talking about can be translated into language activities with children in the classroom.

By now, I guess that just about every teacher in the world has had some practice using the language experience approach to the teaching of reading. This "method" encourages the child to talk about what she has experienced. What she says is written down by a teacher or aide and then read back to her. As she listens to and follows along with what is read the child confirms the fact that talk can be written down.

Using text that has developed out of her own oral language she begins to learn words, phrases, and sentences. She discovers that she can edit, transform, and repeat language patterns in writing. The road to literacy through such a technique is accompanied by powerful feelings of personal worth and satisfaction. The child starts to think of herself as someone who has something important to say; important enough that others will listen to it, record it, and preserve it by writing it down.

To some extent, what we've been talking about in this chapter fits rather tidily with those language experiences in the reading and writing development of children. Except that here we are really looking at another dimension of language: taking little pieces of our own experiences and transforming them into stories for sharing with an audience.

I'd like to suggest that we augment the traditional language experience reading and writing program in the classroom with storytelling. Why not encourage children to record their experiences on tape, or write them down if they are that far along in their academic development? These stories can then be shaped, altered, edited, and pruned so that they are, as Charles Finger puts it, " ... nature improved upon by art."

As the result of this suggestion, one of my students—herself a sixth-grade teacher—initiated a story-hour in her classroom. Children began sharing their experiences with one another. They studied what makes for a good story and shaped their stories so that they would be more interesting. They developed dialogue for characters, practiced voice changes to suit persons in the story, and told bits of the story into a tape recorder for self-appraisal. Gradually, they began to include old traditional tales, songs, and dances their teacher taught them, and offered their talents to the rest of the school as wandering troubadours.

When I visited them, they were costumed for a performance. Tomás was dressed in a wet suit, packing his surf board. He was telling a story about surfing in five-foot waves that struck our coastline during a recent storm. Alex, wearing denims and cowboy boots, had spent the summer with her uncle and aunt in the high country of Oregon. She was going to discuss steer roping. Nguyen, Suzanne, and Imber had taken a craft class at a local recreation center and planned to demonstrate several folk toys they had whittled during that time. They had the makings of another toy— a buzz saw—they planned to teach some third graders to make. (I had always called the same toy a moon-spinner, and had made one myself years ago.)

What these young people were doing was fresh and natural and bubbling with vitality. I began to imagine similar classrooms all over America participating in a kind of renaissance among the young, plying the ancient art and craft of tale telling, enriching their own lives and the lives of others as they shared in the magic of story-telling.

NOTES

1. Kenneth and Mary Clarke, *The Harvest and The Reapers: Oral Traditions of Kentucky* (Louisville: The University Press of Kentucky, 1974), p. 3.

2.Carl Sandburg, *Abe Lincoln Grows Up* (New York: Harcourt Brace Jovanovich, 1928), p. 66.

3. Charles J. Finger, *Seven Horizons* (Garden City, New York: Doubleday, Doran, 1930), pp. 294-95.

ACTIVITIES

1. If you have not yet written down the fifteen or so experiences out of your past that have struck you as important, do so now. What aspects of those experiences served as yeast? Was it a quality of kindness or cruelty? A ghostliness or a sense of the ludicrous? Try to remember back to each time, your own feelings then, and the quality that was central to the experience.

2. Dreams form key experiences for many of us. I find a vividness and color in my own dreams that stays with me long after the light of day has swept night from the room. Patterns emerge; while the dreams may range widely in content and characters, they seem to play on central themes. You might wish to begin a dream journal, and study the content for story material. You will, I suspect, be struck by the rich and wild imaginings of the unconscious mind at play.

3. Write a paragraph describing a room you remember vividly from your child-hood. You will be surprised at how much you remember. The more you recall, the more springs to mind. Here's my bedroom:

> At the top of the stairs, to the right of the landing, was my room—a jumble of angled walls covered with wide wooden boards, their warped surfaces showing through wall paper freckled with age. A linoleum carpet of white and jade green covered most of the floor. A hassock squatted like a giant plump orange in the middle of the room. I'd bought that hassock at Davis Kaiser's Furniture Emporium with money I earned scything grass in the orchard. Thinking back, I believe it was just about the most handsome piece of furniture I ever owned.
>
> My cot, with its heavy quilts sewn from old suiting, hugged a corner under one of the sloping walls, along with a night stand, high and skinny, littered with books and a lamp and my radio.
>
> Oh, the wonder of that radio! At night, lying in bed, I could listen to voices from all across the country—Denver, San Francisco, Los Angeles. I had a front row seat at Grand Old Opry, in Nashville, where I applauded Minnie Pearl and Hank Williams. I danced, slim and elegant in my tuxedo—the heart-throb of all the girls—to ballroom music at Avalon, on Catalina Island.

My room held another magical construction. Across the floor from my cot was a grated twelve-by-twelve-inch opening that led directly downstairs into the living room. Light, pipe smoke, warmth, the sounds of my mother practicing the piano, the smell of bread baking, the voices of company visiting, Shorty's laugh, my father deep rumble, whispered secrets between my sister and her girl friends—all drifted up to me through that opening. It was the coziest place in the whole world, my bed, lying there halfway between waking and dreams, interpreting those sounds and smells ...

4. Describe your room to a friend and ask her to add other details she thinks might be a part of that room, consistent with what you have already told her. Were you able to start her processes of imagining?

5. Jot down phrases describing a person who has made an impression on you. In addition to physical characteristics, consider mannerisms, voice and speech qualities, carriage, how she "expresses" herself. Tell these characteristics to a friend and then ask the friend to describe the person based on the data you have provided.

6. Plan an experience story based on scientific fact. It might be the account of a polliwog's growth into a frog, or the life cycle of an orange, or the history of a snowflake, or the strange story of the coriander, which begins life as one herb and ends life as another. Try to choose facts you yourself have touched. Perhaps you've stood in a stream trout-fishing and seen salmon fighting their way upstream in water barely deep enough to cover their backs, or studied under a powerful lens the delicate patternings of snowflakes, or watched your cat hypnotize a lizard. The storyteller interested in pursuing further those experiences that involve plants and animals will enjoy reading *A Treasury of Science* (New York: Harper, 1958), edited by Harlow Shapley and others.

7. With a group of four or five others, tell an experience that you have each had. It might be one of the following or any of a dozen others:

> *A joyous or sorrowful time ...*
> *A holiday you remember ...*
> *The hungriest you've ever been ...*
> *A gift you received ...*
> *An exciting adventure or incident ...*

Give each person an allotment of time—no more than five to seven minutes—to sketch briefly the experience as he remembers it. Working together, make suggestions to each person that might help him develop the incident into a story suitable for sharing.

8. Working with an experience story that grows out of one of the activities named above, what shaping and transmuting can you use to give added color and drama to the incident?

9. Using the suggestions made in Chapter 2, help other tellers in the group, and ask for help from those around you.

10. If you're feeling uneasy about editing your experiences, read autobiographies, e.g., Mark Twain's *Life on the Mississippi*. Or listen to Hal Holbrook's recording of *Mark Twain Tonight* (Columbia, OS2019 OL5440). At least you'll know you're in famous company.

11. Listen to the Holbrook recording again. Notice Mr. Holbrook's use of intonation to heighten the impact of phrases and words.

12. Visit with old people as they sit and daydream on park benches. Listen to their tellings. Note phrases and words that are strange to your ear and tongue.

13. Regional storytellers have recorded repertoires which spring from their own lives. Here are a few you might enjoy:

Davis, Donald. *Listening for the Crack of Dawn: A Master Storyteller Recalls the Appalachia of His Youth*. Little Rock: August House Audio, 1991.

Klein, Susan. *Through a Ruby Window: A Martha's Vineyard Childhood*. Martha's Vineyard: Self-published, 1993.

Lieberman, Syd. *A Winner and Other Stories*. Evanston, Illinois: self-published, 1986.

May, Jim. *The Farm on Nippersink Creek: Stories from a Midwestern Childhood*. Little Rock: August House Audio, 1995.

O'Callahan, Jay. *Pill Hill Stories: Coming Home to Someplace New*. Marshfield, Massachusetts: Artana Productions, 1990.

Stivender, Ed. *Raised Catholic (Can You Tell?)*. Little Rock: August House Audio, 1994.

5. Migratory Tales: The Glimpse Inside

The essential of all folklore study is collecting and
attempting to understand that which has been collected.[1]
—Stith Thompson

Tom tied a kettle to the tail of a cat;
Jill put a stone in the blind man's hat;
Bob threw his grandmother down the stairs—
And they all grew up ugly and nobody cares.

—Anonymous

On a street corner in an old part of Walla Walla stood a time-worn wooden mansion, tall, ochre-colored, trimmed in dull black. I used to walk by that house on my way to catch the bus home from high school. Silver maples towered over it. In the winter months dead leaves piled up along the mortared foundations. Green shades covered the lower windows. Old rose bushes and hollyhocks tangled the front path.

Each day as I walked past I scrutinized the house for some sign of life. Had a chair on the front porch been moved? Was someone watching me from behind an upstairs window? In my mind I fancied all sorts of stories about the house and its occupants. Then one day my Uncle George, who knew everyone in town, told me the following story:

One rainy night, some years ago, the preacher from the Baptist Church was driving home when he saw a young girl, pale, dressed in a long white gown, standing at the corner of Main and Rose. He stopped to see if she wanted a lift. She nodded and got into the back seat. He handed his raincoat to her, so she could warm herself, and asked where she lived. She told him. He tried to make conversation, asking a few questions, but she didn't answer.

Finally, they came to the address she'd given him. He pulled over and looked back to ask her if this was the right place.

She was gone.

He couldn't believe it. He got out of the car and opened the back door, thinking maybe she'd collapsed. But she wasn't there. He looked up at the house. He saw a light on, and decided to see if anyone there knew the girl. He walked up the path and knocked on the front door. After a long time, he heard the shuffle of feet inside, moving down the hall.

The door opened. There stood a frail old woman, her hair all wispy.

He apologized for bothering her. He told her of the girl on the street corner. Did she know her?

When he finished there was a long silence.

At last the old woman spoke. "That was my daughter," she said. "She was killed at that corner where you picked her up, exactly twenty-five years ago."

You've heard the story before, of course. So have I—many times. Or one something like it. It's one of the migratory tales that has crisscrossed the world in one form or another, always told as absolutely true—but truth that one never seems quite able to pin down.

But that doesn't make any difference. Every time I go back to Walla Walla, I drive out of my way to see that house. It's been freshly painted—white, with shiny black shutters. A brass knocker gleams on the front door. The rose bushes have been trimmed. The lawn, cropped and green, shimmers in the damp morning light. The ghosts have been, perhaps, banished.

But I hope not.

Earlier, we spoke of storytelling as a gift-giving enterprise, with the tale itself a kind of offering that one person makes to another.

That's true, of course. But there's more to a story—any story—than the story itself. For stories—the best stories—rise out of complex human experiences, and are replete with meanings of one sort or another. Exploring those meanings enriches our telling—even though not one word of what we might have thought enters into the telling itself. Take, for example, "The Lady in White."

We generally agree that underlying our rational everyday world are depths of thought and experience of which we may have little conscious awareness. Dreams are one daily reminder of that unconscious life. So are the childhood memories, infantile impressions, traumas, golden hours, and minor tragedies that make up our personal experiences. A friend, for example, can't stand ice cream because of its association with a childhood tonsillectomy.

These thoughts and experiences are what Carl Jung refers to as the "personal unconscious." The personal unconscious is fairly close to the surface, yielding readily to a little detective work: Ice cream ... tonsils ... pain ... hospital ... blood ... it all seems fairly obvious. But beneath the personal unconscious is a deeper and more elementary mental storehouse. Here abide the "primary images," collective in nature, common to all of us. As Jung puts it:

The primary image, which I have termed "archetype," is always collective, i.e., common to at least whole peoples or periods of history. [It] is a memory deposit, an engram, derived from a condensation of innumerable similar experiences; the psychic expression of an anatomically, physiologically determined natural tendency.[2]

This deeper and more elementary storehouse Jung has named the "collective unconscious." In its depths are the archetypes—realities of the accumulated past—that each of us continues to seek and occasionally recognize in our daily lives. These archetypes have been formed out of centuries of experiences by a group—a tribe—of people, and thus create a part of the wisdom of the race. Often these archetypes take human form. We recognize many of them: the Virgin Princess, the Fool, the Lost Child, the Wise Old Man, the Savior (from whatever religion), the Hero, the Earth Mother—these are among the beings who play their roles in the dreams and fantasies our unconscious spins out, and who populate folk and fairy tales.

Archetypes may also manifest themselves in behaviors and situations that the race has developed throughout its history. War, separation, lost love, parental conflict, the struggle for achievement, war—these are archetypal life themes; classic events with which all of us are familiar.

We recognize, too, objects in our lives other than human that assume archetypal proportions. The yearning to be off down the road is a constant theme in the old fairy tales and folktales. The magic carpet and the flying ship have been replaced, perhaps, with the automobile. But certainly the car is a manifestation of an archetype. Like the genie of the lantern, or Pegasus, or a magic carpet, it carries us to foreign destinations. It is a willing servant who in turn demands from us our care and tribute. The Christmas tree, bread rising in the oven, the coyote who lives at the edge of civilization—these and a thousand other animals, plants and objects possess archetypal significance, even though our conscious minds may pretend not to recognize them.

Which brings us back to "The Lady in White." Let's look at that story again.

First of all, the woman in the story is dressed in white. That color conveys a sense of youth, purity, virginity—the innocence of a life just beginning. But the color white has another meaning. In the Christian account of Easter, Christ is wrapped in a white shroud and carried to a cave after he has been lifted down from the cross. Thus, the choice of color here is no accident, for it describes symbolically the freshness of youth and the paradox of death. Think how it would change this story had she been dressed in red. Or black!

And what are we to make of the relationship between the young girl and the man who picked her up? Those males among us who grew up in small towns and rural communities—perhaps we were no different than our counterparts in big cities—carried with us the fantasy of the beautiful young woman who just happened along and offered herself to us. She was an exotic creature from a distant and glamorous place—Seattle, or San Francisco, suddenly and mysteriously appearing, showering her gifts on us, then disappearing into the night, forever young, forever beautiful and beckoning.

But, confusing the issue, the man in Uncle George's version of the story is a preacher—a man of God—a person generally regarded to be of high moral character. Would a preacher lie, and make up this story? And would a preacher share those same male fantasies the rest of us enjoyed?

Or what of the house? Is there a town in America without a dwelling that is reputed to be haunted? Down a side street, sitting under a canopy of trees in the dusty countryside, or wedged between two warehouses, we find those houses, and if we inquire about them, inevitably we hear stories of birth and life and secret awful death.

Why do these houses fascinate us so? Perhaps because, like ourselves, a house is alive. It has a skeleton and a skin. It possesses complex systems that light it, heat it, carry sustenance in and waste products away. It sparkles with new life, then moves into middle age, and finally into creaking and groaning decline, gray and weathered with the years. But even before a house reaches those gray days it may feel lifeless and decrepit, as, for example, when it has been converted into a gift shop or a museum. The soul has moved away and without it the house lacks the pulse and energy of life.

We are, paradoxically, fascinated by such houses. We enter them and fancy we hear the cries of children at play, the clink of china dishes and the clatter of footsteps on the stairs; we smell the aroma of cigars, the odors of roast beef, smoke from a fire blazing in the fireplace.

Those are all memories now, figments of our imagination. The house stands alone and silent, triggering our unconscious longings, representing childhood dwellings, relationships with others, lapsed friendships, sources of energy we can no longer tap, or those buildings we've never entered, but for which we possess a strange feeling of kinship, as if we had known them in another time and place.

And so, the house in the "Lady in White" legend calls up the image of all those haunted houses from our past. And, furthermore, it has in its dim interior a woman—an old woman—feeble and faint, but tenacious in her frail hold on life. Who is this woman and what does she represent? Perhaps she is memory—our own memory—clinging to the past, so frail that its power amounts to little more than predicting the unvarying cycle of events, such as the yearly reappearance of the young girl.

All I have said is, of course, only interpretation. My sense of the meanings of "The Lady" may differ from yours. But for each of us, that legend, and countless others as well, remain strong and vital through the years because they hold, in their spacious interiors, messages for us, the tellers and listeners.

One of the curious and confounding qualities associated with these messages is that they shift about from day to day and telling to telling. Someone once said, "No man wades into the same river twice, for neither he nor the river is the same."

And it's not just the person telling the story who changes, and, changing, changes the story. It's the listeners as well. For, after all, storytelling—at its innermost core—is a group enterprise, even though only one person may appear to be doing the telling. And, complicating the matter further, within the group no two people see the story in exactly the same way.

If that's true, why fret about what lies behind a story? Let the listener find his own meaning, providing there's any to be found. If you recall, that comes close to what Ruth Sawyer said, when she wrote, of her nurse, Johanna:

> *[She] pointed no moral and drew no application. There was the tale—I could take it or leave it; and always I took it.*[3]

But Ruth Sawyer was not arguing against trying to understand what a story signified. She was arguing against using a tale as a take-off point for a sermon or a scold. And that's different. Digging into a story, trying to understand the various layers of meaning associated with it, enriches one's life. And enriches the story, as well, even though in your telling you say not one word about the symbols and signs you know to be there.

There's another reason—a related reason—why tales and stories remain so much a part of our culture. When we hear, and tell the stories, many of them take place in our own neighborhood. Back in Walla Walla, at that same high school, a friend passed on to me the story of "The Iron Hook." According to him, the event had taken place up Mill Creek, just outside Walla Walla, in a fine old stand of cottonwood trees, referred to locally as Miller's Grove. You remember the story ...

A Whitman College student and his girl friend were courting in his car up at Miller's Grove late one night, the radio playing. Suddenly the music was interrupted by an announcement. A maniac, extremely dangerous, had escaped from the penitentiary and was loose in the countryside. He could be recognized by the iron hook he wore in place of his missing left hand.

The girl was terrified. What if the man was just outside their car, lurking in the darkness?

"... Ah, come on, honey," her boy friend told her. "No crazy man would be this far away from town." But just to keep her from worrying, he'd lock the doors. "See! That's better, isn't it?"

No, he must take her home. She couldn't stand this creepy place! Look at those dark and awful trees! Besides, she'd seen something moving, out there in the dark. Hadn't he seen it?

The boy reached for his door handle. He'd show her. She was imagining things. He started to open the door.

She stopped him.

"Don't!"

She pushed the lock button back down.

"Take me home! Right now! I know there's someone out there!" She began to cry.

Peeved, he started up the car, "peeling rubber" in his haste, bounced across the meadow and onto the winding road that led back to the lights of the town.

When they got back to the girl's house, she opened the door. That's when she screamed. Hanging on the door handle of her side of the car was … The Hook!

We always paused just before we said those last two words to prime the listener for the dénouement. And it had happened, just like the story said. Really! Lennie heard it from Bill, whose brother was in the same fraternity at Whitman as the guy in the story. Sigma Chi, he thought it was. And a Sigma Chi wouldn't lie.

Fifteen years later, when I was a graduate student at the University of Oregon, I heard the same story, but this time it had taken place up on Skinner's Butte, not far from downtown Eugene. And when I moved to San Diego, the story was repeated, but this time it happened on Mount Helix, among the hills where I now live.

The question we might ask ourselves is this: Why should this tale appear and be credited with having occurred in three widely separated towns? And, incidentally, these are not the only locales to which the tale has been attributed. Students in my classes, sharing migratory legends, all know a version of "The Iron Hook," no matter what part of the country they might be from.

We see in this story, of course, the archetypal themes with which we all identify regardless of where we make our homes; the nameless terror that lurks in the dark outside every door, the sinister left hand, the latent sexual content of the story. But laying those aside for a bit, what other reasons can we find for the curious fact that this story is alive and flourishing, like Santa Claus or a well-known melody, in so many different places at one and the same time?

Part of the answer, I suspect, has to do with our need for livening up our own world. Whether we like to admit it or not, our home towns generally aren't terribly exciting places. The fast cars, beautiful women, handsome men, parties that never end, dawns that break clear and golden—all lie in a glamorous city somewhere else. Home, on the other hand, is predictable family, unexciting friends, jobs that don't change a lot over the years, and rain a little too often on the weekends.

So what do we do to give our own area—and ourselves, by association—a little glamour and color? We pass along the stories we've heard that tell of strange, grisly, mysterious or portentous events that have occurred locally. By so doing, we brings a sharpness of detail and a vividness of association to an otherwise undistinguished region. Linda Degh tells of a well known legend in Indiana, known as the "House of Blue Lights." According to that legend, there is a house on the north side of Indianapolis whose porch for a time displayed a coffin lined with blue lights. It contained the body of the lady of the house, dead by her husband's hand. Degh says that the tale is known to thousands of high school and college students, who often drive by the house for a closer look.[4]

Sometimes the tales tell of local heroes. In the cattle country surrounding Walla Walla, when I was growing up, there were stories of men who, in less than ten minutes, could tame wild mustangs that had refused to be touched with a saddle. "Elmer seen him do it," Shorty told me. "Tamed that cayuse so's it'd stand right there, quiet as a kitten, whilst he put the bit in its mouth. Done it in less'n five minutes. Said he'd never seen nothin' like it."

Or the tales may bring depth and drama to the local landscape. My father pointed out to me, once, when we were driving down from the mountains to the valley floor, a gnarled cottonwood tree sitting squarely in the center of a stony meadow. "They hung a horse thief there," he told me. "Once." I asked him to tell me more. "Don't know any more," he said. "But I know it's true." That's all he'd say. But I never traveled that road again without seeing that image.

There may be another reason for the vigorous existence of these tales. There's a tendency for people in a conversation to build on remarks made by the previous speaker. One person tells a story, and listeners remember a second and third and fourth story prompted by key words and phrases from episodes in the first story. This process is sometimes referred to as "seconding." Counselors often use this technique in group therapy. One person shares experiences. Others realize they've had a similar experience, and come to feel that they are part of a larger whole.

Much the same thing, it appears, happens with the migratory tale. Its power for us flows out of the collective experience that seconding generates. We hear the tale of the girl with the lacquered bouffant hair and the black widow spider that somehow makes its home there, spins its web, and bites and kills her. Or the two girls who stay behind in the sorority house during the Christmas holidays, and the thump, thump of footsteps climbing the stairs from the darkened kitchen late at night. Or the grandmother who dies while on a camping trip with the family in Mexico, or Spain, or Alabama, and the family wants to take her home to bury her, so they put her on top of the car, wrapped in a tent, and while they're having a quick cup of coffee in a restaurant, somebody steals the car. And Grandma!

We tell these tales to one another, and as soon as one story is complete, here comes another: the Parked Car, the Blue Light, the Lady in White, the Choking Dog, the Sausage Maker. During those tale tellings, everyone becomes a storyteller, for everyone has a version to share. For a brief time, we're a family, sharing fears, tremblings, hopes and humor. "What if it really *did* happen?" we ask ourselves. Safe and slow-moving though our own lives may be, through the stories we touch drama, terror, history, hope. Our lives are changed, enriched and more complete because of the sharing.

Tale Collecting

In these last few pages we've glanced at the meanings that lie behind a few apparently simple stories. We've seen how these brief and fragmentary stories hold in themselves forces that resonate with desires, needs, anxieties and fears we share. Now we turn our attention to the act of collecting these stories. Not from books, magazines, newspapers—rather, from families and acquaintances.

The reason for collecting stories from people as well as books is, I hope, evident. There's an intrinsic difference in retelling a tale you read, and retelling a tale you heard from Aunt Nettie, or Frank who lives down the street, or the stranger who sat beside you at the lunch counter sharing a cup of coffee and a good yarn.

When you hear a story first hand, you sense the relationship between the story and its environment; its ecology, so to speak. There's an added dimension to the tale that comes from having in mind where you were when you first heard it told, what the occasion was, who told you the story, and how that story fitted in with the rest of the talk.

There's another reason for turning to collecting as part of the storyteller's art. We are all gatherers. Whether we collect shells from the seashore, stamps, clothes, real estate, rare books, Disney films, or matchbook covers the tendency to gather lies deep within our being. It doesn't require much imagination to understand that gathering the old legends and the old migratory tales is a way of filling our psychological closets—our souls, if you will. We enrich our sense of who we are and where we came from when we possess a store of these varied aspects of our heritage.

How does one go about this collecting of migratory legends? Obviously, we have neither the scholarly tools of an anthropologist or sociologist. And, as we've seen, our reasons for gathering are somewhat more personal than theirs: we are not so much concerned with extending a body of knowledge as we are with enriching our own lives and the lives of those immediately associated with us.

At the same time, we may wish to put into practice field work procedures used by scholars. By so doing, we add to our understanding of the totality of the stories we collect, and place them in a setting that illuminates for us their various meanings.

Collecting takes the general form of an interview. True, it may not be an interview in the formal sense of the word. We may be sitting with a friend during dinner when she begins to tell us a story we want to add to our collection, or we may be having lunch in a restaurant and inadvertently overhear a conversation at an adjoining booth. Whatever the situation, however, I would suggest obtaining as completely as possible the following information:

- Name, age, and occupation of person telling story.

- Date, time, and place where story was told.

- Social context in which the story was told—a class, a meeting of friends, a party, a storytelling hour ...

- Physical setting—out-of-doors, a friend's home ...

- General circumstances, including talk that preceded the story, attitude of the person telling the tale, and audience response.

- Title of the story as known to the person telling it.

- How the person learned the story—from family members, friends, a book ...

- How long the person has known the story.

- What changes, if any, the person has made in the story.

- What the meaning of the story is to the person telling it.

- What the person's aesthetic impression of the story is.

Understandably, we won't collect all this information for every story we gather. Responses will vary depending on the occasion, on the sensitivity and maturity of the person telling the story, and on a host of variables, many of which are unpredictable. Even so, each bit of additional data we collect adds to our own sense of the story; its beginnings, history, setting, and underlying currents of meaning.

Where may we begin our collections? We err in assuming that the really good stories and legends are off somewhere far away from home. Kenneth and Mary Clarke tell of the college professor who picked up two young hitchhikers from Oregon who had traveled to Kentucky to record folk songs. As the Clarkes put it, "They 'knew,' just as 'everyone knows,' that people in the mountains of Kentucky sit out on front porches, pick banjos or pluck mountain dulcimers, and sing ancient ballads in a pure (or maybe nearly pure) Elizabethan dialect."[5]

Not surprisingly, the best place for tale collecting may be one's own home and neighborhood. From the experiences of my students and myself, I would suggest trying some of the following:

- Nursing homes and homes for shut-ins.

- Older relatives: parents, grandparents, uncles and aunts.

- Storytelling parties, where part of the entertainment involves remembering variations of the migratory tales.

- Classrooms.

- Informal visits with strangers at bus stops, bars, coffee shops, and the like. We have had good luck interviewing people in these places. Once they know we're innocent collectors of stories, they open up to us.

- Workplaces: garages, warehouses, junk yards, antique shops, gymnasiums ...

It's hard to predict when a story or song or new game or riddle will make its way to you. You'll find them while traveling across country, or on a camping trip; sitting across from strangers at a cafeteria, or cropping up in sedate conversation. Once you begin collecting, though, the tingle of anticipation is always there.

Often when collecting we find it ncessary to help those persons telling us the tales to realize how much they know. "I don't remember any stories," is often their first response. Suggest titles and themes of stories. Tell a story or two yourself. Make inquiries using a "Finder's List"—an index of some of the most common legends and tales one may use to stir memories. Such a list may be compiled from titles and first lines of old songs, story titles, and general themes; baby sitter stories, grandmother stories, parked car stories, and the like.

In *The Vanishing Hitchhiker: Urban Legends and Their Meanings* (New York: Norton, 1981) and *The Choking Doberman and Other "New" Urban Legends* (New York: Norton, 1984), Jan Harold Brunvard identifies various tales, ranging from automobile and RV legends to sex scandals, and gives different versions of them.

Or go to the index of a book on folklore, such as Richard M. Dorson's *American Folklore* (Chicago: University of Chicago Press, 1959) or Duncan Emrich's *Folklore on the American Land* (Boston: Little, Brown, 1972).

When collecting, we find a tape recorder helpful. Small and portable, it frees you to ask questions, respond to the story, share in the enjoyment it gives you and the teller, and at the same time lets you obtain an accurate version of the tale, including speech patterns, colorful usage of language, and response to questions regarding the story as given to you by the informant.

And If You Are a Teacher ...

If you're a teacher, story collecting offers numerous opportunities for language growth. Children participate with great satisfaction in the collecting process, sharing aloud versions of the tales they have heard, writing them out for inclusion in a class anthology. Characteristics of various genres may be studied, including their immediacy, brevity, sense of the inexplicable, and their here-and-now qualities. I have myself collected stories and regional sayings from first and second graders, as well as from college students and adults, and know the keen delight and zest with which all of them approached these activities.

NOTES

1. Stith Thompson, cited in Kenneth and Mary Clarke, *Introducing Folklore* (New York: Holt, Rinehart and Winston, Inc., 1963), p. 1.

2. Carl Jung cited in Joseph Campbell, *The Masks of God: Primitive Mythology* (New York: Viking Compass Books, 1959, 1969, 1970), p. 32.

3. Ruth Sawyer, *The Way of the Storyteller* (New York: Viking Press, 1962), pp. 17-18.

4. Linda Degh, "The 'Belief Legend' in Modern Society: Form, Function, and Relationship to Other Genres." In *American Folk Legend: A Symposium*, ed. by Wayland D. Hand (Berkeley: University of California Press, 1971), pp. 55-68.

5. Kenneth and Mary Clarke. *The Harvest and The Reapers: Oral Traditions of Kentucky* (Louisville: The University Press of Kentucky, 1974), pp. 3, 45.

ACTIVITIES

1. Begin telling one of the migratory tales to a group. Stop midway through and ask persons in the group for endings they have heard. Compare.

2. Collect migratory tales from people you know. What cycles do you find? Duncan Emrich, in *Folklore on the American Land*, tells several "Blue Book" stories from colleges across America. Many children have told me variations of the little girl and the ghostly voice. Entire cycles exist dealing with various groups who don't drive well. What other cycles can you identify?

3. I've offered some hunches as to the why of migratory tales—why they started in the first place; why they have such persistent lives. Can you think of other reasons?

4. Some of the migratory tales have been made into ballads and songs. "Frankie and Johnnie," for example, began life as a tale and then became a song. Can you think of other songs that started as stories?

5. Here's a migratory tale a student told me recently. As you read it, can you think of similar stories or stories with some of the same elements? What fears and predjudices may lie behind this story?

> A sorority girl at San Diego State got asked out by this real cool guy. She wanted to buy a new dress, but was short on money, so she went to this store where they sell fancy used clothing real cheap and bought this beautiful dress that fit her like a glove. The saleslady said it had only been worn once and then returned.
>
> She got all ready. She took a long hot shower. She shaved her armpits. She put on the beautiful dress. Her date picked her up and they went to this big dance. The room was very warm. Her arms started to get numb. It got so bad she couldn't even lift a cup. As the evening wore on she got to feeling worse and worse. Finally she fainted. They rushed her to the hospital, where she died. When they did an autopsy, they found embalming fluid all through her body. The people who had bought the dress before her had used it to dress a dead relative for her funeral. After the funeral was over they returned it. That dress was just full of embalming fluid.

6. One benefit of tale collecting is the colorful language, much of it scatological, that people share in the telling. "So dumb his brains rattled around like BB's in a boxcar" and "Mouth as dry as a bucket of ashes" are a couple of the less vulgar phrases my students and I have collected. What are examples of proverbial and rural speech you find during the gathering process?

6. Telling Together

> I am Thou, and Thou art I; and wheresoever Thou mayest be I
> am there. In all am I scattered, and whensoever Thou willest,
> Thou gatherest me; and gathering me, Thou gatherest Thyself.
>
> —EPIPHANIUS, *ADVERSUS HAERESES*

Years ago, when I was in the army, stationed for basic training at Camp San Luis Obispo, our platoon, during field maneuvers, would march ten, fifteen, and twenty miles through rolling brown hills. While we marched, Sergeant Guitano, abreast of us and to our left, would sing:

> *I don't know but I've been told ...*

Marching in time, we'd shout the lines back to him. Then he'd sing the next line:

> *Living alone gets mighty old ...*

We'd repeat that line—or less socially acceptable variations of it—and then would come the refrain:

> *Sound off (Sound off)*
> *Sound off (Sound off)*
> *One, two, three, four*
> *One, two—three, four!*

It all sounds so flat when I write it down. And yet, when I recall those marches; remember the dark Pacific fog at five o'clock in the morning; remember the afternoon odors of eucalyptus in the air, remember the hot smells of dust and oil and naphtha, the clanking of canteens and rifles, the eighty pairs of boots slapping the pavement; I remember, too, the singing. The singing sustained us. It provided a fabric that we could knit ourselves into, and, for a while, laid tedium, fatigue and homesickness to rest.

That experience was but one of the countless times I have raised my voice with others. Caroling at Christmas time, reading in unison at religious services, cheering at a football game, chanting silly rhymes around the campfire, playing Aunty Aunty Over and Red Rover—all have given me that same sense of pleasure and fulfillment.

I have tried to put my finger on what makes choral speaking so satisfying. Perhaps the pleasure of choral speaking has something to do with the altered form of consciousness that repeating well-known words brings about. In the esoteric traditions of the music in the Middle and Far East, it is the sound of the music, rather than its melody, that is important. These sounds are thought to stimulate parts of the brain that are normally unmoved by music.

The same is true with the mantra of yoga. The meaning of the mantra—the "Magic Word"—lies in its cumulative sound, rather than with the coded spoken symbol. That is to say, when one repeats a mantra over and over again—say it is the word "zoom"—the meaning has nothing to do with our usual notion of that word as it relates to motion and speed, but rather is concerned with the altered state of awareness the repeated uttering of that word brings about.

Benjamin Whorf writes, regarding the mantra, or mantram:

> *On the simplest cultural level, the mantram is merely an incantation of primitive magic, such as the crudest cultures have. In the high culture it may have a different, a very intellectual meaning, dealing with the inner affinity of language and the cosmic order. At a still higher level, it becomes "Mantra Yoga." Therein the mantram becomes a manifold of conscious patterns, contrived to assist the consciousness into the noumenal-pattern world—whereupon it is "in the driver's seat." It can then set the human organism to transmit, control and amplify a thousandfold forces which that organism normally transmits only at unobservably low intensities.*[1]

Much the same sort of consciousness altering that occurs from repeating a mantra over and over again happens during choral speaking. We have come to recognize over the last few years that the two hemispheres of the brain treat the world differently. The left hemisphere—the part of the brain normally associated with language—may be characterized as logical, orderly, analytic, verbal, mathematical, and sequential. The right brain can be thought of as holistic, relational, spatial, intuitive, and artistic.

When Whorf says that the mantram "assists consciousness into the noumenal-pattern world" he is speaking of the shift from the rational and analytic left-brain treatment of language to an intuitive and holistic right-brained use of words. When that shift occurs, language is not so much a conveyor of logical thought as it is the means by which larger and more complex experiences are absorbed into our consciousness.

When we participate in choral speaking, that same sort of shift occurs. The language we use links us with one another. But, it also links us with our own unexplored, intuitive and artistic selves.

A Brief Look Backward

Promptly at 8:30 every weekday morning when I was a child, Mrs. McDowell, our teacher, would emerge from behind the splintered doors of Springdale School. Clutching her cloth coat around her, she'd stand at the top of the broad steps, ringing a brass bell she held. The entire student-body—all twenty-eight of us—would line up in front of the flag and recite the Pledge of Allegiance, our breath hanging in clouds if the day was cold:

> *I pledge allegiance to the flag*
> *of the United States of America ...*

That choral speaking tradition still exists today, all over America. But there were other occasions, as well, in the past when choral speaking was used. At Springdale, as in many rural schools where often there were too few books to go around, our teacher would cluster three or four of us around a single text, and we would read in unison. While the results were less than artistic, there was help for the less capable reader who followed along, reading words a split second behind his more successful schoolmates.

As our schools grew richer, every child had a book, and the earlier sort of choral reading died, unlamented. Round-the-circle reading, with each student reciting alone in his personal moment of truth, became the accepted practice. Our poor readers, had they known the securities the past had held, might well have swapped places with those who went before them.

During those years, too, there were the "memory gems"—bits of didactic verse that teachers used to inculcate the young with the virtues of truth, honesty, goodness, proper behavior, and the like. "Casabianca," with the boy standing on the burning deck until death because of his father's orders, "Abou' Ben Adhem," "The House by the Side of the Road," and "Hearts Like Doors Will Open with Ease" are examples of popular choral speaking selections.

With such dreary fare, it is small wonder that choral speaking fell into bad repute. But the fault was not as much that of choral speaking as it was with the uses the school made of it. A shortage of books, or a desire to inculcate moralistic generalizations hardly seem like responsible uses for a worthy art form.

Not that other institutions have treated choral speaking any better. In churches I've attended, a sort of sleepy enchantment surrounds this activity. The minister recites his part of a responsive reading, the congregation drones its way through a few lines, the minister returns to the fray, and the dismal process repeats itself.

What would happen if, one Sunday morning, congregations broke out of that enchantment? Roused from their Rip Van Winkle mumblings, church-goers might discover new vitality and rhythmic grace in these writings. Take Psalm 150, "Praise Ye the Lord":

> *Praise ye the Lord. Praise God in his sanctuary;*
> *Praise him in the firmament of his power.*
> *Praise him for his mighty acts;*
> *Praise him according to his excellent greatness.*
> *Praise him with the sound of the trumpet;*
> *Praise him with the psaltery and harp.*
> *Praise him with the timbrel and dance;*
> *Praise him with stringed instruments and organs.*
> *Praise him upon the loud cymbals;*
> *Praise him upon the high sounding cymbals.*
> *Let everything that hath breath Praise the Lord.*
> *Praise ye the Lord.*

What a grand piece of writing, and what delight it gives to speak it aloud. Take the word "Praise," with its elastic medial diphthong that can be stretched out forever, or snapped into place quickly and easily between the consonants. And note how the word "praise" is immediately followed by those vivid images: "The psaltery and harp" ... "The timbrel and dance ..."

How might this psalm be arranged for speaking aloud? The minister could read the first line, the men the next two lines, followed by the reading of the next two lines by the women, and so on. Or the choir might read the first couplet, the congregation the second, the choir the third, and so forth. Or if the church seating is divided into sections, readings could be assigned to different areas within the church. Or the entire congregation could read the first four lines, which are somewhat general in their exaltation, solo voices could read lines five through ten, and the congregation come thundering in with the last two lines.

Nor is there any reason why the psalm couldn't be read through several times, so as to get acquainted with the text, and to appreciate various meanings.

Getting Started with Choral Speaking

One of the simplest forms of choral speaking is echoic verse: the storyteller says a line and the audience repeats it word for word, intonation for intonation, and action for action. One of the major advantages of echoic verse is that no reading is necessary. The participants, freed from the printed page, can concentrate on matching as closely as possible what the storyteller says and does.

"The Lion Hunt" is a fine example of echoic verse, taught to me years ago by Professor Kingsley Povenmire, with the admonishment that I was never to say it twice in exactly the same way.[2] Incidentally, when leading "The Lion Hunt" I generally sit on a stool or the edge of a table. It's very difficult to demonstrate the gestures appropriately when standing.

Do you want to go on a lion hunt?	**Wide-eyed ... excited ... This is going to be fun!**
All right! Here we go!	**Strike thighs lightly with hands to simulate walking sound ...**
Not so fast. After all, this is Africa!	
Hot, isn't it?	**Wipe brow ...**
It's not the heat. It's the humididity.	**"Humididity"—that's fun to say ...**
There's a bridge.	**Beat hands on chest. (Good bridge sound) ...**
Ooh! Look how far down the river is.	**Look down, frightened ...**
And how skinny the ropes are.	
Nothing to worry about.	
This hill will slow us down.	**Very slow striking on thighs ... increasing tempo as we start back down ...**
Easier on the other side.	
Oh, oh! Another crick.	**Stop striking ...**
And no bridge.	
We'll just have to jump it.	**Begin striking thighs again, slowly ... slowly ... then very fast.**
Back up! Way back!	
Ready? Let's make a run for it.	**Raise arm to signal long jump ... Big slap to indicate landing ...**
Here we go ...	
Pee U. I got goo on my left shoe!	**Look down at shoe ...**
Grass is getting tall.	**Move arms in front of you to part tall grass ...**
Very tall!	**Raise arms higher. Continue parting gestures ...**
Very, very tall!	
Here's a tree!	
How'd you see the tree?	
Wid my nose!	**Sudden stop ... Hold nose. This is painful!**
Let's climb it.	**Hand over hand motions ...**
Maybe we can see something.	**Eye shading. Peering about ...**
Nope. Nothing but tall grass!	**Shake head. Alas.**
Go on up.	**More climbing motions ...**
More tall grass.	**And ... more eye shading ...**
Well, looky here. Here's a baby buzzard's nest.	**Surprise and delight ...**
	Peering in. Don't you just love babies!
And two bitty baby buzzards in the baby buzzard's nest.	**Poke in the nest with your finger ... Isn't this fun ...**
Hello, Bitty Baby Buzzards.	**Sugary baby talk ... Aren't they just the cutest things!**

And here's the mother buzzard.
Hello, Mother Buzzard!
Help! Jump!
She was not a friendly mother buzzard!
Getting swampy.
Very swampy.
Very, very swampy!
Here's a boat! And about time!
Hop in. I'll row!
Oh, isn't this pleasant.
And look! Here's a crackidaddle!
A crackidaddle? What's a crackidaddle?
A crackidaddle is a hippopotamus's grandpappy.
Hello, Mr. Crackidaddle.
Look at that grin!
Friendly fellow, isn't he?
OUCH!!!!!!!!
Very funny. Very funny!
Oh oh! Boat's leaking! It's that danged crackidaddle!
We'll have to swim for it!
Say! This looks like lion country!
Lion Country?
Yep. Lion Country. Anybody scared?
I am!
See that cave?
Looks like a lion cave.
Let's go in!
Dark in here ...
Shhhhhhhhhhhhh ...
See those eyes?
Look like lion's eyes.
See that nose?
Looks like a lion's nose.
See those teeth?
Yup. Lion's teeth.
Excuse me, Mr. Lion, while we continue the examination ...
A little wider please ...
Wow! Feel that tongue.
Rough, isn't it?

And look. Here's Mother. Oh, goodie! It's a party!
A friendly wave ... which becomes sudden panic ...
And solemn pronouncement ...
How does one show swampiness? Lift one's legs and arms very slowly? Make slurpy sounds?

Ah, relief in sight ...
Rowing motions. (Or, you can paddle, if it turns out to be a canoe) Looking around ... so lovely ...
And company, too!

The puzzled greenhorn asks ...

Any fool would know that answer! Repeat it if necessary to get it right ...
So nice to have company!
Admiringly ...
Lean far over ...
Grab your nose ...

Hold nose while speaking these lines ...

A quick glance behind confirms suspicions ...

Swimming motions ...
And ... shaking off water.
Looking around at distant vistas ...
The greenhorn speaks ...
Pompous affirmation ... Of course! And a question ...
Terror-stricken ...
Points. This is getting exciting ...
Head-nodding. It's got to be ...

Opening mouth to form O and snapping fingers against cheeks makes a wonderful hollow cave sound. (And also stings.)
Appropriate shushing gestures ... Pointing ...
Head nodding ...
Pointing again ...
And, continued agreement ...

Peer upward and touch, gingerly, finger to tooth, one by one ...

Getting braver ... opening mouth ... "Erch ... Erch ... Erch ..."

A good, hard shove ... this is one hard mouth to get open ...
Imagine spreading mayonnaise ...

Yup. Lion's tongue, all right!   **No question about it ...**
Look at those tonsils.   **Lean 'way inside ... This is the true test ...**
Uhhuh. Lion's tonsils ...   **Nodding sagely...**
LION'S TONSILS!!!
LET'S GET OUT OF HERE ...   **And then, realization dawns ...**

                                   Repeat all gestures backwards... out of cave,
Everybody safe?   **crossing plain, swimming, rowing ... etc.**

Over the years, I have taken pre-schoolers, teenagers, and adults on a lion hunt. The last time we were out we didn't make it back. The final lines—delivered on that hasty trek back to camp—went something like this:

> *Oh, oh! He got Neshan!* (a boy in the group)
> *Oops! There went Solange!*
> *Tough luck. He just caught Ingrid ...*
> *He's getting closer! But he'll not get ...*

I spoke earlier of the tendency of choral verse to set in motion our intuitive, holistic right-brain selves. "The Lion Hunt," it seems to me, does just that. Occasionally, after going on a lion hunt, I'll ask a group of adults—usually teachers—what they got out of this seemingly nonsensical activity. They'll mention the usual educational gains for children; sequencing, vocal and physical matching with what the leader has said and done, an opportunity for everyone to participate.

But then they go on to talk about other benefits that aren't so readily obvious:

- "I felt like I was really there ..."

- "This is the best thing that's happened to me today ..."

- "It was such fun ... Could we do it again? ..."

- "Usually, I'm shy. But this wasn't embarrassing. Because everyone was helping out ..."

And, it's not just what they say. It's their body language—the way they sit in their chairs. I see them unbend. I see them unwind.

I think we need to heed these responses. Clearly the group enterprise is at work here while, at the same time, each individual is given an opportunity to interpret words and actions in her own way.

Telling Together and the Oral Tradition

Tradition dictates, if we let it, the ways open to us to enjoy a song, play, essay, or poem. Tradition also may dull our hearing of words and ideas. Back at Grove, when John and I were teaching school together, some fifth graders in my class set themselves to compose a musical score for the Gettysburg Address. I was impressed. The task seemed, at best, daunting. But these children, unhampered by tradition, wrote a tone poem of genuine beauty, with odd dissonances and unexpected progressions, that they used as accompaniment to a verse choir of their own organization. (Thinking back on that event, I realize they were my first teachers in the art we're now considering.)

Those of us who heard their performance were fortunate, for we received a new aural image of Lincoln's words. In like fashion, it is possible for us to hear, as if for the first time, other literary works. Consider "America the Beautiful":

> *O beautiful for spacious skies,*
> *For amber waves of grain.*
> *For purple mountain majesties*
> *Above the fruited plain.*
> *America, America,*
> *God shed His grace on thee;*
> *And crown thy good*
> *With brotherhood,*
> *From sea to shining sea.*

Convention dictates that we sing this song. But during one storytelling session a participant suggested that we act it out. One person was designated to be O. Beautiful. Another two were spacious skies. (They stood on a table.) There were three or four amber waves of grain, with some fruited plains lying on the floor in front of them. There was considerable vying for the role of God, which carried with it certain perks: a throne (a chair, on top of the table, surrounded by spacious skies), a sceptor, and a robe (in an earlier incarnation, a sheet). At each end of this spectacle was a shining sea.

When all was ready a chorus chanted the words while a second chorus hummed the tune and the players in the pageant acted out their respective roles.

It was a hit!—so much fun, in fact, that everyone insisted on changing roles and doing it again.

But it wasn't just fun. It started us thinking of the words in different ways. The role of God was played by a woman—"God shed *Her* grace on thee ..." The whole splendid image of a bucolic America, with its amber waves of grain and fruited plains, was called forth—for some of us—for the first time ever.

"America the Beautiful," like so many of our traditional songs, lies dormant, waiting to be heard, waiting to be enjoyed.

And, of course, with so many of these, no printed text is necessary. Participants know the words; they just haven't thought what the words might mean. Taking a ballad out of its musical setting gives us much greater latitude for interpretation than we possess when the tune is there. No longer are we bound by the specified rhythm and melody line of a song, but are free to make our own melody in human speech. Remember that old traditional song, "Billy Boy"?

> *Oh where have you been, Billy Boy, Billy Boy?*
> *Oh where have you been, Charming Billy?*
> *I've been to seek a wife,*
> *She's the joy of my life,*
> *She's a young thing and cannot leave her mother.*

And the later verses:

> *Did she ask you to come in? etc.*
> *Did she take from you your coat? etc.*
> *Did she set for you a chair? etc.*
> *Did she offer you a drink? etc.*
> *How old is she? etc.*

There are, of course, many ways to divide this old song for choral speaking. One of our most successful adventures included acting it out, with the family —Cousin Sally, Uncle Bob, Grandma, Grandpa, Little Henry, Baby Beth, Ma and Pa—all sitting in the living room, waiting up for a surprised Billy Boy, who tiptoes in, shoes in hand, after a late night of spooning. Grandpa asks the first question:

> *Oh, where have you been, Billy Boy, Billy Boy?*
> *Oh, where have you been, Charming Billy?*

Billy gives his answer. Baby Beth asks the next question. Billy Boy, eager to reach his room, gives his answer. This family grilling continues until the final question:

> *How old is she, Billy Boy, Billy Boy?*
> *How old is she, Charming Billy?*

And Billy's answer:

> *Three times six, four times seven*
> *Twenty-eight, and eleven.*
> *She's a young thing,*
> *And cannot leave her mother.*

Whereupon the family starts trying to figure out how old the young thing really is.
　　Once we wrote new verses for this song; someone proposed a new first line:

> *Did she wash your dirty shirt? ...*
> *Did she charge you any rent? ...*
> *Was she gussied up all fine? ...*

And we collectively developed an answer, matching rhyme, length of line, and number of syllables to the original.

In like fashion, we've chanted and acted out a variety of nursery rhymes and childhood poems: "Hickory Dickory Dock" (half the group did the tick-tocks); "Baa, Baa, Black Sheep"; "Ding, Dong, Dell": "Three Little Kittens" (with a narrator/storyteller, a mother cat, and three kittens); "I Had a Dog, and His Name was Rover"; "Fox Went Out on a Chilly Night"; and "Little Miss Muffet."

These old rhymes and songs provide rich opportunities for democratic storytelling. No matter how a group chooses to perform them, one can be sure that for many this will be the first time these words take on meaning, and for all participants, meanings will be enriched, with opportunities for conveying a range of emotions: joy, sadness, dismay, despair, and overwhelming delight.

Telling Together and the Printed Page

Nursery rhymes, old songs, childhood poems are a part of our collective knowledge. But choral speaking can be done just as well with printed text. Let's begin with a light-hearted poem that is particularly fun to use with young children:

The Goblin

> *A goblin lives in our house,*
> *In our house,*
> *In our house,*
> *A goblin lives in our house,*
> *All year 'round.*
> *He jumps!*
> *He thumps!*
> *He stumps!*
> *He bumps!*
> *He knocks!*
> *He rocks!*
> *He rattles at the locks!*
> *A goblin lives in our house,*
> *In our house,*
> *In our house,*
> *A goblin lives in our house,*
> *All year 'round!*

This old French folk rhyme is a good starting point for "choral reading," since the reading itself is so easy. The same words and phrses are used again and again, ("in our house, in our house ..."). New words rhyme ("thumps" and "bumps"; "rocks" and "locks.") And the swing and rhythm of the verse carry the reader along. After one or two times through, he'll have the poem memorized. And, besides, the subject matter is of interest. Goblins and monsters have been around for a long time, one way or another, in both our conscious and unconscious lives.

How might "The Goblin" be dramatized? A chorus might read the first lines, "A goblin lives in our house, in our house, in our house," and soloists read the action lines. ("He thumps ... He bumps ...")

Or one soloist might read the entire poem with individuals acting out the lines.

Or half the group read the lines, while the other half acts them out ...

Or a goblin, dressed in appropriate garb—there goes that sheet again!—could haunt the room, emitting goblin sounds, acting the poem out, while the entire group solemnly and slowly chants the entire poem ...

But you get the point. It doesn't matter how you divide a group to read the poem. The concern is not with matching high and low voices, or dark and light voices, but simply with giving an audience an opportunity to create an experience through choral speech.

Here's another poem, "Trains," by James Tippett:

> *Over the mountains,*
> *Over the plains,*
> *Over the rivers,*
> *Here come the trains.*
> *Carrying passengers,*
> *Carrying mail,*
> *Bringing their precious loads*
> *In without fail.*
> *Thousands of freight cars*
> *All rushing on,*
> *Through day and darkness,*
> *Through dusk and dawn.*
> *Over the mountains,*
> *Over the plains,*
> *Over the rivers,*
> *Here come the trains.*[3]

"Trains" is a fine poem, trimmed of excess words, balanced, and suggestive of the rhythmic surge and headlong rush of a great steam engine.

What contributes to that headlong rush? We could talk about the repetition of the word *over;* the short lines, ranging from four to six syllables in length; the introduction of a rhyme every four lines ...

But to talk about the headlong rush of "Trains" is bland stuff when compared with reading those same lines aloud as a group.

I say reading—but typically I recite the poem to the group, and then say it again, urging them to join in with me as they become familiar with the lines. Three or four times, and they know it. If they are having difficulty I'll put cue letters on a blackboard, if one's available; e.g:

OM
OP
OR
HCT ...

We talk about trains—talk about using this poem to re-create the sounds and the sense of a great steam engine and its cargo striking out across a continent. Someone imitates the sound of a train whistle, another takes the part of the conductor bawling out, "All aboard ... La Mesa, El Cajon, Julian ... Brawley ..." (or whatever towns lie within the region). One group produces the sound of wheels on track—*clickety clack, clickety clack*—while another generates the sound of escaping steam, at first in slow, gusty whooshes, then faster and faster as the train gathers momentum.

Meanwhile, we've lined up a dozen persons in a column in the front of the audience, facing left. They're the train. Perhaps there's a headlight ... a cow-catcher ... a caboose ... The rest are holding the left elbow of the person in front of them with their left hand.

"Trains" gets underway with a toot from the whistle, then the conductor's cry, followed by the first ponderous whooshes of steam driving the pistons (those elbows—remember?) back and forth, and the ever-quickening clack of wheels on iron rails. When the background of train sounds is well established by half the group, the other half recites the poem itself, gradually building to a crescendo ...

Thousands of freight cars
All rushing on,
Through day and darkness
Through dusk and dawn ...

and then fading away, just as a train itself leaves our sight and hearing.

Using "Trains" for choral speaking gives an audience a chance to participate in a mood and a feeling, in the course of which they begin to discover some of the power and variety available to them as language interpreters.

We've done scary poems. Here's Ian Serraillier's "The Visitor":

A crumbling churchyard, the sea and the moon;
The waves had gouged out grave and bone;
A man was walking, late and alone ...

He saw a skeleton white on the ground
A ring on a bony hand he found.

He ran home to his wife and gave her the ring.
"Oh, where did you get it?" He said not a thing.

"It's the prettiest ring in the world," she said,
As it glowed on her finger. They skipped off to bed.

At midnight they woke. In the dark outside,
"Give me my ring!" a chill voice cried.

"What was that, William? What did it say?"
"Don't worry, my dear. It'll soon go away."

"I'm coming!" A skeleton opened the door.
"Give me my ring!" It was crossing the floor.

"What was that, William? What did it say?"
"Don't worry, my dear. It'll soon go away."

"I'm touching you now! I'm climbing the bed."
The wife pulled the sheet right over her head.

It was torn from her grasp and tossed in the air:
"I'll drag you out of your bed by the hair!"

"What was that, William? What did it say?"
"Throw the ring through the window! THROW IT AWAY!"

She threw it. The skeleton leapt from the sill,
Scooped up the ring and clattered downhill,
Fainter ... and fainter ... Then all was still.[4]

After giving a group time to read through this poem silently, suggestions for various ways of presenting it are invited. One performance I remember involved a narrator/storyteller, William, the wife, and the skeleton. The narrator read the entire text with the exception of specific dialogue read by the wife, William, and the skeleton. While the narrator was reading, however, the story was being enacted. (Incidentally, the bed sheet which served so well as God's robe—and the goblin's gloomy garb—got put to a more conventional use here.)

C.P. Cavafy's "Waiting for the Barbarians" has been a much discussed poem among those college students and adults who have read it together in a storytelling session:

What are we waiting for, packed in the forum?

The Barbarians are due here today.

Why isn't anything going on in the senate?
Why have the senators given up legislating?

Because the barbarians are coming today.
What's the point of senators and their laws now?
When the barbarians get here, they'll do the legislating.

Why did our emperor set out so early
to sit on his throne at the city's main gate
in state, wearing the crown?

Because the barbarians are coming today
and the emperor's waiting to receive their leader
He's even got a citation to give him
loaded with titles and imposing names.

Why have our two consuls and praetors shown up today
        wearing their embroidered, their scarlet togas?
Why have they put on bracelets with so many amethysts,
rings sparking with all those emeralds?
Why are they carrying elegant canes
so beautifully worked in silver and gold?

Because the barbarians are coming today
and things like that dazzle barbarians.

And why don't our distinguished orators push forward
        as usual
to make their speeches, say what they have to say?

> *Because the barbarians are coming today*
> *and they're bored by rhetoric and public speaking.*
>
> *Why this sudden bewilderment, this confusion?*
> *[How serious everyone looks.]*
> *Why are the streets and squares rapidly emptying,*
> *everyone going home so lost in thought?*
>
> *Because it's night and the barbarians haven't come.*
> *And some people just in from the border say*
> *there are no barbarians any longer.*
>
> *Now what's going to happen to us without them?*
> *The barbarians were a kind of solution.*[5]

We've performed this poem in a number of ways, but I think the one I liked best occurred on an occasion when no lines were assigned, but after a first silent reading and some discussion about the setting of the poem, a group of fifteen or twenty persons were invited up to the stage area. They milled about. Finally, a male voice—irritated, abrasive—read the first line:

> *What are we waiting for, packed in the forum?*

There was a pause, and then a woman's voice—quiet, reasonable—answered:

> *The barbarians are due here today.*

Slowly, the poem unfolded. There were lapses and lulls in the conversation. Then it would start up again. Occasionally two or more people would begin a line at the same time, and read it together. By the time the poem reached its inevitable question and tragically human answer,

> *Now what's going to happen to us without them?*
> *The barbarians were a kind of solution.*

we had been transported. We were in the forum, all of us, and night was falling, and we were face to face with the truth—that our enemies were all too often imagined.

Enjoying Prose Together

There's plenty of prose in our written and oral tradition that lends itself to informal choral speaking. "The Gettysburg Address" and "The Declaration of

Independence" come immediately to mind. The Twenty-third Psalm is another. But there are other, less stately bits of language as well which promise good fun for children and adults:

> *Q: Where did George Washington keep his armies?*
> *A: Up his sleevies. (Sorry)*

> *Q: What will happen if you eat yeast and shoe polish before*
> *   retiring for the night?*
> *A: In the morning you'll rise and shine.*

> *Knock Knock.*
> *Who's there?*
> *Sam and Janet.*
> *Sam and Janet who?*
> *Sam and Janet evening, you will meet a stranger ...*
> *(It helps if you've seen "South Pacific")*

> *Urchin:*   *Boo-hoo.*
> *Mature Adult:*   *There there. What the matter?*
> *U:*   *I lost my penny.*
> *MA:*   *Lost your penny! Don't cry. Here's another.*
> *U:*   *Boo-hoo ... Boo-hoo-hoo-hoo.*
> *MA:*   *Now what's the matter?*
> *U:*   *If I hadn't lost my penny, I'd have two!*

Tiny stories, like those above, give an opportunity for members of the audience to participate as performers in a storytelling hour. Here's a slightly longer piece, "The Best Liar," taken from *Three Rolls and One Doughnut*, Mirra Ginsburg's translations of Russian folktales:

> *Once upon a time there lived a king who was very, very bored. To amuse himself he sent out criers to every town and village in his land to find the best liar.*
> *"Here ye, hear ye!" shouted the criers. "The king will give a golden apple to the man who tells him the biggest lie!"*
> *People began to come to the king from all ends of the land; princes, merchants, officials. But nobody could please the king.*
> *At last a poor shepherd came to the palace with a large pot in his hands.*

"What do you want?" asked the king.

"Good morning, your Majesty," said the shepherd. "I've come for my money. You owe me a potful of gold."

"A potful of gold?" cried the king. "Ridiculous. I do not owe you anything."

"Oh, yes you do. I lent it to you last year."

"Liar! That is the biggest lie I've ever heard."

"It is? Then give me the golden apple."

The king saw that the shepherd had tricked him.

"Well, it is not really a lie."

"It isn't. Then pay your debt."

The king had to admit that the shepherd had won. He gave him the golden apple and sent him home in peace.[6]

Often, with a piece like this, we'll take a few minutes scripting it, and then ask a group to present it as readers' theater. Scripting might consist of nothing more than giving everyone a xeroxed copy of the text and determining who will read what. For instance, in "The Best Liar" one might wish to assign two narrators, and position them at either side of the impromptu stage, with the action taking place between them. The first narrator might read:

Once upon a time there lived a king who was very, very bored.

A second narrator then reads:

To amuse himself he sent out criers to every town and village in his land to find the best liar.

Aha! We need criers for the next lines—as many as we want to use; and one of the narrators to read the speech tag telling us they're criers (later in the text, we'll probably cut out those speech tags, but here they give useful information); and then back to one of the narrators ...

Incidentally, one iron-clad rule we always follow when we've scripted a piece, and then watch it being performed impromptu on stage by members of the audience is this:

Only those "actors" on stage may read from the text. The audience must not "follow along," but must give their full attention to the play.

Longer pieces work well, too. Several years ago Arnold Lobel wrote and illustrated a picture book, *Fables,*[7] which has become a classic. One of my favorite stories from that book is "The Hippopotamus at Dinner," which tells of a hippopotamus entering a restaurant, sitting down at his favorite table, and ordering a meal. When the waiter brings him his food the hippopotamus throws a fit. The portions are too small. He wants a real dinner, with a bathtub of bean soup, mountains of mashed potatoes, and a bucket of Brussels sprouts. He's hungry!

The waiter obliges, and the hippopotamus eats, and eats, and eats. He eats so much, in fact, that he cannot move. The other diners leave the restaurant. The waiter clears the table. The lights dim. And still the hippopotamus sits there. Perhaps, he decides, he ate a few too many Brussels sprouts ...

We've had wonderful fun with "Hippopotamus"—each group performing it differently. Sometimes there are only three characters—the narrator/storyteller, the waiter, and the hippopotamus. Occasionally several persons will handle the narration, so that one gets the feeling of patrons in a restaurant telling the story. Almost always everyone in the cast—and the remainder of the audience—joins in with the "moral."

As often as possible we use impromptu properties: a chair, a table, a checkered cloth, a bib, a lunch tray, a paper plate and knife and fork. These add sparkle to the performance. But beware of over-preparing. The emphasis here should be on quick, informal audience theater.

Lobel's *Fables* remind me of those written by James Thurber, although certainly Thurber's contained more cynicism and acerbic humor. Here's Thurber's "The Rabbits Who Caused All the Trouble," which has been the source of innumerable variations and theatrical adventures (including commentary delivered as asides) when used as a choral speaking story:

> Within the memory of the youngest child there was a family of rabbits who lived near a pack of wolves. One day, the wolves announced that they did not like the way the rabbits were living. The wolves were crazy about the way they themselves were living, because it was the only way to live.
>
> One night several wolves were killed in an earthquake. This was blamed on the rabbits, for it is well known that rabbits pound on the ground with their hind legs and cause earthquakes. On another night one of the wolves was killed by a bolt of lightning and this was also blamed on the rabbits, for it is well known that lettuce-eaters cause lightning.
>
> The wolves threatened to civilize the rabbits if they didn't behave, and the rabbits decided to run away to a desert island. But the other animals, who lived at a great distance, shamed them, saying, "You must stay where you are and be brave. This is no world for escapists. If the wolves attack you, we will come to your aid, in all probability."
>
> So the rabbits continued to live near the wolves and one day there was a terrible flood which drowned a great many wolves. This was blamed on the rabbits, for it is well known that carrot nibblers with long ears cause floods. The wolves descended on the rabbits, for their own good, and imprisoned them in a dark cave, for their own protection.
>
> When nothing was heard about the rabbits for some weeks, the other

animals demanded to know what had happened to them. The wolves replied that the rabbits had been eaten and since they had been eaten the affair was a purely internal matter. But the other animals warned that they might possibly unite against the wolves unless some reason was given for the destruction of the rabbits. So the wolves gave them one. "They were trying to escape," said the wolves, "And, as you know, this is no world for escapists."

Moral: Run, don't walk, to the nearest desert island.[8]

How might a group arrange this piece for group work? Let me suggest one possibility. Divide the audience into two groups: Wolves and Rabbits. Divide the text so that portions of it are read by Wolves, and the other by Rabbits. For example, in the first paragraph, the Wolves might read:

> *Within the memory of the youngest child there was a family of rabbits*

(Can't you just hear the disgust in their voices when the Wolves talk about those Rabbits?)

And the Rabbits finish the line:

> *who lived near a pack of wolves.*

Here's another possibility. Assign a single reader for the first phrase:

> *Within the memory of the youngest child* (Oh, so timidly!)

And the Rabbits read:

> *there was a family of rabbits*

And the Wolves read:

> *who lived near a pack of wolves.*

The generalization to bear in mind when working with a piece like this is that there's nothing wrong with assigning various parts of a line to different speakers or groups of speakers. Indeed, doing so often helps clarify meanings—or brings new meanings—to a text.

And, finally, here's a piece for an older audience. It's taken on a different look every time it's been performed. It's Ned Guymon's "World's Shortest Detective Story." (Printed here in two columns to save space; read down the entire first column before reading the second column.) Try this with a friend—make that two friends—you'll need a telephone operator—and have fun!

"No!"	*"I knew!"*
"Yes!"	*"How long?"*
"You didn't!"	*"Long enough."*
"I did."	*"What now?"*
"When?"	*"Guess."*
"Just now."	*"Police?"*
"Where?"	*"Later."*
"Bedroom."	*"Why later?"*
"Dead?"	*"Guess again."*
"Yes."	*"Tell me!"*
"Why?"	*"Look!"*
"You know."	*"Oh, no!"*
"I don't!"	*"Oh, yes."*
"You do!"	*"You can't!"*
"Unfaithful?"	*"I can."*
"Yes."	*"Please!"*
"With whom?"	*"Don't beg."*
"With you."	*"Forgive me!"*
"No."	*"Too late."*
"Yes."	*"Good God!"*
"She didn't ..."	*"Goodbye."*
"She did!"	....
"We didn't ...!"	*"Operator?"*
"You did."	*"Yes?"*
"You knew?"	*"The Police."*[9]

On With the Show: A Baker's Dozen Helpful Hints

Thus far we've looked at some of the reasons choral speaking is such a powerful technique for the storyteller. Various sources of material have been suggested. What follows are thirteen practical suggestions for implementing choral speaking and readers' theater in the story hour.

1. When considering texts for choral speaking and readers' theater, look for pieces with lively, well-written text; whether they're poems or stories or scientific accounts or historical documents.

2. Begin with pieces already in the oral tradition of those participating: nursery rhymes, old songs, familiar poems, sayings.

3. When teaching a new selection (one not already known to the group), make copies so that each person will have a copy to read from. Then, if a reader wishes to pencil in marks or notes, or wants to underline certain words for emphasis, she may do so.

4. Before introducing a work for choral speaking, have in mind how it might be arranged for reading aloud. Once a piece has been studied by the audience, changes in the way of presenting it are not only acceptable, but desirable, so long as those changes clarify and enhance the potential meanings available in a text.

5. When "conducting" a group in unison reading, simple hand and lip cues will usually keep voices together.

6. For most choral speaking during the story-hour, use simple divisions suggested by the group itself; persons sitting in different parts of the room can take different parts. Persons wearing blue dresses, or persons with red hair, or persons with birthdays in the winter months can be a group.

7. Ask for volunteers from the audience to give examples of how a line might be read. Ask members of the audience to rephrase a line or phrase in their own words, and then use that voice when speaking the original line.

8. When an action is being described by a narrator, persons taking various roles should respond appropriately. Thus, in "The Hippopotamus At Dinner" the waiter has no lines, but his role is an important one.

9. Keep it short. As a rule of thumb, a poem should be no longer than a page; a prose selection, one which can be read aloud in five to seven minutes.

10. Pieces written in the first person should generally be read in unison.

11. Dialogue should generally be assigned to individuals.

12. Standing, sitting, lying down; using chairs, tables, benches as minimal sets—all are appropriate during a performance if they enhance and extend meanings.

13. Start a costume trunk, with items from the attic and garage sales and second hand stores—scarves, hats, neckties, gowns, canes, boas, wigs, old coats. Invite participants to make use of these, as well as whatever is available in the environment, to add to the pleasures of choral speaking and readers' theater.

And If You Are a Teacher ...

Playing with words as we did with "The Lion Hunt" may seem like little more than a pleasant pastime, but anyone who has taught children to read recognizes how difficult it is to use an intonational pattern correctly unless one understands the meanings that phrases and sentences take on when spoken in a given way. Clearly, choral speech helps students develop a sense of words and what lies behind them.

Or consider basic sight vocabulary. "The Goblin" repeats certain words and letter patterns again and again. Indeed, the sentence

> *A goblin lives in our house*

uses words which are among those most frequently used in the language: *lives, in, our,* and *house.* And then there are the ending rhymes—*jumps* and *thumps, knocks* and *locks*—all common word patterns, painlessly acquired as sight vocabulary when read chorally.

Perhaps students need help with phrase and sentence reading. Phrases from a choral reading can be typed separately, or printed on sentence strip paper, and students can place these in correct order to match those on the printed page. Consider, for example:

> *Over the mountains ...*
> *all rushing on ...*
> *here come the trains ...*

These are vigorous and dramatic phrases, full of impact for the child. Compare them with phrases like "Look at Billy" or "See the funny thing!" Giving a child plenty of practice reading these phrases in a choral setting provides him with the security he needs to build fluency. When he's ready, he can read those same phrases on his own.

Choral reading benefits a child's speech development. He gets practice saying the same phrases over and over again, and the fluency in tongue, lip, and throat movements he learns with those phrases is transferable to other words and phrases in the language; a fact that becomes particularly significant if the language being taught is a second or third one for the child.

Choral reading has other values in addition to the academic. The shy person takes heart from those around her and participates with greater ease in a choral setting. The extrovert learns to participate and share. And, of course, choral reading gives variety and a change of pace to the story-hour. It is an activity where the rewards are almost immediate. In five minutes' time a group can be experiencing together the twin satisfactions of speaking: the artistic pleasure of bringing life to the printed page, and the social joy of participating with others in a mutual endeavor.

I have been in classrooms where readers' theater and choral speaking is used, and have seen the pride and sense of ownership students feel when they take a literary piece—a poem or prose selection, rewrite it for choral speaking, and then direct and perform it. Their efforts make that literature their own.

NOTES

1. J. B. Carroll, ed., *Language, Thought and Reality: Selected Writings of Benjamin Lee Whorf* (Cambridge, Massachusetts: M.I.T Press, 1956). See the essay "Language, Mind, and Reality," p. 27.

2. For further reading, see E. Kingsley Povenmire, *Choral Speaking and the Verse Choir* (Cranbury, New Jersey: A. S. Barnes, 1975). This book is a compendium of ideas, resources, and practical suggestions regarding verse choir and choral speech.

3. James S. Tippett, "Trains." In *I Go a-Traveling* (New York: Harper & Row, 1973).

4. Ian Serraillier, "The Visitor." In *A Second Poetry Book*, ed. John Foster (New York: Oxford University Press, 1980), p. 30.

5. C.P. Cavafy, "Waiting for the Barbarians." In *Selected Poems of C.P. Cavafy*, transl. Edmund Keeley and Phillip Sherrard (Princeton, New Jersey: Princeton University Press, 1972), p. 6.

6. Mirra Ginsburg, "The Best Liar." In *Three Rolls and One Doughnut* (New York: Dial Press, 1970), p. 13.

7. Arnold Lobel, "The Hippopotamus at Dinner." In *Fables* (New York: Harper & Row, 1980), p. 38.

8. James Thurber, "The Rabbits Who Caused all the Trouble." In *Fables for Our Time and Famous Poems, Illustrated* (New York: Harper & Row, 1939, 1940), p. 69.

9. Ned Guyman, "The Shortest Detective Story in the World." [Publisher unknown.]

ACTIVITIES

1. Some bits of prose and poetry are gem-like in their elegance of expression. Here are some I highly recommend:

"I Am Apis." From *The Diary of Vaslav Nijinsky,* ed. Romola Nijinsky (Berkeley & Los Angeles: University of California Press, 1936), p. 20.

"Primer Lesson." From Carl Sandburg, *Slabs of the Sunburnt West* (Orlando, Florida: Harcourt Brace Jovanovich. 1922.)

"My People." From Langston Hughes, *Selected Poems of Langston Hughes* (New York: Alfred A. Knopf, Inc., 1926), p. 13.

2. "Sing-song" reading of poetry has fallen into ill repute. And yet few of us can deny the deep pleasure we feel in accepting and becoming part of the natural rhythm of certain poems. Take, for example, Vachel Lindsay's "The Potatoes' Dance" (in *Collected Poems by Vachel Lindsay* [New York: Macmillan Publishing Co., 1917, 1945], pp. 126-127.) Try this with a group, chanting the lines as you read them, emphasizing the poem's rhythmic qualities.

Another excellent example of rhythmic verse that almost demands "sing-song" is Rudyard Kipling's "Boots." Remember the first line?

"We're foot-slog—slog—slog—slogging over Africa ..."

3. Young children particularly enjoy poems involving body movement activities. "Itsy Bitsy Spider" is one example.

> *Itsy, bitsy spider*
> *went up the water spout.*
> (Fingers of right hand crawl up left arm)
> *Down came the rain,*
> *and washed the spider out.*
> (Fingers slide back down arm)
> *Out came the sun and*
> *dried up all the rain.*
> (Arms over head, let fall to side)
> *And that itsy, bitsy spider*
> *went up the spout again.*
> (Walking back up again, dauntless!)

4. Listen to a recording of Vachel Lindsay reading his own poems. "Mysterious Cat," "The Congo," "Flower-fed Buffaloes," and others are on the recording *Vachel Lindsay Reading "The Congo"* (Caedmon recording TC1041).

5. Young children can have fun with sentences in which all the words begin with the same consonant or vowel sound. Here are some samples; others can be easily created.

> *Adam's adam's apple*
> *Ached awfully,*
> *Antagonizing Adam's adamant*
> *Aunt Abigail.*

> *Pretty Polly*
> *Pending prison,*
> *Pleaded plaintively,*
> *Piously,*
> *Piteously,*
> *Persistently—and un-*
> *Productively.*

Cheerful Charlie
Chewed chocolates,
Challenging chambered chancellors.

6. Here's part of an old mountain song, "Bright Morning Stars are Rising." How might it be arranged for choral speaking?

Bright morning stars are rising,
Bright morning stars are rising,
Bright morning stars are rising,
And day is breaking in my soul.
    Oh where are our dear fathers (2x)
    They're in the valley praying,
    And day is breaking in my soul ...
        And where are our dear mothers (2x)
        They're gone to heaven before us,
        And day is breaking in my soul ...

What other verses might you add? (e.g., *Where are our dear brothers? ... sisters? ... cousins? ...*)

7. How many poems do you know? One? Two? Fifty? Think of all the nursery rhymes, Christmas carols, old songs, and early poems you learned. The number will surprise you. All these are material for choral reading, since they are part of a common heritage with which most of us are familiar.

7. The Story Board

Surprisingly nimble, Biggest Billy Goat Gruff pranced his way across the bridge and picked his way up the hill, where Middle Billy Goat and Little Billy Goat Gruff were cropping the sweet green grass.

And the Troll? He climbed back down under the bridge, and sat on a rock and thought for a long time about winning and losing, and about which was which.

And so, as they said in the olden days, "Snip, snap, snout, this tale's told out!"

—ADAPTED FROM THE BROTHERS GRIMM

The last of the little felt figures joins its fellows on the board. The story ends. Silence. Then a voice pipes, "Tell it again!"

The story board is, at one and the same time, among the most exasperating and the most pleasing of the media a storyteller may use. Exasperating because there are so many opportunities for things to go wrong: the easel toppling over; the figures falling to the ground; the most important character disappearing just when needed.

And yet, there's something about these bright bits of glowing color that charms the eye and mind. Viewers forget the hand that moves the figures off and on the board. They overlook the primitive stiffness of the scraps of material used to fashion the characters. They take in the limited symbols the storyteller provides—three goats, a troll, a crude bridge, a pointed mountain—and from these basic elements conjure swift-flowing streams, flowered slopes, grassy paths, fierce contests, righteous victors, melancholy losers.

Perhaps it is the simplicity of the symbols used which supplies their charm. The human tendency to make full and finished the faintly limned picture has been observed by linguists and psychologists. Incomplete drawings capture a child's attention and stimulate him to add the lines that will make the picture whole. Given the vague or indistinct image, the poem, the minimally etched piece of sculpture—the person taking in that particular bit of communication must work harder. He receives fewer literal, concrete, specific cues. Because there is less done for him, he must do more for himself.

Occasionally I have shown graduate students a series of simple line drawings—a circle adjacent to a diamond, wavy lines crossing one another, a line of dots—and asked them to name the figures.

"First Meeting," "Opposites Attract," "Clown Eyes," and "Modern Art" were some of their responses to the first drawing. Other drawings prompted equally diverse and imaginative responses. It may be the same with board stories. They ask the viewer to take a hint, a suggestion, and from it create a gestalt—a unified whole. Frail as these stories may be when compared with, say, the electronic figures that people the television screen—the audience breathes life into them.

Where to begin our study of this creative media? We'll talk first about the materials we need, then move on to suggestions for making and telling the stories. As you work with these materials and techniques, imagine these stories as they might appear to a child.

The Board

While flannel is the usual covering for a storytelling board, I would not recommend it. Flannel wrinkles and stretches, picks up dirt and dust with the same facility that it holds felt figures, and is difficult to clean.

My own board is covered with inexpensive indoor-outdoor carpeting—the pressed material that reminds me of the inner-soles we used to put inside our hunting boots in cold weather. This carpeting is made in various tones of brown, blue, rust, and green. It comes in six foot widths, but can also be purchased in foor-square tiles. It is not expensive; enough to cover a small fiber-backed bulletin board—18 by 24 inches—can be purchased for about five dollars. Felt figures cling well to this surface. It can be sponged clean, possesses a soft appearance of depth, and is wrinkle free.

But the greatest advantage of this particular covering for the story-board aficionado lies in its remarkable attraction for the hooked portion of the cloth fastener material known as Velcro. More about Velcro in a minute.

The Figures

The bad name story boards have earned over the years probably has a lot to do with the use of paper cut-out figures colored with crayon and backed with sandpaper. The edges of these figures curl and fray, and, no matter how much sandpaper you use, they drift and tumble to the floor right at a critical point in the story. Nor do I recommend pellon or other lightweight stiff fabrics. They lack depth and substance and their colors are not clear.

One of my favorite materials is felt. It has bright, glowing colors, is easy to work with, and is inexpensive and simple to obtain. Most fabric shops sell foot-square patches of felt in a wide choice of colors. Felt scraps may be glued to larger felt shapes with fabric cement to outline pockets, buttons, hats, stripes, eyes, and other details. Additional details, ranging from shading to fine accent lines, may be added with a felt pen. Sequins and tiny buttons and bits of leather and other fabrics may be glued to felt.

Another advantage of felt is that both the front and back of a figure can be shown. Paper cutouts, with their sandpaper backing, can only be placed in one position on the board. Felt figures, on the other hand, can be shown in profile facing left and right, or, when shown full face, can be turned around so that their back shows. Thus, characters can appear to walk in both directions or, like ancient Greek theater masks, feature both a smile and a frown.

Other Materials

Steel wool is useful in story board stories. When stretched out, it resembles dark clouds for night scenes. It makes fine hair for grandfathers, and good smoke for factory smokestacks. From cotton one may form light fluffy clouds, beards, soft down for bird nests, bodies of rabbits and lambs, a snowy field. Brightly colored yarns, particularly those big fuzzy ones sometimes used for hair ties, are useful. A brown yarn, extended across the width of the board, can represent a hot, dusty plain; a blue yarn, the ocean. Green yarn placed in a zigzag fashion can simulate mountains. Or yarn can be used to make simple outlines of houses, animals, and faces.

With the aid of Velcro, small objects can be placed on the story board. Glue a patch of the hooked tape about the size of a thumb nail to the back of the object, and it will cling to the carpeting until pulled off. Wooden blocks, carved bits of foam rubber, pressed leaves, dried weeds and ferns, beads, sequins, feathers, scraps of fur and bark and leather, toys, mirrors—all of these may join your story-board collection with the addition of a bit of Velcro.

Creating the Figures

Typically books or chapters on the story board include actual figures to trace. I do not recommend using those. Tracing inhibits the imagination and does not allow for size variation. Most storytellers, given a few basic suggestions, can create characters and properties which will be both original and pleasing. Working with a smaller or larger board means that the figures must be proportioned accordingly.

There are, of course, many sources of ideas. Encyclopedias and visual dictionaries may provide simple line drawings that can serve as a starting point for your own drawings. Picture books and children's books are an excellent source. But best of all, perhaps, is sitting down with a pencil and paper and making some sketches that catch the essence of the object you wish to present. What, for example, is a troll? Huge sharp teeth and a wild eye; fingers that grasp and tear; long unkempt hair that blows every which way. These few elements, I would submit, are far more powerful for the viewer than any stereotyped drawing.

Prepare preliminary drawings before beginning your work with felt or foam rubber or any of the other materials you use. And, of course, make changes after you've tried out your new story a few times.

Leaving In and Taking Out

The little figures and objects used in board stories are, it seems to me, symbolic. The troll may be no more than a hank of fake fur with a fierce eye gleaming from its center, and Big Billy Goat Gruff a rack of curved and gleaming horns (fashioned conveniently out of foam rubber, with shiny paste pearls on their ends, backed with a bit of Velcro). The full cast may consist of the troll, three goats, a bridge, and little more. Perhaps a bit of yarn could represent a meadow and another longer piece could be used to show mountains that stretch to the sky. But neither trees, river, flowers, nor the sun are essential—the listener will create them from his own imagination.

The reason, in short, for using a story board is not to help members of an audience visualize the story, since for the most part it is fully capable of doing that on their own. Rather, it is to create pleasing and beautiful little pictures as an accompaniment to your telling. However, we shall have more to say on that topic as we move into the stories themselves.

Incidentally, sometimes one may wish to set up the scene for a story in advance, much as a stage is set before a play, so that only the main characters are added during the actual telling. If, for instance, one were telling "Goldilocks," the interior of the house could be already arranged, with corrugated board, painted red, for roof tiles, and yarn outlining the perimeter of the house. Dishes, chairs, and beds could be simple felt cut-outs or toys or bits of other fabric backed with Velcro.

Storing the Figures

I use little baskets and wood or tin boxes to store board figures. At a performance, I hold the box on my lap, peep inside, stir the contents around a bit, and then draw each character forth as needed and place it on the board. The front of the box serves as a dressing room for those characters not yet playing their little roles, and there's a nice bit of magic in knowing they've been slumbering in that aggregation of corners, waiting their turn to strut and parade.

Placing the Flannel Board

Telling stories with a story board is an intimate form of the storyteller's art. The audience needs to see the figures clearly as the action changes and unfolds. If you are standing while telling the story, you may place the board on an easel and put the box with the unused figures on a small table nearby.

With a classroom group sitting on a rug, I'll often lean the board on the back of a wooden chair and then sit in another chair right next to it, with the box on my lap. As I tell the story, I remove the figures from the box (where they have been arranged so as to appear in appropriate order), and place them on the board.

If there's an upright piano in the classroom or auditorium, one can lean the board against its front, put the box of figures on top, and tell the story while standing.

What Stories to Tell

It's difficult here to make any hard and fast generalizations. Just when I think a tale is inappropriate, one of my students will bring it to class and show it off, and I'll realize that I was wrong again. In general, however, we have found there are three classes of stories that lend themselves to telling with this medium:

- the folktale, with its limited cast of characters and settings and more talk than action;

- the scientific account, where pictures supplement words to explain a phenomenon or the functioning of an object or organism. It may be that the teller wishes to compare the size of a gray whale and man, or wants to show the chronology of certain events, or wishes to demonstrate the circuit electricity makes as it travels to a light bulb and back again to the source of power; and

- the accumulative tale or song, where detail after detail is added to the story while at the same time figures are added to the picture being created on the board.

In the following pages, examples of the uses of the story board described above will be shown, together with suggestions for their preparation and telling. Figures used in the stories are modeled after those I have used in my own telling, and are meant to serve as illustrations only.

Folktales

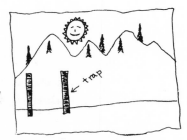

The Tiger, The Brahman, and the Jackal

In far-off India the mountains are high and green. Far below them stretches the hot, brown plain.

Here the sun shines down with all its might, so that few creatures venture out from the shade of tree or house.

On such a blazing day, when no one was about, a Tiger foolishly walked into a trap. Oh, how Tiger carried on! He moaned and cried. He roared with rage. He flung himself against the walls of the trap, but no good came of it. He could not escape.

A Brahman—a holy man—came walking down the road and saw the imprisoned tiger. He stopped and considered him.

When Tiger saw Brahman looking at him, he put on his sweetest smile. "Oh, kind Brahman," he said, "Be so good as to release me from this trap."

But Brahman shook his head. "Release you? And lose my life? Not I. I know the fondness you Tigers have for eating, and I fear that you may have developed an extraordinary appetite after your imprisonment."

Tiger made his voice sweet. "Hungry? Me? No, I am not hungry. I long only to be free, so that I may return to my good wife and cubs."

Brahman, soft-hearted as he was, took pity on Tiger. "Very well," he said, "I'll release you. But promise me this: that you will not eat me."

"Oh, indeed, I promise," said Tiger. And so Brahman opened the cage

Green yarn mountains ... narrow green felt triangles for trees ... brown yarn to indicate plain ... yellow and orange sun ... two upright felt strips on left side of board to indicate cage ...

When Tiger walks into trap, add blue strips to indicate bars ...

Here's the holy man I use. Note that he's finished on both sides so that he can move both to left and right.

and Tiger was free.

No sooner was that wretched animal out of the cage than he fell on poor Brahman and began to roar.

"How hungry I am," he said. "And you look like a tasty morsel. You'll make a fine meal for me after my long fast!"

"Alas," cried Brahman. "I am kind to you, and in return you take my life."

"Why shouldn't I?" asked Tiger. "That's the way of the world."

"Grant me one request," moaned Brahman. "Let me go and ask three others if I have been treated justly. If they agree, then I shall submit without another complaint."

"Very well," said Tiger, "That will only postpone dinner for a few minutes, and I can wait a bit longer. Go and ask three others if you have been treated fairly. But go swiftly, for I am very hungry."

And so Brahman trudged off along the road. The first thing he came to was a Fig Tree. "Why do you look so sad?" asked Fig Tree.

"Woe is me," said Brahman. "I set Tiger free from his cage, and now he wants to make a meal of me in exchange for my kindness. Is that fair?"

"As fair as the world ever is," said Fig Tree. "All day long I stand here, giving shade and food to travelers along this road. They strip branches from me to beat their animals. They accept my shade and my good figs with never a word of kindness. I say to you that you should stop complaining and go to your fate like a man!"

Brahman heard these words with great sadness. He set off down the road again. As he walked, the road beneath his feet began to talk to him.

Children seem to like the ridiculous formality of this pose ... Notice that Tiger is also finished on both sides, so he can now face Brahman ...

This entire conversation takes place while Tiger sits on top of the Brahman.

Move Tiger back near the cage. The Brahman is turned so that he faces to the right of the board, ready to search for supporters ...

Place Fig Tree on the board, to the right of waiting Tiger ...

Remove Fig Tree after its speech ...

"What's the matter, Brahman?" Road asked. "Why are you so sad?"

"Alas, good Road," said Brahman, "I set Tiger free from a cage, and in exchange for my kindness he wishes to eat me. Does that seem fair?"

Lean Brahman over as if addressing Road. The rigidity of the pose adds a nice touch of nonsense ...

"As fair as you could ask for," said Road. "Look at me. All day long travelers walk on me, me, scuffing dust in my face. They roll their heavy wagons over me. They spit on me. And no thanks do I receive. I say that Tiger is acting as he should. Stop your sniveling and meet your fate bravely!"

Poor Brahman! He walked away slowly, sorrowing.

Now a little saddleback jackal came trotting down the road toward him.

"What's the matter, Friend?" asked Jackal.

You may wish to explain that a jackal is a small wild dog that lives in India and other parts of Asia ...

"Ah, I'm a doomed man," said Brahman. "Tiger was caught in a cage, and I set him free, and now he wants to eat me."

"How is that again?" said Jackal. "You were in a cage, and ..."

"No, no," said Brahman. "Tiger was in the cage, and I let him out, and ..."

The little Jackal shook his head, puzzled. "Words! words!" he said, "I just can't understand them. Why don't we go back to the cage so I can see how it was."

And so the two of them set off down the road to where Tiger was waiting.

Here's a nice sinister line ...

"Ahrrrrr," roared Tiger. "I see that dinner has returned, and brought supper as well."

"Ah, good Tiger," said Brahman. "I was trying to explain to this poor creature how it came about that you were

This dialogue must flow easily. Pace, pitch, and tone will help differentiate between the various characters ...

going to eat me. He returned with me so that I could show him exactly how it happened."

Brahman turned to Jackal. "You see," he began, "Tiger was in the cage, and ..."

"Ah, of course," said Jackal eagerly. "Now I understand. The cage was in the Tiger, and Road came walking by, and ... and ... But where were you?"

"You fool!" roared Tiger. "I was in the cage, and Brahman came walking by, and ..."

"You were in the cage?" asked Jackal in disbelief. "But how did you get in the cage?"

Tiger was at the end of his patience. "You stupid fool," he roared. "I got in like this!" And he jumped into the cage and slammed the door shut.

"Ah," said Jackal. "Now I think I understand. *You* were in the cage."

"Yes!" shouted Tiger.

"And Brahman was out here."

"Exactly," said Tiger.

"Perhaps," said Jackal, "if that's how matters were, that's how they should remain!"

And, saying that, Jackal and Brahman set off down the road together.

It's always fun to watch the change of expression on children's faces as the timid Brahman and the enraged Tiger explain all this to poor, addlepated Jackal ...

who turns out to be ...

... not so stupid after all![1]

In the story we just told, notice how words and figure placement form a kind of rhythm:

In far- off India the mountains are high and green ... (Say that line, then pause and create those high green mountains with a length of green yarn. Place narrow triangles of green felt in the mountains to represent trees.)

Far below them stretches the hot, brown plain. (Again, say the line, pause, and place brown yarn across the bottom third of the board to simulate the floor of the plain. On the left-hand side place two upright lengths of felt to show the cage.)

Here the sun shines with all its might (set the sun in the sky) *so that few creatures venture out from the shade of trees or house.*

On such a blazing day, when no one was about, a Tiger ... (place Tiger on the board) *foolishly walked into a trap.* (Move Tiger across board from right to left, place him in the cage, and then entrap him with three cross-pieces of felt.)

One of the sources of pleasure for an audience is the kaleidoscope of arrangements possible with a few bits of felt and a story board. Do not hurry these arrangements. Once the characters in a story are in place, limit their movement. When Tiger roars and wails and throws himself against the bars of his cage, the storyteller does not move him. Each member of the audience supplies, in her own mind, an imagined enactment of that event. During the dialogue between Tiger and Brahman, do not touch the characters.

Scientific Accounts

It was mentioned earlier that scientific accounts form one of the classes of stories particularly suited for the story board. Here is an account of grunion spawning.[2]

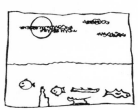

The Grunion

During the months between March and August, when the moon is full and the tides are at their highest, the grunion appear in the surf along the beaches of California.

The tide reaches flood stage. For a brief moment it hesitates.

It is on the waves of this ebbing tide that the fish swim ashore. Their bodies shimmer like silver coins as they lie writhing on the wet sands. They remain there for only a few seconds, however, for on the wash of the next high wave they leap back into the water and are carried out to sea.

This goes on for perhaps an hour with thousands and thousands of grunion swimming up onto the beach,

Place felt moon, steel wool clouds, and blue yarn water on the board, matching their placement so that a rhythmic balance of words and pictures is achieved ... Brightly colored sea creatures are added to the seascape. (Sequins and beads are useful ...)

Introduce a pair of grunion into the water—mine are about three inches long—pale blue felt, touched up with silver paint ... Deft manipulation of the yarn can show how the grunion leave the water when it is at its highest to lie briefly in the sand

... Move the yarn up and down to demonstrate the rising and lowering of the tides ...

Repeat action to demonstrate the fact that many grunion leave the water and then return.

leaving the water, and then returning to it.

During that brief moment, there on the wet sand, the female has shed her eggs, and the male has fertilized them.

The eggs are safe, for each succeeding wave advances a little lower on the beach than the one that preceded it.

Nor will the high tide of the following night disturb the eggs, for after the full of the moon each tide halts a bit lower on the beach.

And so, for about two weeks, the eggs are left undisturbed in the warm, damp, incubating sand.

During that time a miracle occurs. Magically, it seems, each fertilized egg has changed into a larval fishlet—a perfectly formed miniature grunion, imprisoned within the friendly confines of the egg, waiting for its release.

With the tides of the new moon that release comes. The waves sweep in, higher and higher, until they swirl about on the sands, sifting and moving the covering under which the little masses of grunion eggs lie buried.

The sand stirs and washes away. The egg membranes break, and the tiny grunion, feeling the cool water's touch, are borne out into the vast sea.

I tried various items, including a miniature egg carton to show grunion eggs. At last I settled on a pale cluster of circles ...

This can be shown by moving the yarn up and down ...

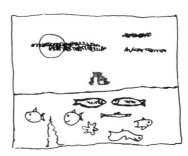

Exchange the full moon for a new one ...

Using the yarn, show how the waves move up, higher and higher, until they touch the eggs and wash over them ...

Remove the egg cluster and place fishlets below the surf line along with other sea life ...

In the account of the grunion, as in "The Tiger, the Brahman, and the Jackal," the storyteller develops a pattern of alternating spoken phrases with physical placing or moving of objects in the story. For instance, the first portion of the story might work out something as follows:

During the months between March and August, when the moon is full (place moon in sky; add steel wool for cloud) *the grunion appear in the surf along the beaches of California.* (Place blue yarn to simulate water level, add bits of colored felt to the lower third of the board to represent tiny sea creatures, then a couple of slender grunion ...)

The tide reaches flood stage. For a brief moment it hesitates. Then it begins to ebb ... (Move the blue yarn up and down slowly to show the advance and retreat of waves ...)

It is on the waves of this ebbing tide that the fish swim ashore ... (Move the grunion from the water portion of the board to the sand portion, above the blue line representing the surf ...)

Their bodies shimmer in the light of the moon as they lie writhing on the wet sands ... (The remainder of the story continues with this same alternating pattern ...)

Accumulative Stories

In the accumulative tale, detail after detail is added to the account—and to the picture on the board—as the plot develops. The following demonstrates this genre. You will find in it characteristics woven into the thread of similar stories emanating from different cultures. (This story is very popular with the K-3 crowd. It also tells well without a board.)

Not Afraid of Anything

Once there was a little girl, and she wasn't afraid of anything!

She wasn't afraid of dark shadows...

Or boogie men ...

Or creepy crawly bugs.

"I'm not afraid of dark shadows, or boogie men, or creepy crawly bugs," she said, and she dropped a creepy crawly bug right down inside her grandmother's dress.

She was a brave child!

Her parents thought she ought to learn a little healthy fear.

Her daddy took out the night light in her room.

Place items on the board as they are named...

Black felt shadows ...

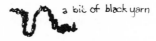
a bit of black yarn

Boogie men ... (Stretch out the word boogie—it's lots of fun to say ...)

Creepy crawly bugs ... (Mine are fake fur, with tiny button eyes ... plastic bugs with velco on the back would also work just fine ...)

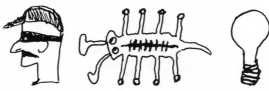

A light bulb ... (Mine is made from felt ...)

"I don't need a night light in my room," she said.

Her mother took her to the biggest department store in town, and that little girl ran away and hid in the dress racks, and stayed there and stayed there until the store closed.

A store, also felt ...

Notice there's no representation of the little girl ...
The siren noise is fun ...

A friendly policeman found her and took her home in his paddy wagon, the siren wailing. Oooooo-hhhhheeee ... On the way home he bought her an ice-cream cone.

An ice cream cone ...

"I like being lost in big department stores," she said. "But they don't scare me!"

She was one brave child!

Can't you just imagine the sassy tone she'd use ...

One night, that little girl was lying in bed, almost asleep, when she heard a sound far off down the road. *Kerwump, kerwump* ... It sounded like empty boots, marching.

***Kerwump, kerwump* ... These happen to be the sounds I like to make here ... you may find others that suit you better ...**

Closer and closer the sound came, louder and louder, up the front path, right through the kitchen door without even opening it, down the long front hall, and into her bedroom.

Practice this part again and again until it just rolls out ...

The little girl raised herself up to see what that awful noise was.

Mime this action ... she's sitting up, scornful ...

And there, next to her bed, was a pair of empty boots; huge, bright yellow, with long purple shoe laces.

Boots ...

She looked at them with disdain.

"And," she said, "I'm not afraid of empty boots that go *kerwump, kerwump!* either!"

That same sassy voice ...

And she lay back down and tried to go to sleep.

But now, far off down the road, she heard another sound; a whistling, hissing sound, whistling and hissing down the road, up the front walk, right through the kitchen door, down the long front

Draw out "whistling and hissing" as you say these words, so that they actually seem to whistle and hiss ...

hall, and right into that little girl's room...

With an annoyed sigh, that little girl raised herself up again and looked to see what was making that dreadful sound.

There, on top of those ugly yellow boots, was a pair of whistling, hissing blue trousers!

The little girl looked at them, her lip curling with disgust, "And I'm not afraid of whistling, hissing trousers, either!"

And she lay back down, tucked the covers around her head so she wouldn't have to listen to any more of this noise, and tried to go to sleep.

And now she heard a flapping, slapping sound. It flapped and slapped, far away, off down that cold, dark street, and then, closer and closer, flapping and slapping up the front walk, and right through the kitchen door. It flapped and slapped down the long hall, and into that little girl's room.

She flounced the covers back and sat up. "Now what!" she muttered.

There, on top of those ugly blue trousers, was a flapping, slapping red shirt, with great, long bony hands sticking out each sleeve, and on each finger of those great long hands, long ugly plastic fingernails, painted purple.

That little girl stared at them with absolute loathing.

"And," she said, "I'm not afraid of flapping slapping red shirts, either! So buzz off!"

And she lay back down, and pulled the covers up, very tightly, and stuck her hands down under the covers—not because she was afraid, you understand

Can you sigh, annoyed, as the little girl might have, as you mime this action?

"Blue" can be drawn out ...
The trousers I made are cut from blue denim, with a sewn patch on the knee, and a tiny leather belt, and a little brass buckle ... about two inches high ...

I sometimes ask, "Have you ever done that—tucked the covers around you?"

Can't you just imagine how she's going to say this?

Much of the fun in this story is the repetition—of words, of actions, but all with slight variations, and always building ...

"... flapping, slapping red shirts ..." How will she say that line?

Generally, there's an aside to the audience here—"You've never done that—have you? Put your hands under the covers ...?"

—but because the room was getting cold, and tried to go to sleep.

And now, far off down the street, she heard a howling, growing sound. It howled and growled, closer and closer, up the front walk, and right through the kitchen door, and down the long hall, and into her bedroom.

It was a howling growling head. Oh, it was ugly! It was huge, big as a milk-fed pumpkin, with a great long green nose, and eyes big as china plates, and fat pink ears, and a bristling orange mustache, and hair the color of lemon meringue pie.

That head bounced and bopped its way right up on top of the red shirt. It stared down at that little girl.

She reared up in bed. "What do you want?" she said. Boy! She was mad!

That head didn't say anything. Boots moved a little closer. *Kerwump! Kerwump!*

"What do you want?" She didn't sound quite so brave this time.

Head didn't say anything. Boots moved a little closer. *Kerwump, kerwump!*

And then, right then, that little girl started to cry. "Ba-woop! Ba-woop! Ba-woo-woo-woo-woo-woop!"

"What do you want?"

"YOU!"

That little girl was out of her bed that fast. Down the long front hall. Through the living room. Right into her parent's bedroom!

They were sleeping close together on this big, high bed. She climbed up, clutching the quilt with both hands. She shoved her daddy to one side. She shoved her mother over to the other side. She

And of course the audience knows what it's going to be ... "A head! A head!" they're saying. "That's right," I acknowledge ... "It's a head, just like you said!"

Small children like this part; they shriek in dismay each time a new facial feature is named ...

I demonstrate the staring ...

Aren't you proud of that little girl? She's got starch!

A hint of panic entering in ...

Those happen to be the crying noises I make ... you will want to invent your own ... It's pathetic, the way she's caved in ...

Nice and loud!

Hand gestures to show her shoving her father and mother aside ...

slid down between them and pulled the covers up, tight, shaking all over like jello.

A little quivering of your own would be in order ...

She slept with them that night. And the next night. And the next. She slept with them for five nights in a row!

And from that time on, she was a different child. She had to have a night light in her room. Her daddy had to look under her bed every night for boogie men.

And on only very special occasions did she drop a creepy crawly bug down inside her grandmother's dress.

And that's the truth!

After telling this story, if it's a small group, I may ask, "What kinds of things are you afraid of?"

"I'm not afraid of anything," someone will say.

"Why, you're just like that little girl."

Someone else will burst out, "I'm not afraid of anything either, but I don't like loud noises!"

Another child will mention something she doesn't like too well, either, and another, and before long all of us—including me—are telling about the things we aren't keen on: creaky noises in the house, or snakes, or the long walk from the garage to the kitchen door at night, or the family going away.

And a Modern Tale ...

As I mentioned earlier, when working with a story board one has to decide: "Which parts of the story do I show and which parts do I tell?" In some stories this decision is not a difficult one. In "The Tiger, the Brahman, and the Jackal" the number of characters and objects was limited; the fig tree, the cage, the hot, dusty plain, the animals—one could show them all. In the second story, "The Grunion," it was necessary to be somewhat more selective; thousands of grunion leap ashore in California during those nights, but are represented with two little scraps of felt. Millions of eggs are laid in the sand, shown by a single egg mass. In "Not Afraid of Anything," illustrations focused only on the things the little girl was afraid of. Father, mother, grandmother, dark and gloomy streets, the kitchen door, even the little girl herself, were not shown.

In the following tale of a man who adds room after room to his house to accomodate long-staying guests, a similar decision was made. I first planned to show all the visitors who came and stayed—the bicycle-riding goat, the sleeping dog, the goose, the donkey, as well as the central character, Paco. But in the end, I decided to show only the house, and let the listener imagine the other elements. I think the decision was a good one.

Incidentally, some may think this story had its origin in the Watts Towers of Los Angeles—those fantastic creations fashioned from cement and old pipe and broken bits of glass. But I think a more likely source of the story is my childhood observations of my father—a man unfailing in his generosity.

Paco

Once there was a man, and his name was Paco.

He lived all alone out by the city dump in a little house he had built for himself out of scraps and bits.

Every morning Paco would get up. He'd start a fire, and fix himself some breakfast: *tortillas, huevos rancheros,* a cup of coffee.

Then he'd go outside and sit in his old yellow chair and sun himself.

Sometimes he'd tend his geraniums.

And sometimes he'd just sit and watch the big trucks haul in junk and dump it in huge piles.

He was a happy man. He bothered no one. And no one bothered him.

Oh, sometimes he felt a little lonely.

But not often.

Then, one day, while Paco was sunning himself, an old donkey came ambling down the road, sadly swinging his tail from side to side.

"*¿A donde vá, Señor?*" asked Paco. "Where are you going?"

The house is a soft tan, with a purple chimney, and a few bricks showing through ...

Chimney smoke in different colors; a new puff of smoke for every food item named ...

One may add a chair and a geranium patch ...

"Nowhere," Donkey answered in a melancholy voice. "No one wants me any more. So I'm just walking until I can't walk any further; then I'll stop there."

"*Pero no, Señor*," said Paco. "You must stop with me."

"But where'll I stay?"

"*¡No problema!* We find old lumber at the dump, and I build you a place. You'll see! *¡Venga!* Come on!"

And that's just what they did. They found boards, and partly filled cans of paint, and they built another room on Paco's house. And because they had to build it up high, they put in a stairway.

And Paco settled back to enjoy life again.

Every morning he fixed his breakfast of *tortillas y café con leche*—coffee with milk. Donkey nibbled a little dried grass. The two of them tended the geraniums. Then while Paco sat and watched the big trucks, Donkey practiced stair climbing.

Occasionally they discussed politics. Sometimes they played checkers.

Fué una vida dulce—It was a sweet life.

And then, one day, they heard a honking noise.

HONK! HONK! It was a lame goose, gray, with an orange bill, honking its way slowly down the road.

"*Es una cantina bonita*," said Paco. "A beautiful song."

"That's right! Make fun! Make fun!" said Goose, marching on. "I'll soon be out of your hearing, and won't be bothering you again."

"No, no," said Paco. "The sound is pleasant. Permit us the pleasure of your practice."

Throughout this dialogue, nothing is added to the board ...

Now we add Donkey's room, red with white trim, and a stairway going up ...

"But where would I stay?" asked Goose. "*¡No problema¡*" said Paco. "We'll have a fine room for you in no time."

No sooner said than started. Before nightfall, there was a fine, swimming pool; white, with brass trimming and clawed feet and red roses painted on the side. Perfect for practicing scales.

And, of course, another stairway to get one there.

Then the three of them settled in. In the morning Paco would fix himself his breakfast. He'd go outdoors to sun himself. After her bath, Goose would come downstairs and hunt for snails in the geranium beds. Donkey would graze a bit, then join Paco for a game of checkers.

And life went on; day following day.

Then one evening two pigeons flew by and settled down on the rim of Goose's bathtub. They cooed throaty sounds, and seemed reluctant to go on.

Goose did not appreciate being disturbed while bathing.

"Please leave at once," she said in her haughtiest voice.

"We've come a long way and are weary," said one pigeon. "And my wife is expecting. Could we perhaps stay a few days and recover?"

"Hmmmpf!" sniffed Goose. "Certainly not with me! But talk to Paco. Perhaps he could arrange something. And now, if you please, I'm getting ready to rehearse."

So the pigeons flew down and talked to Paco, and the next morning he and Donkey and Goose went searching in the dump, and in a couple of days they'd

This particular bathtub is of shiny white cardboard, with painted red roses and gold claw feet ...

Goose is quintessentially the *artiste;* flighty, self-centered; irritable ...

But she does recognize Paco's generosity ...

built a fine airy cote, with a King's X flag flying from the roof to let everyone know this was a sanctuary—a safe place.

Mrs. Pigeon laid her eggs there, and soon three featherless little pigeon babies, appeared.

In much the same way, an old stray dog came looking for a home, and a kangaroo who had run away from the circus, and a goat who could ride a unicorn.

Everyone who came wanted to stay, and Paco and Donkey and whoever else could help would find bits and pieces over at the dump, and with them they'd build more house: a sun porch for Dog, a tower for Kangaroo, and a fine little cabin for Goat, who said it reminded him of the Rockie Mountains, where he'd lived when young.

And the days passed, all of them content with themselves and the world.

And then one morning when Paco went outside after breakfast to sit in the sun, a big official-looking man was standing there, studying a book and scratching his head and mumbling to himself.

"This your house, *amigo*?" he asked Paco.

"*Si, Señor*. It is a fine house, *no?*"

"*Si*," said the big man. "A fine house; a beautiful house. That's the good news. The bad news is this: I'm from the Los Angeles Building Department, and you're going to have to tear it down."

"Tear it down? But why?"

"Now understand, *amigo*, I don't want to do this," said the big man. "But in the first place, you've got no permits. And besides, it's not done according to the law. Any of it. Take those stairs, stuck out in the open like that—so nice

You may wish to explain that a cote is a small shed for keeping birds ... this one is perched atop a long pole ...

Dog's house, with nice big windows ... and Kangaroo's tower ... a cabin for Goat ... all these elaborately decorated pieces are added as mentioned ...

And here's the completed house! No additional pieces are added to the flannel board from this point on.

The big man is giving Paco bad news, but still, he's a sympathetic character. To build suspense, you'll want to not let too much of that sympathy show too early ...

and airy. But you can't have 'em. Says so right here on page 129, subsection A.

"Or take that bathtub ..."

"*Pero señor*, that is not a bathtub. *Es una alberca*—a swimming pool—for *Señorita* Goose."

"You know that. I know that," said the big man, very patiently. "You could tell me it's a swimming pool for the president of the United States. But it don't matter. According to the book it's a bathtub, and if it's a bathtub, it's got to be in a bathroom."

The big man sighed. "Oh, I could go on," he said. "But you see what I mean. You're going to have to tear it down. And I'm awful sorry, because I don't remember ever seeing a house I liked better!"

He finished writing, and snapped his book shut. He got in his big blue truck and drove away. He didn't even look back!

Paco couldn't believe it! His fine house to be torn down! His friends—practically family—sent away!

Just then he heard Donkey, coming down the stairs.

"What's up?"Donkey asked. "Thought I heard voices."

"*Fué nada,*" said Paco, trying to act cheerful. "It was nothing. Tell you what, though, let's have a party tonight!"

And that's what they did. They had watermelon, and strong cheese. They had *tortillas y frijoles*. They had orange soda pop and *cervesa*. They had bird seed for the pigeon babies. They sang and danced until the first light of dawn. Paco seemed to be having the best time of all.

Finally they all went to bed.

But Paco did not sleep well. The

next morning, before anyone else was up,
he brewed himself a cup of coffee, black,
and went outside with his hammer to
begin tearing down the house.

And there was the big man with the
blue truck, again. And next to the truck,
a long fancy black car, with four important looking people standing by it, staring at the house.

"*Buenos días,*" said Paco, sadly. He
did not feel at all well.

"*Buenos días, amigo,*" said the big
man. "I brought some *gente muy impor-
tante para ver su casa.*" He turned to
them. "Well, what do you think?"

"*Fantástico,*" said the first man.

"Incredible sense of line and
dimension," said a tiny woman, peering
through thick spectacles.

"Innovative in its variety of materials," said another woman, very tall and
thin.

"A unique statement of the personal philosophy of the artist," said the last
man.

"A winner!" all of them said
together.

"What is this winner business?"
asked Paco.

"It's like this, *amigo,*" said the big
man. "If your house is just a house, you
have to tear it down. But if it's a Work of
Art, that's different. These folks are from
the Los Angeles County Art Board. And
if they say your house is Art, why then,
it's safe. That's why I invited them over."

"You mean I don't have to tear it
down?"

"Tear it down?" the woman with
the glasses gasped. "This precious Work
of Art! Over my dead body!"

"It must be protected for all time,"

**Develop various voices and mannerisms for
these characters ...**

said the tall, thin woman. "You will be the curator—the caretaker. The city will pay you to live here."

There was handshaking and congratulating. The tall thin lady gave Paco a kiss on the cheek.

Then they all drove away, promising to return soon with a plaque.

And that's how Paco and his friends spent the rest of their days living in the biggest Work of Art in all of Los Angeles County.

And the last time I drove by, the blue truck was parked there, and the long, fancy black car.

And I heard singing!

Isn't it wonderful, when Art prevails!

Audience Participation

One may give an audience the opportunity to participate through the use of old ballads and poems. Distribute token symbols to persons in the audience. While the rest sing, the items are brought forward as they appear and placed on the board.

Here's a version of "Billy Boy," together with suggested pieces for use with the story board.

Where Have You Been, Billy Boy

Oh, where have you been, Billy Boy, Billy Boy?

Oh, where have you been, charming Billy?

I have been to seek a wife, she's the joy of my life,

She's a young thing and cannot leave her mother!

Did she ask you to come in, Billy Boy, Billy Boy?

Did she ask you to come in, charming Billy?

Yes, she asked me to come in, there's a dimple in her chin,

Remember an earlier suggestion for acting out this song as readers' theater?

She's a young thing and cannot leave her mother!

Did she take from you your hat, Billy Boy, Billy Boy?

Did she take from you your hat, charming Billy?

Yes, she took from me my hat, and she threw it at the cat,

She's a young thing and cannot leave her mother!

Did she set for you a chair, Billy Boy, Billy Boy?

Did she set for you a chair, charming Billy?

Yes, she set for me a chair, but the bottom wasn't there,

She's a young thing and cannot leave her mother!

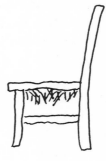

Did she offer you a drink, Billy boy, Billy Boy?

Did she offer you a drink, charming Billy?

Yes, she offered me a drink, then she threw it down the sink,

She's a young thing and cannot leave her mother!

Can she make a cherry pie, Billy boy, Billy Boy?

Can she make a cherry pie, charming Billy?

She can make a cherry pie, Quick as a cat can wink its eye,

But she's a young thing, and cannot leave her mother!

How tall is she, Billy Boy, Billy Boy?

How tall is she, charming Billy?

She's as tall as a pine, and as skinny as a vine,

She's a young thing and cannot leave her mother!

How old is she, Billy Boy, Billy

Boy?

How old is she, charming Billy?

Three times six, four times seven, twenty-eight and eleven,

She's a young thing and cannot leave her mother!

With adults and older children it's also fun to first place the token on the board and ask for the audience to create new verses. Some of these are guaranteed to surprise and delight.

And If You Are a Teacher ...

We must not overlook the pleasure and learning potential for children in handling these little figures. Often, after telling a story, I will invite children to retell the story in their own way, using the figures and pieces. Invariably, they make the story their own, adding original touches and rearranging the pieces. The puffs of smoke in "Paco" were added by Susan after she first heard the story. She also put the house together in a new way, substituted a pink pig for the goat. Kangaroo and dog shared a room so the pigeon babies could have their own place. The changes made the story hers.

Occasionally, at home, I'll find stories left for me by the daughters on the story board or the old Persian rug in the study—bits of yarn and scraps of felt to tell about the cat and her new kittens, or magenta and yellow mushroom houses on a street lined with pink and green palm trees reaching far into the sky. (I *think* that's what those stories were about. I may have been wrong.)

In the classroom the little figures help children visualize concepts that might be difficult to grasp without graphic illustration. Sequencing, too, can be developed with the story board.

I would recommend, after a classroom telling, the characters and figures be made available to children so that they might touch them and hold them and, if they choose, use them to recapture briefly all or part of the story.

And I would urge the teacher/storyteller to keep a box of felt scraps and a board in the classroom. Given the raw materials, children can create their own characters and figures and become story board tellers, sharing their art with others.

My students and I have used the story board when working with children who have limited reading abilities.[3] We tell the child a board story, then invite him to tell us a story back, using the same characters. As he proceeds with his telling, the teacher writes down what is said, with story length not to exceed a page of hand-printed manuscript. (This is done so that teacher and child won't have an excessive amount of text to work with. It also promotes brevity and story structure.)

When the child has finished telling his story, he is asked to read through the printed manuscript, underlining all the words he recognizes. Generally he astonishes himself, knowing more words than he thought he did. True, he may mark the same words—*the* and *big* and *Billy Goat Gruff* again and again—but that doesn't matter—they're words he recognizes, and he can receive legitimate praise for his efforts.

At that point, teacher and child read the story together; the child reading the words he knows and the teacher reading what's left. For example, a typical marked sentence in such a story might look like this:

Big <u>Billy</u> <u>Goat</u> <u>Gruff</u> says, "I'll eat you <u>up!</u>"

In that sentence, the child has indicated that he recognizes *Billy, Goat, Gruff,* and *up.* The teacher supplies *Big, says, I'll,* and *eat.*

It's fun! Child and teacher trip over each other in their reading. It turns out that the child knows more words than he's marked down. Teacher scolds him for knowing too many words—"Don't I get a chance?" They try the story again. This time the child knows an additional ten words or so. More scolding. Before a half hour has passed, he can read the entire story without mishap.

The teacher then puts sentences from the story on cards and scrambles them. The child must arrange the sentences in the same order in which they occurred in the story. From there they proceed to word cards; the teacher writes out single words, the child matches them, and then reads them aloud. He creates new sentences from the words he knows, then goes to a story book and find the same words there. He and the teacher, working together, note word patterns: *goat* and *coat, boat* and *float,* and *shoat* and *moat,* for instance.

Notes

1. "The Tiger, the Brahman, and the Jackal" is an Indian fable, believed by some to be more than three thousand years old. Imagine the listeners it has delighted over those centuries!

2. For a more precise account of grunion spawning, cf. Rachel L. Carson, *The Sea Around Us* (New York: Oxford University Press, 1951), pp. 164-165.

3. For a more extensive treatment of the story board as a tool for teaching reading, see my article, "Frank and Frannie and the Flannel Board," in *The Reading Teacher* (October 1973), pp. 43-47.

Activities

1. Old songs and rhymes are excellent for creating group participation board stories. For example, how might you use "The Farmer in the Dell," or "Old McDonald Had a Farm," or "She'll be Comin' 'Round the Mountain"?

2. I have found, to my surprise, that older audiences as well as the young enjoy board stories. One excellent source of material for stories for a more mature group is James Thurber's *Fables for Our Time and Famous Poems, Illustrated* (New York: Harper & Row, 1939, 1940). "The Moth and the Star," for example, makes an elegant board story. Also, as I mentioned earlier, adults have a good time creating new rhymes for "Billy Boy" and other well-known songs.

3. The story board works well for illustrating components of an object. For example, one can show the parts of a flower, or the process of pollination. One of my students created a fine story showing the change from egg to polliwog to tadpole to frog using a few simple board creations. Visual dictionaries—e.g., *The Macmillan Visual Dictionary* (New York: Macmillan, 1992)—are useful sources for these stories.

4. You might also try telling some of the board stories you know in traditional fashion. What reaction do you have? Which does your audience prefer?

8. *Storytelling with Puppets*

The hunchback will, at various points in the performance, throw his baby out a window, kill a policeman, and confront the devil; this is a comedy.

—Steve Tillis[1]

There are people who weep; people who are sad and aroused watching puppets, though they know they are merely carved pieces of leather manipulated and made to speak. These people live in a world of illusion; they do not realize the magic hallucinations they see are not real.

—King Airlanga, *Meditation of Ardjuna*[2]

We do not know for certain when or how puppets first began. Herodotus, writing in the fifth century B.C., describes figures of "great antiquity" that were caused to move with strings and wires. Masks of straw and clay have been found in caves, suggesting that primitive man, thousands of years earlier, sensed the potential for wonder in those unmoving features.

It is not only the fact that we are unable to trace back puppets to their beginnings that creates their mystery. Mystery lies, also, in the effect puppets have on those of us who animate them. We watch them come alive in our hand, and are so captivated that for a brief time we suspend disbelief as they ply us with their ancient sorcery.

How does that happen? Joseph Campbell tells of the mask in a primitive festival that is venerated as if it were indeed the actual god it represents. Even though a member of the tribe created the mask and another member wears it while dancing in the ceremonies, the mask has acquired sacred qualities that are not part of this world.

Indeed, as Campbell points out, the masked dancer himself is transported: "He does not merely represent the god; he is the god."[3] In other words, there has been a shift of view on the part of the participants with regard to reality. While conventional logic tells them that man and spirit are separate, and that "make believe" and play are external and unrelated to the everyday world, here they accept and experience the masked creature as fully alive and incorporated into their consciousness.

Puppets, it seems to me, play this same role in our lives. If we look rationally at the composition of a puppet, what do we see? Bits of fake fur, buttons, pieces of felt and fabric, foam rubber, beads and trinkets stitched into place and bearing little resemblance to creatures we normally associate with our world. True, it may have a long yellow beak and a black furry neck, but by our rational standards it is not a bird; it has no body, no legs, no tail or wings. Its eyes are old buttons.

And yet, when the puppeteer *believes* in the puppet, it comes to life. To him this object on the end of his arm, manipulated by fingers and wrist, made to speak by the animator's voice, is no mere object. Rather, it is a separate and significant being, alive and vibrant and filled with its own special essence and will. And that's true of the audience as well. They accept the puppet in the same way the participants in the festival accepted the masked dancer. They see no connection between puppeteer and puppet, which they perceive as possessing a life and spirit entirely its own.

I mentioned the special essence and will of a puppet. If there is a single quality puppets possess, it is their irrepressibility. Puppets lack the self-doubts, questionings and timid retreats to conventionality and reason we humans suffer. Instead, they can be bold and brash, zany and full of wicked humor—quite the opposite of we who hold them and support them and, at least superficially, give them movement and voice.

In one of my classes, Lars, an anthropology student, made a fierce Viking puppet, complete with helmet and sword. Lars himself was shy, intellectual. His parents had migrated to the United States from Norway when he was a small child. All his schooling had been in the States, where his father was a school administrator. When Lars disappeared behind the puppet stage, however, we could not believe what we were seeing or hearing. A harsh voice speaking a strange tongue assaulted us. A Viking appeared, brandishing his sword, singing a drinking song, half English, half Norwegian. Visions of snowy mountains and sacked villages; winter storms and high prowed ships came to mind.

And then it was over. Mild Lars reappeared, shaking his head in wonder. "I learned that song when I was four years old," he said. "I haven't sung it since, that I can remember."

In that same class a sweet, demure young woman disappeared behind the stage, and a venomous witch appeared, scolding us, singing a bawdy song, her voice as discordant as a long disused instrument. The young woman, too, expressed surprise when her performance was over. "I don't know where that came from," she said.

Carl Jung speaks of the "shadow"—one's obscure, dark side, seldom recognized, rarely revealed to others, and often unacknowledged by the individual. It is this shadow element that makes us complete and whole as persons. But how do we make contact with that unacknowledged presence, so different in behavior, appearance, manner, and values from the self that sits in the sunlight for all to see?

It may be that puppets have the power to activate those impulses and tendencies that we normally reject. They put us in touch with the shadow self, and in so doing, enlarge and enhance our understandings of who we are. "Harmless and amusing little fellows," we think as we watch their antics. "Where did they ever learn to behave like that?" And then we realize their actions and behaviors are a mirror, revealing to us—ourselves.

Puppets and the Story Hour

We face a minor dilemma when we introduce puppets into our storytelling. Until the moment we herald their entrance, they lie mute—shoddy dolls in our storyteller's bag. Once we bring them to light, however, they become rivals—performers who may dominate the hour. While we want to give them their full share of attention and glory, at the same time we wish to remain something more than the "storyteller with the puppets."

To achieve a sense of balance in the story hour, I often begin by sharing some of the homemade toys I have constructed: moon spinners, gee-haw whimmy diddles, flipper dingers, and bull roarers. Handling these toys, talking about their origins, and playing with them provides a comfortable way to get acquainted with an audience.

Once I've shown a few toys to the group, I may ask children to tell me about toys they've made. And then, I create a puppet—an instant puppet—and animate it. To make this basic puppet, one needs only a small styrofoam cup, a couple of silk scarves (one a bit smaller than the other), and two rubber bands.

1. Poke (carefully now!) a little hole in the bottom of the cup, just large enough to accommodate your forefinger.

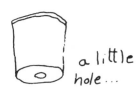

2. Fold the smaller of the scarves diagonally as if for a handkerchief. Place this across the top of the cup and poke part of the lower portion of the scarf up into the hole. The cup will now appear as a faceless head wearing a scarf.

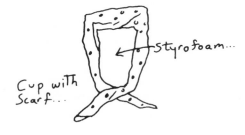

3. Center the larger scarf over your dominant hand, with the forefinger pointing up.
Gather a bit of cloth around the middle
finger and secure it in place with a rubber
band. Repeat with a bit of cloth around the
thumb. At this point you will have a puppet
body with two wriggly arms and a neck.
(Note that the ring finger and little finger
are pressed against the palm of the hand to
give the puppet a belly.)

4. Place the styrofoam head on the neck
(your forefinger). The puppet is now complete.

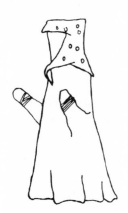

There's something uncanny about seeing a puppet created in a minute or two
before one's eyes. But perhaps even more uncanny is watching these common
things—a cup and scarf, a couple of rubber bands—begin to stretch and move and
yawn and come alive.

I often invite children to help with the waking up process. "Wake up, Puppet,
wake up, Puppet ..." we chant, and as we say those magic words, the puppet slowly
raises its head, looks around, seems to drift off to sleep again, lifts its head once
more, slowly and timidly peers out at the group, and then begins to nod its head as if
recognizing us. It may begin to move its arms. It may dance or clap its hands together.
Perhaps it clings to me as if frightened, then peers out and shyly waves an arm. Or it
may begin to jabber a high, quick, sharp puppet sound, and we discover to our astonishment that it's a witch, watching us and letting us know that we must be careful not
to cause its anger by mocking it with our laughter.

"But the puppet has no face," a rational critic observes. "How can it be a shy
newborn, or a witch, or a ballerina?" And yet, it's this very lack of features which lets
the puppet be whatever it wants.

There are endless variations available for this simple and elegant little puppet. With facial tissue and yarn, one can create the traditional headdress of an Arab. Or tie the smaller of the two scarves in a single loose knot and, while a member of the audience holds the puppet head by its neck—"Not so tight, Jodi, you'll give the puppet a head ache!"—tie the scarf around the top of the puppet's head to form a fortuneteller's turban. One can make a roughly triangular opening about the size of a quarter on one side of the cup and wedge a bit of foam rubber into the opening to serve as a nose. A mustache is easily added by inserting a thin strip of fake fur under the nose. Eyes can be drawn in with a felt pen. With the addition of an earring and a jauntily tilted head scarf, a pirate appears.

The spontaneity of this puppet is part of its charm. Often, when showing its construction to adults, I borrow items from the audience, such as earrings, jewelry, beads, scarves. Neither the audience nor I are quite sure how the puppet will turn out, what it will do or say, or how it will act.

In the activity just described, making a puppet becomes part of the story hour. But there are other times when the storyteller becomes the puppeteer and the play is more or less pre-set. In such a situation, the audience (and the puppeteer) are both required to suspend disbelief. After all, the storyteller sits in plain sight. He makes no attempt to use ventriloquism or other techniques that might tend to remove him from audience awareness. If the event is successful, however, everyone accepts for a little time the required shift in size, space, and general rules of logic, and the tiny drama unfolds.

For one such puppet play, I use a miniature theater that makes out into a tiny stage in front of me. The stage itself is a hinged board covered with black felt, so that the puppets' bright costumes show up well. I wear a black sweater. Such a technique, incidentally, owes a debt to traditional Japanese bunraku theater, with its masked and dark-gowned animators who move human-sized puppets in front of them during the

course of a play.

I use two puppets for this play. One is a finger puppet constructed from material that fits over the first two fingers of a black glove that conceals the rest of my hand. The two free fingers permit the puppet to engage in a full repertoire of physical shenanigans. The second is what I refer to as a mitten puppet. Constructed of bright yellow fake fur, with a cellulose nose and fierce jet eyes, it fits easily over my left hand. Its mouth is very flexible, permitting a variety of expressions, ranging from sinister to crafty good humor.

A bit of business always precedes the little play. I place the string holding the puppet stage around my neck and open the little stage. I introduce Roberto, the glove puppet, and put him on my right hand; then Woogle—the mitten puppet and Roberto's best friend—on my left. If the audience is very young—kindergartners through second-graders—I coach them on three important pieces of information they'll need to know during the play. How much are two and two? What are the last three letters of the alphabet? Who was the first president of the United States? These questions occur later in the play, and it's always *such* comfort when they know the answers and Woogle doesn't!

Once the preliminary fun is over—and it takes longer to tell about than to do—the play begins.

R: Poopti Poopiti Poopti Poop, Poopti Poopiti Poop! Nice day to be out for a walk. Momma send me out for mushrooms ... say to watch out for woogles. But I not afraid of woogles.
Who's afraid of the big bad Woogle?
The big bad Woogle,
The big bad Woogle.
Who's afraid of the big bad—
Oooh, Who you?
W: Me ... Woogle.
R: Woogle! Woogle! What you doing here?
W: Woogle looking for breakfast.
R: Breakfast? Breakfast? What do Woogle like for breakfast?
W: Woogle like something soft and squishy and chewy.
R: Soft? Squishy? Momma say I soft and squishy. I wonder if I chewy? ...I wonder if bad Woogle plan to eat me? ... I know, I play trick on him ... Woogle!
W: Yes?
R: If you answer three questions, I help you find breakfast.
W: Three question. Three question. Hmmm. Woogle know lots of answer. Go on. First question.
R: First question. Yes. First question is ... What are last three letters of alphabet?
W: Last three letters of alphabet! Last three letters of alphabet! Is hard question! Last three letters of alphabet is ... L ... Q ... P! I did it! I did it! I answer first question!
R: Oh Woogle! I so sorry! Last three letters of alphabet not L ... Q ... P! Last three letters of alphabet X ... Y ... Z! Why, every child know that! Well, you no answer first question. But two more to come. And here second question: How much is two and two?

Roberto walks onto stage from right, singing, then talking to himself. Woogle is lurking off stage left, on my lap ...

And begins slowly making his way up to the stage ... as Roberto sings to the tune of "Who's Afraid of the Big Bad Wolf ..."

Roberto abruptly stops singing when he spies Woogle slithering onto the proscenium.

Woogle's voice is nicely sinister ...

A little panic ... but not much ...

Until he hears of Woogle's mission ...

Woogle draws out the words "soft," "squishy," and "chewy."

Roberto does this as an aside to the audience ... giving himself time to think ...

And comes up with an idea ...

Which he proposes to Woogle, who probably isn't too bright anyway ...

And Woogle agrees ... (Note that both Roberto and Woogle speak an eclipsed speech, omitting articles and endings ...)

Roberto's back in control now ...

And Woogle's starting slowly, but gaining confidence. He knows! He knows! He *thinks* he knows!

Except he's wrong. And, adding insult to injury, after Roberto tells him he's "so sorry," he kicks Woogle across the nose, much as an irritable schoolmaster might cuff a reluctant scholar ... And follows up with the second question ...

Math is *not* Woogles's best subject ...

W: How much is two and two? How much is two and two? Is hard question. Very hard question. Arithmetic not my best subject. But two and two ... me think. Two and one is ... seventeen. Divide seventeen by one hundred and six. That thirty-nine. So. Two and two is ... Ninety-one! I did it! I did it! I answer hard arithmetic question!

But he's willing to try ... and comes up with ...

an answer!

R: Oh, Woogle! Poor Woogle! Try so hard! But is not right answer! Two and two is four! Every child know that! One more chance. We try history. Tell me, Woogle, who is first president of United States?

Which is ... alas, not quite right ...

And leads to another cuff on the nose ...

And a third question ..

W: First president! First president! Is not fair. Too hard. But wait. I know ... First president is ... is ...

First president is ... is ...

Christopher Columbus!

The audience, of course, is supplying the answer ... George Washington! George Washington!

R: Oh, Woogle! Missed again! Is very bad luck. I so sorry. First president is George Washington! Every child know that! Well, you no answer three question, so I no can help you find breakfast. Too bad. Must be going. Think I hear Momma calling ... So long ... *Adios* ... ... See you later, Alligator ... *Auf weidersehen* ...

... But hapless Woogle gets it wrong. (A current celebrity works well here!)

And now the tough part. Robert's got to get away before Woogle knows what's happening ... He's jitterbugging his way across stage while saying his goodbyes ...

He's going to make it! He's going to ...

W: Raughhhhhhhhh! Now Woogle ask three questions. What do Woogle like for breakfast? Little kids! What kind of little kids? Smart little kids with all the answers! When do Woogle like his breakfast? Now! ...

Alas ... Woogle makes his move ...

...And the story ends ...

We gasp in dismay when Woogle grabs Roberto right in the middle of his fancy footwork. We've pinned our hopes, all of us, on Roberto. He'll get away. But he doesn't. We can't believe it.

"Do it again," a child says. "Let him get away this time."

But I can't. I've tried replaying the drama, changing the ending and tricking the Woogle, but the whole matter seems out of my hands. The best I can do is provide reassurance. It's just a play. Roberto and Woogle are good friends; they sleep together in the old puppet bag between shows. Once when I looked inside, I saw the Woogle putting a little blanket over Roberto when he thought he might have developed a chill.

Roberto and Woogle come alive as we think about them, play with them, talk about them, talk to them. The same is true of the other puppets. Sometimes, after I've made a cup puppet and Roberto and Woogle have put on their show, I'll bring out a few other puppets and briefly demonstrate a few simple rules for working with them:

- When a puppet talks, his head or body moves—not a lot, but enough to cause us to focus our attention on him.

- When one puppet is talking, the other puppets listen by turning their gaze to the one talking.

- When a puppet has a movable mouth, as Woogle has, it opens and closes a bit for every syllable uttered, and closes completely at the end of each sentence.

- In general, a puppet's off-stage focus should be directed at audience eye-level.

Once we've settled on those few simple rules, I ask if there's anyone who'd like to befriend a few puppets who haven't yet had an opportunity to perform. Needless to say, my invitation rarely goes unaccepted.

We might then all practice singing a well known song. Once we've gotten to the point where we're singing it together, puppets are distributed to members of the audience. Two people are pressed into service as curtain operators. Their role is to hold up a sheet—the one harking back to readers' theater days—we use as a make-shift stage above which the puppets will appear. A person is assigned to announce the performance, another to direct the puppets in their singing. By the time we've finished assigning parts I may be the only one left in the audience.

These "song fests" are a delight. Puppets are always on the verge of dancing anyway, and they move and sway and wriggle to the music as they sing. Occasionally we'll follow up the group singing with a recorded dance number so the puppets can concentrate on moving to the rhythm.

After this first performance, children may want to put on a puppet play. To get things started, I'll suggest a situation which could lead to a conversation between two puppets. Perhaps one of them is Jack (of beanstalk fame) and the other the Giant. Thirty years have passed since Jack stole the hen and the money and the golden harp. They're sitting at a bus stop, busy with their own thoughts. But now the Giant happens to notice that this skinny guy next to him reminds him an awful lot of that boy who stole all his pretties such a long time ago. What will he say? How will Jack answer him? And what happens then?

We take a minute or two for a couple of volunteers to decide which puppets they want to use. We urge brevity (no more than a minute for a play) and spontaneity (follow where the puppets lead). Our puppeteers slip behind the curtain and the show begins.

None of us knows what course the action will take. Will Jack and the Giant reminisce about those long ago days? Will the Giant try once again to catch Jack? Will Jack steal the Giant's bus ticket? Several volunteers may be given an opportunity to perform the same play, which turns out differently each time.

Occasionally, I hand out slips of paper containing single lines—"Has anyone seen my mother?" or "Is that water I hear?" or "Someone's at the door!"—and encourage people to find a friend with whom they'd like to put on a puppet play. In that way we have several bits of theater brewing at the same time and can balance our performances with different situations. At the end of this chapter, I suggest a half-dozen other situations that have provoked interesting little plays.

I will mention briefly one puppet that has come to figure prominently in my own storytelling. Several years ago, early in the morning of Father's Day, the front doorbell rang. There, lying on the front stoop, wrapped in a little quilt, lay a tiny monkey—a hand puppet—to which was pinned a note: *Please take care of me*. It was not difficult to identify the gift-givers; the daughters were giggling and tee-heeing behind the old Monterey pine.

Since that day, Monkey has been part of the family. Often he closes the story hour with a bit of rollicking nonsense. I may tell the audience that I have one last puppet I'd like them to meet, that there was a big party at our house last night and this puppet ate too much banana cream pie, but that perhaps, with some coaxing he'll come out for a minute.

As the children wait, I reach into the bag where he sleeps and adjust the quilt around him so he's snug and warm. Finally he appears, shyly peeping over the edge of the little quilt, rubbing his eyes, scratching sleepily behind his ears. I talk to him. "See all these people, Monkey? They want to say hello. Come on, don't be scared." I mention names of persons in the audience he might know. "Chance is here ... and Rachel. And look, there's Mrs. Baumgartener! She's the principal of this entire school. You'll want to say hello to her, won't you?"

Reluctantly, oh so reluctantly, he emerges, peers around, snuggles up against me, hides his face, and then looks out at everyone again.

"Now," I say, "I want you to show everyone how well you can wave." I wait. Nothing happens. More coaxing. Finally, one single sweeping arm gesture, and that's it.

"Come on," I chide him, "You can wave better than that."

I ask the audience to show him how to wave. "Notice the flexible wrist movements, the extended fingers, the happy smiles," I tell him. "Come on, you can do it!"

At last, another wave, not much better than the first.

As a last resort, I threaten him. "Now wave properly or there's no more banana cream pie."

That prompts such waving as you have never witnessed. He waves and waves and waves and waves ... I view this at first with immense satisfaction, then restrained tolerance, and finally, downright disapproval. He's mocking me!

"Stop it," I tell him. But the waving continues.

I'm annoyed.

"Stop," I repeat. "That's enough!"

I grab his little arm with my free hand and hold it. I make him promise that he won't wave again. I lecture him on the sacredness of a promise. At last he quiets down. His tiny hand trembles, barely in control, but at least he's not waving. Whew!

I turn to the audience to tell them good-bye. I thank them for their kind attention. I praise their manners. But they laugh.

"No, no," I assert. "It's true. You've been a wonderful audience."

They laugh again. I'm puzzled.

"It's Monkey," one little girl squeals. "He's waving."

I reassure her. She's wrong. Monkey would not be waving. Monkey could not be waving. Monkey promised.

But then, the whole audience explodes, and a look at Monkey confirms my worse fears. He's waving—feverishly, gloriously! Completely insouciant, a rebel to the last!

Making Puppets Your Own ...

I have found—with Monkey the exception—that those puppets which best come to life for me are the ones I've made. For that reason, I would like to suggest materials and procedures for creating simple puppets. But first, let me propose a few general principles to keep in mind.

Puppets are not scaled-down versions of people or animals. On the contrary, they represent magnifications, physically and psychologically. In life, a soprano may strain slightly to reach high C; a puppet, however, stretches its neck to twice its original length when it strives to hit a high note. A couple may exchange occasional sharp words, but Punch and Judy exchange sharp blows—constantly. The kitten that sleeps on your lap at the breakfast table seems cuddly and lovable; but the puppet kitten is solicitous beyond compare, whispering in your ear, straightening your tie, snuggling up for puppet kisses.

Because of this tendency of the puppet to comment on foibles and excesses, the puppet maker must identify the most pertinent elements in a character and exaggerate them. If the giant you imagine has large eyes, then the puppet's will be larger still. If the self-important dowager has pursed lips and a bouffant hairdo, then the puppet representing her will have hair puffed out twice as far, and a mouth a pickle manufacturer would envy.

And then there's the question of what to put in and leave out. Perhaps the most important elements of a puppet are those you omit; for their omission serves to accentuate the details you choose to include.

This magnification of character requires boldness in the use of color and line. It's often useful, when a puppet is being constructed, to pose it under the light of a swivel-necked desk lamp, then step away and observe it as if you were sitting in an audience. Can you distinguish the elements you've chosen to amplify? Change the pose and study the puppet again. Such experiments help point out where you may wish to make changes in design.

Nor does this concern with essential character stop at the head of the puppet. Materials, body configuration, extremities—all must be consistent. Pin costumes on the puppet and subject them to study before sewing or gluing them in place.

There are innumerable materials from which puppet heads for hand puppets can be made. Gourds are light-weight and take paint well, and become wonderful abstract puppets. Remember the old tale "Five Chinese Brothers"? I have seen these puppets beautifully constructed of smooth gourds, with black pumpkin seed eyes and plaited black yarn pigtails. Their clothes were black silk; their hands white fabric.

Styrofoam is excellent for scupting puppet heads. Craft stores carry this substance in balls of various sizes. The styrofoam can be left as it is, or shaped with hand pressure, sandpaper, and small knives. Once carved, a tube of heavy paper—sized to fit one's pointer finger—inserted at the base of the head forms a neck and opening for the animator.

Foam rubber, which is available in many upholstery fabric stores, is one of the most versatile materials I have found for puppet construction. It can be carved and shaped into lightweight and mobile heads. Stuffed inside garments, it fleshes out arms and legs. Cut into long thin spaghetti-like strands, it makes wriggly antennae and quivering whiskers. With various contact and hot glues, one can weld bits of foam together into odd and unusual shapes. Also, foam is supple, so that a puppet constructed of it is capable of expressive movement, as well as being comforting in its softness.

Fake fur, which comes in various bright colors, is wonderful for puppets. This material fastens together easily with various glues. Seams are easily hidden because of the length of the fibers. Puppets made in this way have a fine comic appearance. Incidentally, Steve Tillis, commenting on choice of materials and the signals those materials convey, notes that if Bert and Ernie, of Muppet fame, were constructed of a lustrous metal, or leather, or wood, rather than softer materials, their effect on an audience would be substantially altered.[4]

Burlap sacking, frayed at the edges, achieves the rough texture of a boy's hair. A fringe of soft cotton encircles an old man's pate, with matching eyebrows and mustache. Steel gray yarn laid in a crisscross pattern and pulled together into a bun in the back forms the hair of an elderly matron. A French drummer has hair of black felt, sleek and wig-like in appearance, which shows only at the temples and in back, since he wears a bright red military cap with gold trimming. Rough-edged pipe stem cleaners, cut in half and bent double like hairpins, then forced into a styrofoam head, can hold loops of yarn—hair "transplants"—to give a puppet a fine bushy mop of hair that may be braided, fluffed out or teased into a halo.

Outgrown infant garments—tiny T-shirts, overalls, or tennis shoes—make good puppet clothing, and can be purchased inexpensively at second-hand stores and bargain basements. They, too, have a comforting, familiar feel that appeals to children.

As must be clear, there is no limit to the materials one can use when creating puppets: fruits and vegetables, paper tubing, papier-mache, balsa wood, tin cans, balloons, rubber balls, tennis balls, dolls' heads, silk stockings, furry slippers, old stuffed toys, buttons, beads, bits of felt, ping pong balls, egg cartons, clam shells, corks—the list is endless.

It's helpful, though, to choose lightweight materials

whenever possible. The head of a papier mache puppet might seem reasonably light at the beginning of a performance, but as the minutes pass, the hand grows weary. For this reason I recommend styrofoam, light fabrics, foam rubber, and cardboard.

One caution: care must be taken when choosing paints. Oil and lacquer-based paints will dissolve styrofoam. Latex products, on the other hand, will not. They dry quickly, and stretch and fill to form a nice, grainy undersurface. Once a surface has been established, water-based acrylics, with their bright, true colors, work well for painting features and obtaining natural skin tones. Tempera is less satisfactory, as it becomes brittle with age, and rubs off onto other puppets.

One personal prejudice: avoid brown paper bag puppets. They crackle and rattle in an unseemly way; their origins are so obvious that it requires a forgiving eye to find them beautiful; and their bleak lack of aesthetic appeal hampers an audience's ability to imagine them alive.

While my students and I have fashioned many different kinds of puppets over the years, three of them have been most popular. The first, of course, is the little cup puppet, which can be made for almost nothing—scarves, a styrofoam cup, a couple of rubber bands, a bit of kitchen sponge, closet castoffs. Furthermore, it can be costumed to play a number of roles: a cape of red cloth, and it's Little Red Riding Hood; a bit of brown yarn and a long gray foam rubber nose, and it's the wolf; a pale bonnet and gauzy netting for the body, and Grandmother appears in her night dress.

The other two puppets share some common elements: they are large, tend to be nonhuman in appearance, have movable mouths and are easy to craft and animate. They are more difficult to make than the cup puppet, but give hours of pleasure both in crafting and later, when they come alive on stage.

The first of these is made of foam rubber. For such a puppet, one will need the following:

- two pieces of foam, each 4 by 4 by 12 inches;

- contact cement (the sort that adheres to foam) or hot glue;

- large buttons for eyes (with smaller buttons for their centers);

- foam spray paint (try a craft store for this product);

- one piece of fake fur, 12 by 24 inches;

- felt for the mouth and tongue.

Step One: Shape the two pieces of foam to form an upper and lower portion of a head. (We often wind up with bird-like puppets, the two foam pieces forming the upper and lower portion of the beak. Crocodiles run a close second. But one can also make block-headed Bert and Ernie-like characters.) Sharp scissors work well for this shaping. So does a bread knife. With a little practice foam rubber sculpts rather well.

foam shaped with scissors to form a beak.

Step Two: With a sharp-pointed serrated knife, make a slit three inches wide and three inches deep in the piece of foam designated for the top portion of the puppet's head.

a slit for your hand

and another for your thumb...

Step Three: Make a narrower slit, an inch and a half wide and three inches deep, in the second piece of foam. These two slits accommodate the puppeteer's hand; the top portion of the head holding the fingers and the lower portion the thumb.

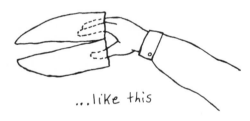

...like this

Step Four: Decide on the color you want this part of the puppet to be. Many foam colors are rather pleasing; soft tans and greens and pinks. But you may also spray the foam with a brightly colored foam spray.

Step Five: Select a pleasing contrasting color of felt for the mouth and glue it into place with contact glue or hot glue. Note that the felt forms a hinge at the back of the puppet. (One can run a glue line across the back to further stabilize the hinge.)

Felt

felt Hinge

A tube of fake fur is fastened....  to the head and...

Step Six: Make a tube of fake fur, sewing or glueing the seam, and glue one end of it to the back of the puppet's head. (This tube hides your arm.)

Step Seven: Experiment with various eye materials; ping-pong balls, corks, columns of foam rubber, buttons ... Don't fasten these into place until you've studied the puppet under a strong light from a distance of several feet away.

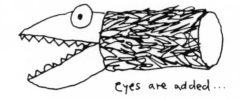

eyes are added...

Step Eight: Augment the puppet's appearance with other items. A tongue and teeth may be added. Little hats, berets, scarves, a neck tie, jangling beads—create different looks.

Step Nine: Test your puppet. Does the mouth move easily? Is your hand comfortable? Ask a friend to animate the puppet for you. How does it look? Make adjustments as required.

   For the box puppet, one needs:

   • a shoe box;

   • hot glue or craft glue;

   • foam rubber scraps;

   • kitchen sponge or cellulose in various colors;

   • buttons, marbles, ping pong balls, for eyes;

   • a piece of fake fur at least 2 by 2 feet;

   • felt for the mouth.

Step One: Cut each side of the box down at the mid-point and fold the box back on itself. This is the basic size of the puppet. If it seems too large, find a smaller shoe box.

Step Two: Glue foam straps across both the top and bottom portion of the box, leaving enough space to insert fingers (on the top half) and thumb (on the bottom half). Without the foam inserts the box will flap uncontrollably on your hand.

Step Three: Cut and shape fake fur so that it fits the box, leaving the mouth free to move easily. One will need several pieces of fake fur for this step.

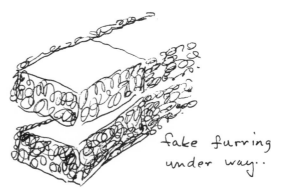

Step Four: Continue with fake fur around the back of the head and down to form a long neck. (This covers your arm.)

Step Five: Glue in felt mouth of contrasting color. (You may also wish to add some foam rubber teeth.)

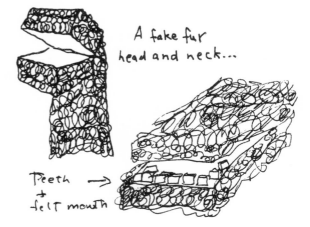

Step Six: Shape cellulose to form a nose and ears if those are appropriate for the puppet you're making. Attach.

Step Seven: Design and attach eyes.

Step Eight: Add other costume pieces; hats, neckties, old stiff collars, and the like.

Step Nine: Ask a friend to animate the puppet while you observe it for changes you might like to consider.

My students and I often include, when we create puppets, some special token or symbol out of our own lives. It may be a button or a bit of fabric handed down from a garment we or a family member or friend has owned for a long time, or leather from an old pair of gloves, or junk jewelry and beads. We tell ourselves, knowing we're being foolish, that perhaps, just perhaps, these fragments from our own lives provide the puppet with a feeling of family and belonging that it might not otherwise possess.

And If You Are a Teacher ...

No one would dispute the magical appeal puppets have for children. Nor is it only the young who are drawn to the unique qualities a puppet holds locked inside itself. Upper-grade children and high-schoolers—not to mention college students and adults—are also attracted to puppets, perhaps because of the forces we spoke of earlier in this chapter.

We are, as teachers, fortunate that this keen interest in puppets prevails, for what other medium offers such opportunities for creative expression? Sculpture, design, dance, music, staging, language development, improvisation and traditional theater, carpentry, mime—the range is limited only by the time available to work with this antique and yet surprisingly modern medium.

Where to begin? One good place is with creating the puppets themselves. While one can always buy puppets for classroom use, there are valid reasons for inviting students to construct their own. The creativity one adopts in crafting a new character is very powerful and carries over to the time when the puppet begins to move and talk and respond to others.

Once the puppets have been constructed, you may begin teaching students simple animation techniques. Those I suggested earlier in this chapter are probably sufficient. Once basic guidelines for animation have been established, move on to warm up activities. Here are some that have worked well:

1. Have the puppets recite together some of the old nursery rhymes: "Three Blind Mice," "Hickory Dickory Dock," or "Baa, Baa Black Sheep." These provide language so well known by most children that they don't have to think about the words, and can concentrate on helping their puppets move their mouths and bodies appropriately.

As a follow-up activity, divide the group into two parts, and have them face one another. Group One puppets say the first line to Group Two, who then say the second line to Group One. This activity gives students and their puppets a chance to watch others during the animation process. Also, it gives puppeteers a chance to test out their puppet voices, which tend to be thinner, higher, and faster paced.

2. Sing old songs: "I've been Working on the Railroad," "Billy Boy," "Bingo," or "Three Blind Mice" gives students an opportunity to watch each other's puppets move.

3. Play popular recordings and encourage puppets to dance to the music.

4. Ask students to name their puppets and create for them a history and occupation. Now it's the puppets' turn. They introduce themselves to another puppet, and then introduce that puppet to another puppet and converse briefly—no more than a minute or so.

Once these improvisational bits of theater have been undertaken, students are ready to try somewhat more formal puppet plays. Retelling old folktales, doing joke routines, singing duets, revising television commercials, conducting interviews, reciting poems—the range is limitless. In general, however, we have found the following to be true when presenting puppet theater:

- Brevity is essential. A highly successful bit of puppet theater for a puppet might take no more than thirty seconds. Five minutes is an absolute maximum.

- Music can weld together a performance. A teacher friend and her children staged an old folktale using hand puppets. The music she chose—recorded bits by a flute and xylophone —helped convey the light, eerie quality of the story. One can also use music to lampoon: a rich Wagnerian overture as a prelude to the appearance of a timid little puppet heightens the sense of humor and potential slap-stick. Two of my students, staging "Three Billy Goats Gruff," used Simon and Garfunkel's "Bridge Over Troubled Waters" as background music to begin and end the play.

- Ceremonies are important. It adds to the sense of theater to darken the room, lighting only the stage area. Final bows and curtain calls, both for puppeteers and their puppets, give a sense of completeness.

- Pre-recording dialogue for a play is not recommended, as much of the charm and delight of classroom puppetry lies in the impromptu and spontaneous.

- A narrator puppet may be designated to introduce the play, describe scenes, and bridge episodes.

- If a video recorder is available, use it at rehearsals so that puppeteers may observe their own performances. Or institute a coach/pupil strategy so that students can help one another with animation and voice.

The Puppet Stage

Over the years, our puppet stages have become increasingly simple. Probably our most popular stage at the present time is a plain bed sheet held in place by a couple of volunteers behind which the puppeteers stand or crouch. The advantages of the sheet are several: one can raise or lower it so that it's always the right height; it can be moved easily; and it requires no storage space. For classroom use, perhaps its greatest advantage is that a half-dozen puppeteers can get behind it at one time.

If a bed sheet is not available, one can turn a table on its side, or tape a sheet of corrugated paper across a doorway.

But should you wish for something a bit more permanent, I would recommend a light-weight stage made from a large recycled cardboard box, such as that which a refrigerator is crated in. Such a box can be opened up and used as a "backyard fence," in which the puppets appear at the top of the fence, with the puppeteers back stage holding them aloft. This stage conceals the puppeteer and provides maximum freedom of movement—making dances, marches, and processions easy.

Or one may cut a proscenium opening, so that puppeteers standing or sitting backstage may hold their puppets in front of them. With such a stage, a scrim of plain, dark thin fabric is required so that the puppeteer may see the audience and watch her puppets as she animates them and speaks their lines, while at the same time remaining invisible to the audience. Since a blank scrim is, essentially, an empty set, it is easy to suggest to the audience, either with a few words or with some simple properties, where the play is taking place. In theaters we have built, we hemmed the top of the scrim and passed a broom handle through so it draped well, then fastened the broom handle from side to side of the stage to serve as a stabilizer. Also, we weighted the bottom of the scrim with a slender metal chain in the hem so it remained stable during performances. Finally, we painted the stage exterior with various designs and colors.

Puppet Theater and the Academic Curriculum

Most of the puppet plays we've discussed thus far are spontaneous. Little time needs be spent planning or executing them. However, there is much learning to be gained from putting together a puppet performance complete with script, scenery, lighting, music, written invitations to parents and friends, programs, posters, appearances on local radio and television, costumes, sets, properties, and the like.

How might one prepare a tale for formal puppet theater? To explore that question, consider the familiar story, "Mrs. Vinegar":

> A fisherman and his wife live in a vinegar jug. One day the man catches a carp with scales of pure gold. The fish begs for release, and the kindly fisherman sets it free. When he returns home and tells his wife of the event, she tells him the carp he caught must have been magic; he should have asked for a boon. "Tell the fish we want a cottage," she says, "I'm tired of living in this miserable vinegar jug!"
>
> The fisherman returns to the shore of the lake and calls out for the fish. When the carp appears, he repeats his wife's request.
>
> "Tell her it shall be as she desires," says the fish.
>
> The fisherman returns home, and there, indeed, is a cottage.
>
> But the wife is not satisfied. Not with the cottage, nor with the mansion she next asks for, nor a castle, nor the palace from which she rules as royal empress.
>
> "More. More. Tell the fish I want more," she says finally. "I wish to stop the sun in its journey."
>
> The fisherman makes the request. The waters turn black and the skies grow dark with thunder clouds. And the fish says, "That foolish woman! Return to her and find her where she belongs!"
>
> The fisherman returns home There is his wife, back in the vinegar jug.

In staging this "fate" tale, one might wish to use two theaters, side by side, with scenes between the fisherman and his wife occurring in one theater, and conversations with the fish in the other.

Scenery need be suggested only. Perhaps the first scene contains the outline of a vinegar jug, thinly veiled, permitting us to see the wife inside their home. The water where the fish swims might be cellophane with a faint blue light showing through to suggest depth.

In later scenes one could identify a single aspect of the various dwellings—the roof outline of a cottage, a mansion's Doric column, the golden-arched window of a palace.

Music can help set the mood for this particular play. Selections from English country dances would be appropriate for the cottage scene. Perhaps a portion from Handel's *Water Music* might fit the first encounter between the fisherman and the golden carp. Other music to consider would be "Pomp and Circumstance" when the wife is an empress, or some of Edvard Grieg's turbulant dissonances during the final scene between the fisherman and the carp. Put the music on tape in the order it is to appear in the play, so that it may be controlled easily from backstage.

As mentioned earlier, darkening a room creates a sense of theater. The light of a projector, flashlight, or small spotlight may be used to illuminate the stage from the front. One can drape Christmas tree lights behind the stage where the various colors blend and give warmth and naturalness to the tiny actors. Two small clamp-on lamps above the puppets and on either side eliminate harsh glare and shadows. Blue and green lighting inside the second stage suggests the seashore where the carp and Mr. Vinegar meet.

Characters for the play might include, in addition to Mr. and Mrs. Vinegar and the carp, a narrator (perhaps a neighbor of the Vinegars, retelling the story) and a chorus that handles some of the sound effects.

To begin work on this play, children could study various versions of this story and discuss them. Questions could be posed for study. What was Mrs. Vinegar's character? How would you describe her husband? As students talk through these characters and situations, they begin to get a sense of what the puppets they are going to create will look like. And, too, the outline of the play takes shape. The first act appears, and the second and third. Lines and dialogue begin to flow from the language of the performers. A written script appears, but with the full understanding that it may change as rehearsals get underway.

What fun puppetry can be! But there's more than fun here—more than games and foolishness and frivolity. Puppets call on something buried deep within us, and we, and our students, respond to that call.

NOTES

1. Tillis, Steve, *Toward an Aesthetics of the Puppet* (Westport, Connecticut: Greenwood Press, 1992), pp. 2-3.

2. Brandon, James R., *On Thrones of Gold: Three Javanese Shadow Plays* (Cambridge, Massachusetts: Harvard University Press, 1970), p. 3.

3. Joseph Campbell, *The Masks of God: Primitive Mythology* (New York: Viking Press, 1959, 1969). Beginning on page 21, Campbell discusses the role of the mask in primitive culture and relates it to our ability to suspend disbelief and experience the transforming experience of sensing another world.

4. Tillis, Steve, *Op Cit.*, p.127.

BIBLIOGRAPHY

The following books will give many helpful suggestions to the beginning puppeteer.

Baird, Bil. *The Art of the Puppet*. New York: Macmillan, 1965. This beautiful book is an inspiration to read and to see. Colored plates illustrate every aspect of puppetry, and the text recounts many of Mr. Baird's own experiences in his career as a puppeteer.

Batchelder, Marjorie. *The Puppet Theater Handbook*. New York: Harper, 1947. This book gives excellent suggestions for the making of all types of puppets, including shadow puppets, hand puppets, rod puppets, marionettes and finger puppets, together with the planning and staging of puppet plays.

Beaumont, Cyril. *Puppets and Puppetry*. New York: The Studio Publications, 1958. A brief history of puppetry is followed by outstanding black and white photographs of puppets from all over the world. Excellent as a source of ideas for puppets.

Bramell, Eric and Christopher C. Somerville. *Expert Puppet Technique*. Boston: Plays, Inc. 1966. This delightful little book gives suggestions for scripting, puppet design, puppet manipulation, stage setting, and performance. While the book could be read to advantage by professional puppeteers, the authors direct their remarks to the amateur.

Champlin, Connie and Nancy Renfro. *Storytelling with Puppets*. Chicago: American Library Association, 1985. Suggestions for building a puppet collection, using puppets in participatory storytelling, and miniature puppet theater are discussed. This text gives abundant suggestions for implementing puppetry in the storytelling hour.

Emberly, Ed. *Punch and Judy: A Play for Puppets*. Boston: Little, Brown, 1965. This charming and historically accurate picture book would serve as a good reference to persons wanting to stage a Punch and Judy production.

Phlomm, Phyllis Noe. *Puppet Plays Plus: Hand Puppet Plays For Two Puppeteers*. Metuchen, New Jersey: The Scarecrow Press, Inc., 1944. Scripts for more than thirty brief plays intended for children three through eight are given, together with production notes. A good source of ideas for the librarian or primary teacher.

Tillis, Steve. *Toward an Aesthetics of the Puppet*. New York: Greenwood Press, 1992. This book establishes fundamental concepts of an aesthetics of puppetry. Rich in scholarly detail, this is a must for those wishing to explore more fully the meanings which lie behind our continuing fascination with puppets.

ACTIVITIES

1. The following improvisational theater starters have worked well for us with puppets. All of them require two puppeteers and puppets:

- Your puppet has a problem. It meets another puppet, tells that puppet its problem. Remember, *that* puppet also has a problem. Puppets help one another.

- One puppet is an interviewer on a TV show. The other is a person who has just returned from a fantastic adventure.

- Select a political news item. One puppet takes a positive view of this news; the other assumes a negative stance. Try to resolve the conflict.

- Find a recording of a famous duet. (Nelson Eddy and Jeanette McDonald singing "Ah, Sweet Mystery of Life" is a good example from the past.) Have puppets lip-sync parts.

- One puppet takes the role of parent. The other is a sixteen-year-old asking for the keys to the car for the first time.

- Working with a friend, think of three or four of the corniest jokes you can remember. Teach these to the puppets and have them retell the jokes with appropriate side comments.

2. Punch and Judy have been popular for hundreds of years. Investigate their origins. Plan and produce a Punch and Judy show. Ed Emberly's *Punch and Judy* will be of help when designing costumes and settings.

3. Locate the puppet theater in your area and attend one or more performances. Ask the puppeteers to show you their art and craft.

4. The Puppeteers of America hold yearly meetings where it is possible to gain many exciting new ideas for creating and animating puppets. Information concerning this organization may be obtained from *The Puppetry Journal*, Macedonia, Ohio.

9. The Singing and the Dance

Sally go 'round the sun,
Sally go 'round the moon,
Sally go 'round the sunshine
Ev'ry afternoon, Boom! Boom!

—Traditional, U.S.

In a cavern, in a canyon, excavating for a mine,
Dwelt a miner, forty-niner, and his daughter, Clementine.
Oh my darling, Oh my darling, Oh my darling Clementine,
You are lost and gone forever,
Dreadful sorry, Clementine.

—Traditional, U.S.

I had a dog, and his name was Blue
And I'll bet you five dollars he's a good one too.
Go on, Blue, I'm a comin' too.

—Traditional, U.S.

Not too long ago I sat in a circle with perhaps fifty teachers; there to share with them some songs, games and dances they could take back to the classroom.

But the time and the setting were all wrong. It was the middle of the day, just after lunch, when that dark odor of fatigue and nervous tension begins to build among those charged with responsibility for teaching the young, day after day, week after week, throughout the year. We were in the cafeteria, and the sharp scent of institutional cooking and disinfectant hung ripe in the air. Globs of Jell-O and macaroni had fallen to the floor and skidded across the tiles under four hundred pairs of feet, leaving behind shiny snail trails of food. From the kitchen issued the clatter of dishes being washed.

I began by singing "A Uni Uni I Ki Ani," a song I learned several years ago from friends in Quebec. After I had sung it through a time or two I urged them to sing along with me, clapping time as we sang. We repeated the song, employing variations of a clapping game.

By the time we had sung the song through three or four times, the kitchen odors had receded from consciousness. The sharp animal scent of alarm on our bodies was being replaced with a fine glow of physical exertion. Earlier, I had suggested that we imagine we were in an Indian Long House, with a roof of cedar bark and a smoky fire with glowing embers in the center of the circle and the rain falling in the forest outside. (That's about as far away as one can get from a school cafeteria in sun-drenched Southern California!)

We paused and talked for a minute about what was happening. "It's like an old-time party," one person said. "I can imagine myself a thousand miles away from here." We talked about the unbroken circle we created when we were touching both our own knee and the knee of the person next to us. Someone mentioned the difference in the texture of the cloth covering her knee and that of her neighbors. Another person noted that our bodies seemed to have different temperatures; this knee felt warmer than that one. Another commented on fat and bony knees. We laughed.

We moved on from that game to "Draw a Bucket of Water," the old English children's game that has sparked so many play parties. We danced "Muh 'Zudio," and I taught them the verse that one of my students had shared with me out of her childhood in rural Florida. We went on a Lion Hunt and did some choral speaking. Two persons taught us an old dance—"Sally Go Round the Sun"—they had known as children, and we wove our way through the simple steps according to their direction.

All too soon, it seemed, the hour was over. People were reluctant to leave. Their step was different. Their bodies were relaxed. They chattered and laughed as if on holiday.

I have thought about that hour, and other hours I've spent with similar groups. These adults, highly skilled and trained, were on the firing line, so to speak, for teaching elementary children is no picnic. And yet for a brief time they managed to find a sense of playfulness and release. It was as if the hour provided a kind of mental and spiritual cleansing. They bathed briefly in the waters of innocence and joy.

Itzak Bentov tells of the vibrations and resonances that fill our world. Every rock and tree and blade of grass and sparrow emits signals, most of them too fine for the ear to hear or the eye to see. But the vibrations and resonances given off by people are another matter. These we may sense rather readily. We know, intuitively, when the vibrations we give off and the vibrations of those we're with are in harmony.[1]

A friend of mine has made a study of what he refers to as "the melody and the dance" of a classroom. How teachers and students walk, touch, speak, move around the room. How they resonate with one another. Is there a sense of harmony, or is the tone one of discord and dissonance? He studies these patterns and suggests that they seem to have a lot to do with how children learn.

That's no surprise. But what does that have to do with singing and dancing and the storytelling hour?

A lot, I think. I am certain that these simple clapping games and songs and rustic dances serve important ritualistic functions for the participants. They provide us with a way of reaching out and touching one another within the structured security of an activity. They give us a little time to get to know one another. They let us use our voices, minds, and bodies in an integrated way. True, we may have sung the same song a dozen or fifty times. But that doesn't matter. The ritual is what counts. Singing the words, singing the tune, moving to the rhythm—we use these to weave ourselves again into the fabric of that ritual.

And when we do, it feels right. Earlier, when we discussed the appeal of choral speaking, I suggested that when one recites well-known verse, he calls on the part of the brain that deals with gestalts, with intuition and the nonrational, with sensual, diffuse, tactile, nonlinear experiences and thought. Because the material spoken is so well known, the languaging side of the brain no longer has sole performance rights.

The same may be true, perhaps to an even greater extent, when applied to making music. When we sing and dance and share the simple clapping games, we do so as whole people. Our intellect is given a chance to play. Our bodies are given an opportunity to move rhythmically. Our innate response to ritual is satisfied.

My own teachers, back in Springdale school, had, I believe, an intuitive awareness of the power of music. Every Friday morning they'd troop the entire student body—all twenty-eight of us—down to the basement, a low-ceilinged dungeon warmed by the big coal-burning furnace that squatted off to one side. We'd seat ourselves on wooden benches. Mrs. McDowell, who was principal, as well as upper-grade teacher, would hand out the blue-backed songbooks, frayed and worn from countless other Fridays. Miss Courtney—primary teacher and graying spinster—would draw up the stool to the piano. Solemnly, she'd open and close her fingers a few times to "work out the kinks," while we watched, fascinated. She'd try a few tentative chords and a scale or two. At last she'd pronounce herself ready.

We'd start with "America." Then "America the Beautiful." We'd sing "The Star Spangled Banner," hoping always we'd hit the high notes without cracking. Then Mrs. McDowell would call for requests. Hands shot up. Someone would always ask for "The Little Brown Church in the Vale," not through any religious inclination, but because we loved the chorus, where the song divided into parts, and the girls sang, "Oh, come to the church in the wild wood ..." while the boys droned, "Oh, come, come, come, come ..." We sang "She'll be Comin' 'Round the Mountain," and "Down in the Valley," followed always by "Red River Valley." We sang doleful songs ("Tenting Tonight on the Old Camp Ground") and lively ones ("Captain Jinks"). We sang rounds: "Row, Row, Row Your Boat" and "Have You Seen the Ghost of John?" Beginning in November, we sang Christmas carols: "Silent Night," "Oh Come All Ye Faithful," "Joy to the World."

I don't remember ever learning any new songs, don't remember our teachers ever varying the routine in any way; and yet the richness of the ritual was such that it shook out the cobwebs of boredom we had accumulated during the week.

Somehow, over the years, I grew away from that friendly affair with music. There were piano lessons, with practice an hour a day every day but Sunday, and college choir, and attendance at concerts, but except for singing "Praise God From Whom All Blessings Flow" at the dinner table with my family, that group pleasure in making music got lost.

Then, several years ago, while camping with friends in Baja California, I rediscovered the fun of group singing and dancing and moving through the steps of folk games.

We had set up sun shades to protect ourselves from the fierce blue skies, and between sorties to the beach for swimming and sailing and clam digging, we'd lounge there, reading, dozing. Pat decided to teach me how to play the guitar. At first, my fingers felt like sausages—fat and jointless—while hers effortlessly found the strings and frets. But before the afternoon was over, chords were coming from my borrowed guitar—chords overladen with noise, but musical sounds nevertheless; chords that could be sung to. I learned "Home on the Range." "Skip to My Lou" followed, and "Red River Valley." A recording device would have revealed the buzz of fingers touching unwanted strings, the slushy edges of notes. But all I heard was myself, making a new kind of music that sounded sweet in the bright desert air.

The music was sweeter still that evening, after supper, when we gathered around the big camp fire and the guitars, mandolins, and banjoes emerged. Song after song was sung, and I cautiously joined in with a chord or two here and there, urged on by friendly help from the other musicians.

Since then, my guitar playing has improved. Not much, but some. At a campground in the scrub pines of Massachusetts one summer evening my family and I were seated around the fire, singing to ourselves, when a man with a banjo stepped into the circle. We shared songs and campers' gossip late into the night. His brothers and sisters have shown up at campgrounds and in homes more times than I can tell.

Music seems to communicate when other language is frustrated by linguistic barriers. One evening I was at a party with a group of educators gathered from all over the world. The pre-dinner talk was formal, cautious, intellectual, cognitive. But after dinner a woman from Brazil sang and played a song from her country for us. Two Jamaicans did a dance that required no translation. The thaw had set in. I sang "The Fox Went Out on a Chilly Night," followed by a prim Australian who led us in "Waltzing Matilda." Before the evening was over, the group was doing an impromptu serpentine out the back door and through the back yard, singing "When the Saints Go Marching In," holding hands like children.

Getting Started ...

A warm, enthusiastic pleasure in the act of singing is the greatest asset one may bring to an audience. If you can carry a tune, know the words to many songs, have a clear voice, and are skilled with an instrument—preferably a portable one—so much the better.

But having said that, let us first identify what you *don't* have to have to share songs and dances with others.

You *don't* have to have a "good voice," as my father used to put it. The more I listen to the storytellers in my classes, the more I am aware that there is no single voice I respond to best. Scratchy growls, sweet trembling sopranos, basso profundos all are, in turn, intriguing. And the same is true of singers. What seems to count much more than the voice itself is the enthusiasm and vitality of the singer.

"But I can't even carry a tune!" Sorry, but that won't let you off, either. It's the song, and not the singer, that's important. Your whole-hearted and genuine pleasure in singing is what counts. Reedy, coarse-edged voices may carry meaning far better than a trained instrument, with its fine attention to volume and tempo. One of my students, who would have rendered "Silent Night" unrecognizable had she hummed it, charmed us all with her talking blues version of "The Soldier's Lament." She had two things going for her; she loved the song and brought her own meanings to it, and she had a sense of rhythm—the beat.

"I could never *learn to play a guitar or a piano or a ..."* Nice try. But singing is often done without accompaniment. And dancers provide their own accompaniment with singing and hand clapping and foot stamping. And there are options for the frustrated instrumentalist. An auto-harp is simple to play, requiring only that one read the letters of the alphabet and stroke the strings while depressing the appropriate keys. Blocks of wood, clapped together, serve as the rhythm base for many songs. Hand clapping and finger snapping are good natural accompaniments to singing. The guitar itself is not insurmountably difficult—at least to the degree of skill with which many play it. Learn three basic chords—say, the D, G, and A—and you can accompany hundreds of songs.

"But I don't know any songs!" That's just not true. You know countless songs: Christmas carols, nursery songs, and counting-out rhymes; old camping songs like "Dixie," "Yankee Doodle," "Way Down Upon the Swannee River," and "Home, Sweet Home"; songs like "Bingo" and "Frére Jacque" and "This Land is Your Land." And there's no reason why you should be limited to memorized songs. Write the words on a blackboard or chart, or ditto copies and distribute them to the audience. Or sing the song, and sing it again, encouraging the audience to join in when ready.

Which Songs to Sing

Why do some songs feel so right, while others seem flat and dull? Perhaps it's the goodness of the song itself—its ability to speak in vigorous language and tune to a wide range of persons. It may be that folk songs live on because people, notably children, like them. But it may also be that songs which have for years been forgotten spring to life again as their words take on fresh meanings. During America's

Revolutionary War a young girl sang of her lover:

> *The cruel war is raging and Johnny has to fight,*
> *I want to be with him from morning till night ...*

And two hundred years later, when the rattle of sabers has been exchanged for the clatter of helicopters, the song sounds as if it had been just been written. War, cruel then, has become, if possible, even more cruel. That young girl's pain reaches across time and touches us. The years have not muffled her anguish.

The songs included here are ones I've known for a long time. They are songs I enjoy singing and hearing sung as much as when I first learned them. I feel toward them as I feel toward old friends; they wear well. They might not be your favorites—at least not yet. But give them time.

Further, I chose these songs because of their storytelling qualities. While recognizing that the traditional view of a story might not be met by such songs as "A Uni Uni I Ki Ani," we can still acknowledge that the mood of that song conveys a scene, a time, a happening. The tale may be nonsensical, as with "Froggie Went a' Courtin'" or "Old Joe Clark." Or may suggest a character. Imagine "Captain Jinks" (of the Horse Marines) who teaches ladies how to dance; who, though he can't afford it, feeds his horse expensive corn and beans; and who is the pet of the army. What a splendidly foolish fellow we imagine him to be!

And, finally, I picked songs which would be, I hoped, at least partially familiar to most persons. Our goal here was to begin using songs as a variety of storytelling, rather than learning new songs. Thus, you will find that most the songs included are ones you may have sung as a child: "Sweet Betsy from Pike," "Wait for the Wagon," "Ain't Gwine Study War No More," and "Red River Valley."

Singing the Songs

Sing the songs simply and easily, with no particular attempt at "expression," no slowing down of tempo at the conclusions of verses, and no special increase or decrease in volume. Allow a good, strong, toe-tapping beat to come through, not hesitating, yourself, to keep time with foot stamping or hand clapping. If the pitch of a song is too high, it can be easily modified, particularly if one is using the guitar or auto-harp as an accompanying instrument.

Learn the words well and sing them clearly. In "Buckeye Jim" part of the sweet strange beauty of the song gets lost if the words aren't clear:

> *'Way up yonder above the moon*
> *A blue jay nests in a silver spoon.*

It takes close listening to appreciate the delicate poetry of these words. The singer must do all she can to help an audience catch them. If the song is unfamiliar it makes sense to provide a bit of background before singing the song, or recite a few lines.

Keep the songs moving. There is a temptation to sing the storytelling song or ballad somewhat slowly. Traditionally these songs are paced at a fairly good clip; perhaps because of concern with completing what may be a rather extensive number of verses. This, of course, does not rule out varying the tempo and experimenting with it. After years of singing "The Fox Went Out on a Chilly Night" at a headlong pace, we tried singing it slowly. And liked it! The song seemed entirely new when the tempo was changed.

As one examines old songs printed in different sources, wordings vary. That's because different singers found certain phrases more comfortable than others. You will want to modify songs to suit the group being sung to. In "Sweet Betsy from Pike," for example, certain verses seem better adapted to adult audiences, and may be omitted when singing the song with children. Or one may sing selected verses if the song seems too long. A synopsis of the omitted verses can be told if necessary.

Seat participants for group singing close together. Courage to sing comes with singing along with others. Besides, most voices sound richer and fuller when they're blended with others. And don't worry about those not singing. Their source of enjoyment may be in listening, rather than performing.

Limit yourself to two or three songs a session. Singing a song several times gives both the storyteller and the audience opportunities to try out changes in tempo, or introduce part singing, or assign solo voices. And, there's pleasure in hearing the improvement that comes about as a result of practice.

When introducing a new song, if copies of the words are not available to the audience, sing the chorus, then repeat it. After two or three times, the audience begins to get a feel for the words and tune and can join in. At this point, sing a verse or two while the audience joins in on the chorus. Invite persons in the audience familiar with the song to sing verses.

The Singing ...

In the next few pages a handful of songs, along with notes and commentaries are included. They're songs out of my own past; songs my friends and I have enjoyed singing. Leafing through them, you'll perhaps remember songs from your own past that have created that same sense of community spirit and pleasure.

A Uni Uni I Ki Ani

Often I begin a storytelling hour with this song. Vigorous, full of fun, suggesting distant places and other times, it draws people together. My students at McGill University taught me the song, asserting that it was an Eskimo chant. Later, when we stopped off to see family in Walla Walla, my sister-in-law listened to the song, and said, derisively, "Campfire Girls!"

To sing it, we arrange ourselves in a compact circle, close enough so that we can easily touch our neighbor. The first time through, the storyteller sings alone while others clap hands with the beat. Once the audience become familiar with the words—usually the second or third repetition—variations of the clapping game are introduced; participants first lightly striking their own knees with open palms, then alternating that with striking the right knee with the left hand while at the same time striking the left knee of the person to one's right with the left hand. Later, that gets varied, striking first one's own knees, then the left knee of the neighbor to the right, back to one's own, and then the right knee of the neighbor to the left. (Somehow, that's easier to do than to write about.) The last time through the song, participants sing under their breath, but the knee slapping begins very slowly and constantly accelerates until the final few bars are clapped at a rapid and rollicking beat, and hands flung up into the air on the words "ni che."

A un - i un - i i ki a - ni,

a un - i un - i i ki a - ni,

i ki yi i ki i ki a moo,

i ki yi i ki i ki a moo,

* Ah Woo! Ah Woo ni che!

* This last line is spoken, or chanted, rather than sung

Old Joe Clark

"Old Joe Clark(e)" has been around now for more than a hundred years. The origins of the song are uncertain; Joe Clark may have been a moonshiner, or a peace officer, or a hermit who lived back in the hills of Kentucky.[2] Some spell his last name with an *e* after the *k*. What is certain is that he's been memorialized in one of the most popular of breakdown songs, for which hundreds of stanzas are given. We never sing this song but that the audience begins, without invitation, to clap to the rhythm.

First sing the chorus, and once that has been established, begin singing the verses, only a few of which I've singled out.

Old Joe Clark, the preach-er's son, Preached all o-ver the plain, The on-ly text he ev-er knew was "High, low, jack and the game."

CHORUS: Fare thee well, Old Joe Clark, Fare thee well I say, He'll fol-ler me ten thou-sand miles, To hear my fid-dle play.

[Refrain:] *Fare thee well, old Joe Clark,*
Fare thee well, I say,
He'll foller me ten thousand miles,
To hear my fiddle play.

2. *Old Joe Clark had a house*
Sixteen stories high,
And every story in that house
Was filled with chicken pie.
    [Refrain]

3. *Old Joe Clark had a cat,*
She would neither sing or pray,
Stuck her head in a buttermilk jar
And washed her sins away.
    [Refrain]

4. *I went down to old Joe's house,*
He invited me to supper.
I stubbed my toe on the table leg,
And stuck my nose in the butter.
    [Refrain]

5. *I went down to old Joe's house,*
Never been there before.
He slept on the feather bed
And I slept on the floor.
    [Refrain]

6. I wish I was in Arkansas
Sittin' on a rail,
A jug of whiskey under my arm
And a possum by the tail.
    [Refrain]

7. Wish I was in Tennessee
Sittin' in a rocking chair,
One arm round my whiskey jug,
and the other around my dear.
    [Refrain]

8. If you see that gal of mine
Tell her when you go,
Before she makes a loaf of bread
She's got to set the dough.
    [Refrain]

Often, after we've sung a few verses of this song, I'll give the first two lines of a new verse, and ask for persons in the audience to complete it:

Never cared for turnip pie
Think it tastes like glue ...

or:

If you die and go to heaven
Tell St. Pete for me ...

By the way, while there aren't as many chorus variants as there are verses, there are several. You'll have no trouble making up your own, but here are a couple:

Rock-a-rock, old Joe Clark,
Rock-a-rock I say,
You'll be rockin' all day long,
Rock till judgment day.

Fly away, old Joe Clark,
Fly until you're gone;
Fly away, old Joe Clark,
With golden slippers on ...

Sweet Betsy from Pike

Perhaps no song tells better the story of the '49ers who crossed the continent in search of gold than does "Sweet Betsy from Pike." Fewer than half of the verses currently in print are given here; all of them tell with robust humor of Betsy and her lover, and the perils they faced. In singing the song, we may have the males—or a solo male voice—in the group sing the lines, "Betsy, get up, you'll get sand in your eyes!" and "You're an angel, but where are your wings?" The girls get their chance with, "Good-by, you big lummox, I'm glad you backed out!" Pike County, incidentally, is in Missouri.

Oh don't you remember sweet Betsy from Pike,
Who crossed the big mountains with her lover Ike,
With two yoke of oxen and a big yellow dog,
A tall Shanghai rooster and a fat spotted hog.

[Refrain:] Singing too-ra-la-loo-ra-la-loo-ra-la-lay,
too-ra-la-loo-ra-la-loo-ra-la-lay.

One evening quite early they camped on the Platte
T'was near by the road on a green shady flat,
And Betsy, quite tired, lay down in repose
While Ike gazed amazed at his Pike County rose.

[Refrain]

Out on the prairie one dark starry night,
They broke out the whiskey and Betsy got tight,
She sang and she shouted and skipped o'er the plain,
And showed her behind to the whole wagon train.
    [Refrain]

They soon reached the desert where Betsy gave out,
Down on the sand she lay rolling about
Poor Ike, with great tears, looked on in surprise,
And said, "Betsy, get up, you'll get sand in your eyes."
    [Refrain]

Long Ike and sweet Betsy attended a dance,
Ike wore a pair of his Pike County pants,
Sweet Betsy was covered with ribbons and rings,
Said Ike, "You're an angel, but where are your wings?"
    [Refrain]

Long Ike and sweet Betsy got married, of course,
Ike became jealous, obtained a divorce;
Sweet Betsy, well satisfied, said with a shout,
"Good-by, you big lummox, I'm glad you backed out!"
    [Refrain]

The Fox Went Out on a Chilly Night

   This fine old song, which dates back to the fifteenth century, tells a quick-paced story, full of clever wit. The line "Old Mother Flipper-Flopper jumped out of bed ..." has always been a personal favorite of my own children. Note that the chorus is a repeat of the last two lines of each verse—good for audience participation Incidentally, "The Fox" has been used by several artists, including Peter Spier, as the text for a picture book.

The fox went out on a chilly night,
Prayed to the moon for to give him light,
For he'd many a mile to go that night
Before he reached the town-oh, town-oh, town-oh,
He'd many a mile to go that night
Before he reached the town-oh.

He ran 'til he came to the great big pen,
Where the ducks and the geese were kept there-in;
A couple of you will grease my chin
Before I leave this town-oh, town-oh, town-oh,
A couple of you will grease my chin
Before I leave this town-oh.

He grabbed the grey goose by the neck,
And he slung a duck across his back;
He didn't mind all their quack, quack, quack,
And their legs all dangling down-oh, down-oh, down-oh,
He didn't mind all their quack, quack, quack
And their legs all dangling down-oh.

Old Mother Flipper-Flopper jumped out of bed,
Out of the window she cocked her head,
Crying "John, John, the grey goose is gone!
And the Fox is in the town-oh, town-oh, town-oh,"
Crying "John, John, the grey goose is gone!
And the Fox is in the town-oh."

Then John he ran to the top of the hill,
And he blew his horn both loud and shrill,
And that Fox, he said "I'd better flee with my kill,
'Cause they'll soon be on my trail-oh, trail-oh, trail-oh,"
And that Fox, he said "I'd better flee with my kill,
'Cause they'll soon be on my trail-oh."

So that Fox he ran to his own den,
There were the little ones: eight, nine, ten,
Crying "Daddy, Daddy, better go back again,
For it must be a mighty fine town-oh, town-oh, town-oh,"
Crying "Daddy, Daddy, better go back again,
For it must be a mighty fine town-oh."

That Fox and his wife, without any strife
Cut up the goose with a carving knife,
And they never had such a supper in their life,
And the little ones chewed on the bones-oh,
*   bones-oh, bones-oh,*
And they never had such a supper in their life,
And the little ones chewed on the bones-oh.

Red River Valley

This song had its origins in New York State as "The Bright Mohawk Valley," but as it moved west it was simplified and purified, until there emerged an easy-going and lazy little song that almost seems to sing itself and, as John and Alan Lomax put it, "drifts straight into your heart like smoke from a lonely cabin rising and disappearing into the prairie sky."[3] When we sing "Red River Valley," we usually follow it with "Down in the Valley," a song that possesses its own sweet melancholy, then move on to "Careless Love" and finish up with "You Are My Sunshine."

From this valley they say you are going
We will miss your bright eyes and sweet smile;
For you take with you all of the sunshine,
That has brightened our pathways awhile.

[Refrain:] Come and sit by my side, if you love me,
Do not hasten to bid me adieu,
Just remember the Red River Valley
And the cowboy who loved you so true.

From this val - ley they say you are go - ing.   We will
miss your bright eyes and sweet smile;   For you take with you all   of the
sun- shine,   That has bright- ened our path - ways a   while.
CHORUS
Come and sit   by my side   if   you love me,   Do not
has - ten to bid   me a - dieu.   Just re - mem - ber the Red   Riv - er
Val - ley,   And the cow - boy that loved you so   true.

I've been thinking a long time, my darling
Of the sweet words you never would say,
Now, alas, must my fond hopes all vanish?
For they say you are going away.
    [Refrain]

Do you think of the valley you're leaving?
Oh, how lonely and how dreary t'will be.
Do you think of the kind hearts you're breaking?
And the pain you are causing to me?
    [Refrain]

They will bury me where you have wandered,
Near the hills where the daffodils grow,
When you're gone from the Red River Valley,
For I can't live without you I know.
    [Refrain]

Skip to My Lou

There are probably hundreds of known stanzas to this old song, and more being added all the time. In fact, they may be made up while singing the song.

Cows in the pasture, moo moo moo ...
Drank a glass of buttermilk, thick as goo ...
Owls in the treetops, Whoo, whoo whoo ...
Flies in the buttermilk, shoo, fly, shoo ...
Lost all my money, what'll I do ...
Chicken and dumplings make good stew ...

And, while last words of the stanzas usually rhyme with *Lou*, other word patterns may be used:

John's got a blue shirt, Mike's is red ...

Simple games are often played with this song. In one version, a child stands in the middle and as the song is sung chooses a partner from the circle of children side-stepping in a circle around him. The two of them then skip around the circle, after which the first child joins the group and the second child chooses a partner to repeat the game. Verse after verse is sung.

In a Southwest version played among young adults, a young man stands in the center of the circle while other couples hold hands and sing, marching in a circle around him. He inspects all the girls and chooses one to march with. Her partner then goes to the middle and the game is repeated:

Lost my partner, what'll I do ...
I'll find another one, prettier than you ...

But it's not always males doing the choosing. Girls can do the inspecting, too:

I'll find another one, handsomer than you ...

One final comment about "Skip to My Lou." It is remarkably easy to play on the guitar, requiring only two chords; D and A7.

Little red wagon painted blue.
Little red wagon painted blue.
Little red wagon painted blue.
Skip to my Lou, my darling.

[Refrain:] Skip, skip, skip to my Lou,
Skip, skip, skip to my Lou,
Skip, skip, skip to my Lou,
Skip to my Lou, my darling.

Buckeye Jim

Occasionally one comes across a song that has about it a sense of absolute purity and beauty—the beauty of still clear waters, of sunlight filtering through pine branches onto spring grass. Such a song is "Buckeye Jim." Children and adults alike are fascinated by this song, with its other-worldly lyrics, and a melody that "weaves and spins" its way into one's heart.

'Way up yonder above the sky
A bluebird lives in a jay-bird's eye.

[Refrain:] Buckeye Jim, you can't go,
Go weave and spin, you can't go, Buckeye Jim.

'Way up yonder above the moon
A blue-jay nests in a silver spoon.
    [Refrain]

'Way down younger in a wooden trough
An old woman died of the whoopin' cough.
    [Refrain]

'Way down yonder on a hollow log
A red bird danced with a green bullfrog.
    [Refrain]

"Froggie Went a'Courtin'" and "The Old Gray Goose is Dead" are two songs which go well with "Buckeye Jim." Interestingly, although this song appears in a number of anthologies, its origins—like the song itself—remain a mystery.

Have You Seen the Ghost of John?

Another of my favorites, this song is itself a paradox; a doleful minor key, and an amusing question posed: Wouldn't John, a ghost, wandering around in skeletal form, be chilly with no skin on? This song is a round—a good one for Hallowe'en singing, though not restricted to that time of year. Entry points are numbered for four groups, but it can be sung with two.

1. *Have you seen the ghost of John?*
2. *Long white bones and the rest all gone,*
3. *Oo—oo——!*
4. *Wouldn't it be chilly with no clothes on?*

Hey, Ho, Nobody Home

Another live round, this song was popularized by Peter, Paul, and Mary.

1. *Hey, ho, nobody home. No [Group two enters after 'No.']*
2. *Meat nor drink nor money have I none ...*
3. *Still I will be merry!*

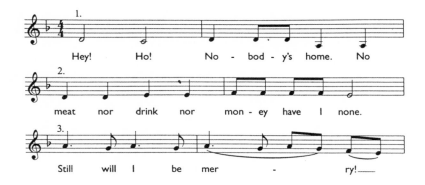

It's good fun to sing "Buckeye Jim," with its haunting melancholy, and then break into "Hey, Ho, Nobody Home." After the entire audience has sung it together a few times, divide the group and sing it as a round.

Ain't Gwine Study War No More

The tune and words to this song vary from source to source. The ones printed here are those I learned from friends. Unfortunately, musical notation barely suggests the richness of this fine Black American spiritual, which tells us something important about this kind of song—it is best learned orally, and not from a written source.

Try singing the lead line, "Gwine to lay down my burden ..." with the rest of the group joining in on "Down by the riverside ..." Once the pattern has been established, invite members of the audience to take solo lines.

> Gwine lay down my burden, down by the riverside,
> Down by the riverside, down by the riverside,
> Gwine lay down my burden, down by the riverside,
> To study war no more.
>
> [Refrain:] Ain't gwine to study war no more,
> Ain't gwine to study war no more,
> Ain't gwine to study war no more.
> Ain't gwine to study war no more,
> Ain't gwine to study war no more,
> Ain't gwine to study war no more.
>
> Gwine to lay down my sword and shield ...
>   [Refrain]
>
> Gwine to put on my long white robe ...
>   [Refrain]
>
> Gwine to try on my starry crown ...
>   [Refrain]

Gwine lay down my bur-den, down by the riv-er-side, down by the riv-er-side, down by the riv-er-side, Gwine lay down my bur-den, down by the riv-er-side, to stud-y war no more.___ Ain't gwine stud-y war no more, ain't gwine stud-y war no more, Ain't gwine stud-y war no more, Ain't gwine stud-y war no more, ain't gwine stud-y war no more, Ain't gwine stud-y war no more.

And the Dance ...

Within our own country, the play party and its simple dances have a long and honorable history. In righteous Protestant communities of frontier America, square dancing, with its clasping of waists and accompanying fiddle music, was looked upon as the Devil's work.

But, as always, when the rules are too strict, young people began to find ways to work inside and around the requirements of the older generation. Fiddle music—"The Devil's work!"—was done away with so that objection could not be raised. Instead, partygoers clapped their hands and sang. No liquor or "spooning" was allowed; that might happen on the way home, but not at the party. The fancy steps and intricate patterns of the square dance were abandoned, and the storytelling songs of children were used: "Skip to My Lou," "Go In and Out the Windows," "Old Gray Goose," and "Buffalo Gals." Rough-clad young men and sparkling-eyed girls in faded calico might be seen together, clasping hands and sashaying to the beat of songs they were themselves singing.

Once started, these play parties began to have their own heart and life. Off the main roads and away from the bright lights of towns, they were still practiced as recently as the 1940s and 1950s. I remember, from my boyhood, dances and play parties at Ferndale Grange, a spare whitewashed wooden structure a mile up the road from our house.

Everyone in the neighborhood would be there: the Steens and the Cauvels, the Powells and the Calhouns, the Babcocks and the Eifforts; the men with their sunburnt faces and white shirts and dark blue trousers and cowboy boots, the women in pretty cotton dresses, the old folks with their canes and shawls, and the infants, wrapped in pink and blue blankets, sleeping peacefully through all the fun. There'd be a potluck supper, with ham loaf and homemade rolls, potato salad and macaroni salad, green beans and baked beans, red gelatin salad with marshmallows and green gelatin salad with canned fruit squares, sixteen varieties of cake and the same number of pie.

After supper, the tables would be pushed to the back of the room. My older cousin, Henry, who was the life of any party, would start things off with a simple choosing-the-partners game, something like, say, "Skip to My Lou," to get folks "loosened up," as he put it. Following that, he might call on Uncle Dale and Aunt Mabel, known as "being good on the dance floor," to demonstrate the steps of a more intricate game—"Old Dan Tucker," perhaps. My sister Carol and Jackie Whipple, in their early teens, were dancing together, off in a corner, whispering, hoping that some handsome boy from Walla Walla would hear the music and drop in. There's be a break for coffee and cake and lemonade, and the games would resume: "The Noble Duke of York," "Pawpaw Patch," "Bingo."

About ten o'clock or so, someone would start to sing the first notes of "Good Night, Ladies." Everyone was on the floor for that one—even the elderly. After that, tables would be cleared and arranged back the way they'd been. The bare wooden floor swept clean. The rudimentary kitchen spiffied up. Folks would load up for the trip home. The lights would be switched off. "See you next time," voices would call through the darkness. "Next time ..."

A couple of the play party games I've described here come from those Ferndale Grange evenings. Others I learned from Richard Chase when he'd come visit us and he and my students and my family and I would gather together out in the front yard under the old Monterey pine. Others were taught to me by students. One or two I made up.

I'm recommending these dances because they're easy to learn and fun to do. They're good ice-breakers among youngsters or adults. And you can move on from them to more intricate dances such as those found in the books named at the end of this chapter.

Draw a Bucket of Water

This old play party game may be played with as few as four players or with multiples of four. It's a fine get acquainted activity. English in origin, and probably more than five hundred years old, the game has been a popular "dance" among young people in the eastern hill country as well as in the American southwest, receiving numerous changes over time.[4]

Introduce this dance by singing the song a couple of times, encouraging the audience to join in. Once they've learned the song, call for volunteers to demonstrate the dance.

To play, two couples stand as in figure A, the boys holding hands with one another and the girls doing the same across the center of the spot designated as the "well." As they sing, players move their arms back and forth in time to the music, pumping with the hands and arms and not with the body. At the end of the verse, players 1 and 3 raise their arms to form an arch and allow player 2 to "pop under," as shown in figure B. The same action continues for each of the players. As each player pops under, the arch is lowered behind her or him.

When all four players are within the arch, the "bucket" is bounced briskly clockwise, as the players chant together three times: "Jump, Jump Jump! All around the pump!"

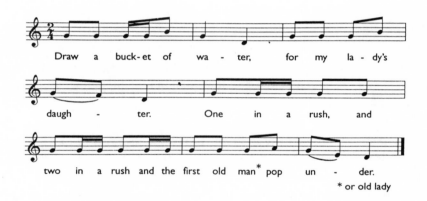

Draw   a   buck-et   of   wa - ter,   for   my   la - dy's

daugh - ter.   One   in   a   rush,   and

two   in   a   rush   and   the   first   old   man* pop   un - der.

* or old lady

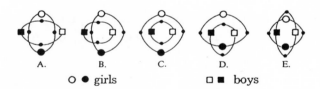

A.   B.   C.   D.   E.

O ● girls   □ ■ boys

Draw a bucket of water,
For my lady's daughter,
One in rush, and two in a rush,
And the first (or second) old man (or lady) pops under.
    [Repeat four times]

Muh 'Zudio

Bits and pieces of this fine old Black American play party dance and game have come my way over the years. The tune to which the dance is performed is much like that of the chorus in the old song, "Shortnin' Bread."

Before playing the game, teach the song (as was done with "Draw a Bucket of Water"). Once participants know the song, move on to the game itself.

This away, Muh 'Zudio, Muh 'Zudio, Muh 'Zudio,
This away, Muh 'Zudio, right on down.

To play, partners (preferably of opposite sex) join hands and stand facing one another, girls in one row and boys in the other. As the song is sung, partners alternately pump hands back and forth, dropping them at the last word, "Down." Next, the following lines are sung, to the same tune:

Step back, Sally, make a little alley ...
Step back, Sally right on down.

As they sing these lines, players drop hands and move apart, leaving an "alley" down the center. Clapping hands to keep time, they then sing:

Here comes Sally, strutting down the alley
Here comes Sally, right on down.

During the singing of those words, "Sally" (the first girl in the row) struts down between the other players, arms moving, hips bumping, hands clapping, doing a "cake-walk," urged on by the others.

Then, the next lines:

> *Here comes another one, just like the other one,*
> *Here comes another one, right on down.*

During these lines, Sally's partner struts his way down the alley in the same fashion, rejoining Sally at the end of the row.

At this point in the game, according to one of my students, all the players chant the following twice:

> *Eenie meenie, gypsy leena,*
> *Ooh, ah, oompa leena*
> *At chi katchi*
> *Lib er atchi*
> *I love you!*

And while chanting it perform a figure eight, returning to their original positions at the end of the chant, at which time the entire sequence begins again, with the couple which had been second in line now occupying the role of head couple:

> *"This a-way Muh 'Zudio ..."*

One last comment regarding "Muh 'Zudio." Having played this game many times, I can attest that it is not for the short-winded. One way to make the dance a little easier from a physical standpoint is to limit the number of couples to six.

Grab Your Partner!

This old game can be labeled a dance only by the wildest stretch of the imagination, and yet it is a wonderful ice-breaker at a play party, giving all participants a chance for vigorous exercise.

To play, couples join hands and "march around, two by two," singing those words to the tune of "Skip to My Lou." At the conclusion of the first verse, those on the inside of the circle continue marching while their partners remain standing in one place in the circle. Additional verses are introduced by the caller, who remains outside the circle:

> *"Lost my partner, what'll I do ..."*
> *"I'll find another one, prettier than you ..."*
> *"Flies in the kitchen, shoo, flies, shoo ..."*
> *"Cows in the pasture, moo moo moo ..."*
> *"Little baby crying, boo hoo hoo ..."*

During those verses, insiders continue to march and outsiders continue to stand in one spot, singing and clapping time to the music.

At an unexpected moment in the singing, the caller shouts out, "Grab your partner!" At that signal all the insiders head back home to find their partners. They grab hands with them and squat where they are. The last couple to reunite are the losers. (But do not leave the circle.) And the game starts over.

Needless to say, there are plenty of collisions and bumps in the game, but that only seems to add to the fun. As a caller, I generally make the first call for "Grab," after only a verse or two have passed and partners are fairly close to one another. After that, I often allow time for singing several verses before shouting out, as this adds to the tension. Also, after a couple of times through, have players change places; insiders becoming outsiders and vice versa.

'Tis the Gift to be Simple

Several years ago my family and some friends were camping just beneath San Jacinto Peak near the little town of Idlewild. When supper was over and the dishes put away, we joined hands, formed a small circle, and danced to the old Quaker song.

'Tis the gift to be simple,
'Tis the gift to be free,
'Tis the gift to come down
Where we ought to be ...

The steps were improvised, but there in the dim sweet light under the pines, it didn't matter. What mattered was the movement, the touching. I describe our steps below, but you may want to refashion them to suit yourself.

'Tis the gift to be simple,
'Tis the gift to be free,
'Tis the gift to come down
Where we ought to be;

And when we have come
To the place that's right
We shall be in the valley
Of love and delight.

When true simplicity is gained
To bow and to bend
We shall not be ashamed,
But to turn and to turn
Shall be our delight,
'Til by turning and turning
We come round right.

Joining hands, form a circle with other dancers. While singing the first two lines, side-step clockwise four steps; on the next two lines, side-step counter-clockwise so that everybody is back at the starting point. Repeat action, side-stepping counter-clockwise four steps, returning to starting point. On *when,* stretch the circle by taking two steps backward, and then moving again toward the original position. When singing *"To bow and to bend ..."* drop hands and bow to left and right. Then, while singing *"But to turn and to turn ..."* slowly turn a full turn clockwise and then counterclockwise.

And If You Are a Teacher ...

Songs, dances, jump rope rhymes, and clapping games come naturally to children. Little coaxing will be required to make these a part of their school day. But, one might ask, are they valid? Can they be defended as a significant part of what a child needs to know?

In my mind, there is little doubt that these old songs and games are important. Earlier I described my experiences with teachers where songs and dances brought us together. The same has been true with children.

But there is another justification for including these fine old tunes and games. They are part of our uniquely American culture and heritage, linking us with our own past. The strains may be traced to England, to Africa, to Germany, to Mexico, to the ancient fertile crescent. The culture may have grown and spread from Carolina or Texas or Oklahoma or Washington State. But the culture is in us—a part of our knowing—and we, as teachers, have both the privilege and the responsibility to share that culture with our young.

And what's in it for the children? They get an enriched sense of their own place in the world; where they came from, what their parents' parents were like. They also get lots of practice playing with words, with language, with rhythm and rhyme.

And, besides, it's fun! Certainly we need not apologize for that.

NOTES

1. Itzhak Bentov, *Stalking the Wild Pendulum* (New York: E.P. Dutton, 1977, and Rochester, Vermont: Destiny Books, 1988).
2. John A. and Alan Lomax, *Best Loved American Folk Songs* (New York: Grosset & Dunlap, 1947), p. 86.
3. *Op cit.*, p. 199.
4. Richard Chase, *Singing Games and Play Party Games* (New York: Dover Publications, 1967), p. 24. Mr. Chase points out that "Draw a Bucket of Water" apparently had its beginning in ancient Celtic well worship.

ACTIVITIES

1. Make a list of songs you already know. Which are your favorites? What makes them so?

2. Most play party dances require very simple actions. Try improvising a dance for one of the songs we sang; "Sweet Betsy from Pike," for instance. You may want to limit the action to some simple steps backward and forward, then perhaps a promenade, or a grand right and left.

3. Plan a storytelling hour that includes singing and dancing as well as more conventional storytelling. One might begin the hour with "A Uni Uni I Ki Ani," then dance "Muh 'Zudio," and finish the hour with a migratory tale or two, or perhaps some improvisational puppet theater involving audience.

4. Ask persons you know what old dances, songs, and games they remember. Have them teach them to you.

FURTHER READING

There are many, many excellent books that describe folk songs and folk dances. Ones I have particularly enjoyed are named below:

Blood, Peter and Annie Patterson. *Rise Up Singing.* Illustrated by Kore Loy McWhirter. Bethlehem, PA: Sing Out Corporation, 1988, 1992. This spiral backed book contains words, chords and sources for twelve hundred songs. It's portable and encyclopedic all at the same time. You'll find here the lyrics for just about every song you can think of—ballads, funny songs, golden oldies, popular tunes, songs celebrating ecology, faith, work, and holidays. As Pete Seeger says in the introduction, "When one person taps out a beat while another leads into the melody, or when three people discover a harmony they never knew existed, or a crowd joins in on a chorus as though to raise the ceiling a few feet higher, then they also know: there's hope for the world." One note: music is not included (except for the rounds).

Chase, Richard. *Op cit.* This delightful little book gives compete instructions for eighteen games, including diagrams for the dance formations and notations for the songs. Mr. Chase has drawn many of these games from Lady Gomme's 1894 collection of the traditional games of England, Scotland, and Ireland.

Fox, Dan, with commentary by Claude Marks. *Go In and Out the Window: An Illustrated Songbook for Young People.* New York: The Metropolitan Museum of Art and Henry Holt & Company, 1987. First of all, this book, with its songs illustrated with paintings and artifacts from the Metropolitan Museum, is very beautiful. But it's also useful. There are over sixty songs. "Bingo" is here, and "I Had a Little Nut Tree." There's the haunting "Skye Boat Song," which the youngest daughter played and sang for her school's talent night when she was a second grader. Dan Fox's piano arrangements are among the most simple and elegant I know.

Kraus, Richard. *A Pocket Guide of Folk and Square Dances and Singing Games the Elementary School.* New York: Grosset & Dunlap, 1947. This fine old book contains over a hundred songs, together with complete information as to their sources, fugitive verses, and musical commentary. The piano arrangements are the work of Charles and Ruth Seeger, and are a delight to play.

McIntosh, David S. *Singing Games and Dances.* New York: Association Press, 1957. This collection of dances and games was selected by Mr. McIntosh from those he learned in southern Illinois. Names and information about the original contributors of the songs are given wherever possible.

Seeger, Ruth Crawford. *American Folk Songs for Children in Home, School, and Nursery School.* Illustrated by Barbara Cooney. Garden City, NY: Doubleday, 1948. In the foreword to this book Carl Sandburg writes, "Ruth Seeger's song book is no sudden notion. It represents many years of a rare mother living with her music and her children. Her collection embodies an extraordinary array of time-tested songs for little ones, many of them so old they have been forgotten and now have the freshness of the new."

10. Reading Aloud

POLONIUS: What do you read, my lord?
HAMLET: Words, words, word.

—SHAKESPEARE, *HAMLET*, ACT II, SCENE 1

But words are things; and a small drop of ink,—
Falling, like dew, upon a thought, produces
That which makes thousands, perhaps millions, think.

—LORD BYRON, *DON JUAN*

The page of a great book does not differ mechanically from
the page of a worthless book—it is merely a sheet of paper
with some black odd-looking specks on it. It remains that, or
it is transformed into wisdom, beauty, joy. But this transfor-
mation depends finally upon the reader—
upon the reader's ability to *read.*"

—LEE WILSON DODD, "ON LEARNING TO READ"[1]

When Jean-Paul Sartre was four years old, and precocious, he demanded to have his own books. His grandfather, a writer, went to the office of his own publisher and returned home with a collection of fairy tales. Sartre took the two little volumes, sniffed them, opened them—"making them creak"—examined the "little dried herbals," knowing they held a mystery, but not knowing what shape the mystery might take. Nothing happened. He tried treating them like dolls; kissing them, rocking them, beating on them. Still nothing. At last, in desperation, he took them to his mother.

Earlier, she had told him these same stories; told them in her own words, with unfinished sentences and faltering cadences, hurried summarizations, and lapses into commentary on the day's events; told them while she bathed him, or rubbed him down with eau de Cologne, or tucked him in bed; much as we've all told night-time stories to our own young.

But now she sat him down opposite her, on his little chair. She bent over the book, lowering her eyelids, so that he thought she'd fallen asleep. And then, a voice—a "plaster" voice, not his mother's—spoke. And the speech—he didn't recognize it, either. It took him a moment to realize that it was the book that was speaking, and not her. Word followed word, with no hesitation—"frightening sentences," Sartre called them, "singing, nasal, broken by pauses and sighs, rich in unknown words, they were enchanted with themselves and their meanderings without bothering about me."[2]

In Sartre's account we see the paradox of reading aloud. The reader is, in a sense, a storyteller. But also she is the medium through which the story passes. The words—these "little dried herbals"—strung together in preordained fashion, march along, "enchanted with themselves and their meanderings." They must be stuck to. That's the rule!

And if that's the rule, it may seem odd to conclude a book on storytelling with a chapter on reading aloud. For the one appears to be the antithesis of the other. The minute a storyteller begins her tale, she is free to cut and shape it as she chooses. But the reader doesn't have that same latitude. The printed words, line after line, across and down the page, dictate. She may speed them up or slow them down, shout them out or whisper them. But the words themselves are unchanged; inflexible. They belong to the book. After she's gone, they're still there.

And so, reading aloud, which at first glance looks easier than telling a story, singing a song, or animating a puppet, may well be more difficult. Elaborating on details when the audience needs or wants them, compressing a story when attention is flagging, modifying language to fit the group; indeed, changing the outcome of the story itself—these rights and obligations belong to the storyteller, but are usually considered outside the realm of the reader.

And yet, clearly, there are times when the storyteller is better-off reading than telling. One such time occurs when the style of the writing is so intrinsically a part of the story that it would be impossible to replicate it when telling. Remember the first chapter of A.A. Milne's *Winnie-the-Pooh*, "In Which We are Introduced to Winnie-The-Pooh and Some Bees, and the Stories Begin"? Pooh talks to himself, sings, climbs a tree, and falls out. That's about it. But the narrative charms us. Change Milne's words, change the order of Milne's words, and the charm vanishes.

So what if one wishes to include *Winnie-the-Pooh* in a storytelling repertoire? Memorizing it, word for word, is a possibility—but a time-consuming one. Reading the story aloud turns out to be the best plan.

A related instance in which reading aloud is preferred to telling happens when the storyteller wishes to introduce a specific book or author to a group. Ashley Bryan, well known for his own original illustrations and stories, does this when he shares the work of others with a audience. He brings their books with him, and "reads" from the book as he recites the poems. I carry a tattered copy of X.J. and Dorothy Kennedys' little anthology, *Knock at a Star*, with me, and read poems from it at storytelling sessions, partly because there's no way I can "tell" those poems better than they're written, and also because I want the audience to know where to look for more. Here's Charles Causley's mysterious "What Has Happened to Lulu?" from the Kennedys' book, a poem that invariably elicits a variety of responses:

> *What has happened to Lulu, mother?*
> *What has happened to Lu?*
> *There's nothing in her bed but an old rag doll*
> *And by its side a shoe.*
>
> *Why is her window wide, mother,*
> *The curtain flapping free,*
> *And only a circle on the dusty shelf*
> *Where her money box used to be?*
>
> *Why do you turn your head, mother,*
> *And why do the tear-drops fall?*
> *And why do you crumple that note on the fire*
> *And say it is nothing at all?*
>
> *I woke to voices late last night,*
> *I heard an engine roar.*
> *Why do you tell me the things I heard*
> *Were a dream and nothing more?*
>
> *I heard somebody cry, mother,*
> *In anger or in pain,*
> *But now I ask you why, mother,*
> *You say it was a gust of rain.*
>
> *Why do you wander about as though*
> *You don't know what to do?*
> *What has happened to Lulu, mother?*
> *What has happened to Lu?*[3]

What do *you* think happened to Lulu? Here's another poem from the Kennedys' book, an anonymous one which they heard from Scottish schoolchildren. Do you recognize the original? Can you think of other takeoffs?

> *We four lads from Liverpool are:*
> *Paul in a taxi, John in a car,*
> *George on a scooter, tootin' his hooter,*
> *Following Ringo Starr!*[4]

Reading aloud is also appropriate when sharing picture books. *Madeline and the Gypsies,* with its brightly-colored sketches of the French countryside, loses much if the pictures are not shown. The same is true for Lynd Ward's *The Biggest Bear,* or Judith Hendershot's and Thomas B. Allen's *In Coal Country,* or Linda Morris's and David DeRan's *Morning Milking,* or Cathi Hepworth's zany alphabetarium, *Antics.* A good part of the pleasure in these books lies in studying their pictures:

"Look at that monster ... Is he going to eat up Max?"

"Naw, he likes him ... See that smile on his face? He just wants to be friends ..."

It would take a courageous teacher to read Maurice Sendak's *Where The Wild Things Are* without showing the illustrations.

And then, of course, there are those books where the illustrations form a counterpoint to the words. In Raldolph Caldecott's *Hey Diddle Diddle and Bye Baby Bunting,* for example, the written text consists of two nursery rhymes which most of us know by heart. But what a surprise the book holds; for the illustrations tell a different story. "... And the dish ran away with the spoon," the text reads. And the illustrations? They show us, first, a lithesome little beribboned spoon and her beau, the handsome and portly dish, dashing away toward conjugal bliss. And then, on the next page, tragedy, as her mother—a fork—and her father—a knife, intervene, and, alas, break up the romance in an alarmingly violent way.

Or consider William Steig's *Caleb and Kate,* with its amusingly high-flown language—"He wheeled and flung her to the floor, hissing broken curses through his beard"—and its disarmingly simple illustrations. The charm of the book is lost unless both are enjoyed together.

Finally, there are those times when you cannot really separate reading and telling. You may tell a portion of a story, and then read selected passages after the setting and situation have been described. Remember in *Island of the Blue Dolphins,* when Karana vows to kill the leader of the pack of wild dogs, and then, after she has wounded him, finds she is unable to do so? It is not possible to improve on the sparse elegance of Scott O'Dell's prose in that moving scene, and reading those passages aloud seems both natural and effective. At the same time, one can set the scene through a capsulated telling of the events leading up to that dramatic episode.

For these reasons, then, reading aloud well is a skill needed by the storyteller. Taking those bits of dry ink—those "little dried herbals"—and breathing life into them requires practice. In the next few pages, we'll consider some of the things you can do to improve your own oral reading.

Voice Quality

Why are some voices so pleasant to listen to, while others we grow weary of in a brief minute or so? Pitch certainly plays a part. But it's not a simple matter of a low-pitched voice being more pleasant than one that is pitched higher. What seems to make the difference is how relaxed one is while reading. Unlike Sartre's mother, with her "plaster" voice, one's reading voice should, insofar as possible, be the same voice one uses when storytelling.

Consider the poem printed below. Read it first as you would normally. Then read it again, pitching your voice higher. Now read the passage a third time, consciously lowering your voice to another register. Which pitch seems more relaxed and comfortable?

> *I had a little pony,*
> *His name was Dapple Gray;*
> *I lent him to a lady,*
> *To ride a mile away.*
> *She whipped him, she lashed him,*
> *She rode him through the mire;*
> *I would not lend my pony now,*
> *For all the lady's hire.*

While for the most part one pitches the voice at a comfortable register, there are times when a different register must be used to give story clues. Consider the following line:

> *"Someone's been eating my porridge!"*

Papa, Mamma, and Baby Bear all speak those same words. Pitch is one sure way for the storyteller to inform an audience which of the bears is making that pronouncement. While reading "The Elephant's Child," would one pitch the crocodile's voice high or low? What of Elephant Child himself? Pitch can be a significant aid in separating the several voices the reader must maintain in handling dialogue well.

Of course, even if general pitch is raised or lowered, it varies throughout a sentence or paragraph; or even, for that matter, throughout a word. The pitch that takes place between words and syllables, the *interval,* and the changes that occur even while the syllables within the words are being uttered, *intonation,* combine to make up the *speech melody*—that flexible and varied pitch pattern which strikes the ear so pleasantly. Take the first line of the poem we just read:

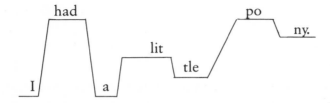

Interpreted, that sentence reveals to the reader a former time and a loss. But consider that same arrangement of words, with a different melody:

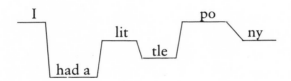

Interior changes in pitch bring a completely different meaning to the sentence, so that the second example suggests a jealous child—"My *brother* had a fine horse, and all I had was this little pony!"

But even the diagrammed examples don't really illustrate what goes on when one speaks. The word *I* in *I had a little pony* is, in reality, a complex series of pitches, as the diphthong moves from a "long" *i* to a "long" *e* and the voice moves up the scale while speaking the word.

These interior melodies come naturally in daily speech. But, as the young Sartre observed when his mother first read to him, one's reading voice often takes on a different quality—less musical, flatter.

As an experiment, read the following sentence, varying interval and intonation pitch so that the statement conforms to the meaning printed in parentheses:

- *He wooed the lighthouse keeper* (rowing across the bay each evening to her lighthouse).

- *He wooed the light housekeeper* (who weighed only eighty-seven pounds).

- *He wooed the light house keeper* (who refused to do any heavy housekeeping).

Another important element in reading aloud is tonal quality. Papa Bear sounds like himself not only because of the low pitch of his voice, but also because of its timbre. Timbre is that set of tonal characteristics that informs us that the voice we're hearing is one person and not another. There are many reasons why each person has the particular tonal characteristics he does. Physical make-up plays a role: adenoids can affect tone adversely; a weak palate, a tendency to tongue thrust, age, a bad cold—all contribute. There are regional differences: the twang of a Kansan; the drawl of a North Carolinian.

And, of course, there are the affective factors. "Put on your galoshes!" the young bride says to her husband. Later, when she repeats those words as the harried mother of a brood of children, the effect is not the same. Fear, anger, hate, shyness, timidity—each of these shapes and alters speech.

As an exercise, my students and I often read a few simple sentences, and then ask others to guess the conditions we have in mind from the way we've read them. Here's one we've used, together with a variety of conditions:

Someone's at the door.
> (Small child, to mother)
> (Burglars)
> (The person outside)
> (Lovers)

Without losing the particular characteristics of one's own voice, it is possible, through proper breathing, tongue placement, and posture, to obtain a more pleasing sound. Improper breathing may be one of the most noticeable of the errors a reader makes. Plan ahead so you have plenty of air to read a phrase or sentence comfortably, without having to force out the last words. Try reading the following sentences, inhaling just enough air at the beginning of each to carry you comfortably through:

1. *Gently Peter lowered the kitten to the bed of clean rags.*

2. *"There, now," he said. "You're going to be all right here, safe from those wicked dogs."*

3. *The little kitten lay at first in a daze, but gradually the warm milk began to course its way through the tiny body, so that, even while Peter watched, it began to purr and stretch its legs luxuriously among the soft clothes.*

One ought to be able to read the third sentence without pausing for breath or resorting to that pinched tone that indicates a shortage of air. Standing or sitting up straight and drawing deep breaths will usually provide plenty of carrying power for working through even the longest phrase or sentence. Of course, that doesn't mean that one should not take a breath within a long sentence. But those breaths should be dictated by meaning, and not by necessity.

Volume is another aspect of voice quality to consider. Most often the problem reader does not speak loudly enough, tiring the audience needlessly. Equally distressing, though, is the loud, booming voice that causes listeners to retreat mentally. Ask a friend to listen to you read, moving so that you are various distances apart. Does the sound come through clearly, requiring little physical effort on her part?

Focusing one's voice, as well as volume, determines how well words will be understood. Consider, for instance, a few lines from Matthew Arnold's "The Forsaken Merman," reprinted below. These lines, I would submit, are a real test of making one's meaning understood when reading aloud. "Let us away" can rather readily turn into "lettuce sway." "Now the salt tides seawards flow ..." is a real tongue-twister. A passage like this takes work. Read it through several times to see where pauses and breaks aid articulation, then tape record it and replay the recording to hear how well you're doing.

The Forsaken Merman

Come, dear children, let us away;
Down and away below!
Now my brothers call from the bay,
Now the great winds shorewards blow,
Now the salt tides seawards flow,
Now the wild white horses play,
Champ and chafe and toss in the spray,
Children dear, let us away!
This way, this way! ...[5]

Rate

When Ruth Sawyer told "The Peddler of Ballaghadereen," she spoke at an unhurried 150 words per minute. Whether telling or reading, one would do well to emulate that pace. This advice is fairly easy to heed when telling a story; but when reading—ah, that's another matter. The words are there, and one is often inclined to move through them as quickly as possible.

Not that rate should be constant. There are times when the words need to tumble out. Remember Robert Browning's "The Pied Piper of Hamelin"? When the piper first steps into the street, the rate is deliberate; the stage is being set. But then, gradually, the narrative builds, both in volume and tempo, until when one reaches the lines beginning "Great rats, small rats, lean rats, brawny rats ..." the words come spilling out.

... Into the street the Piper stepped,
Smiling first a little smile,
As if he knew what magic slept
In his quiet pipe the while;
Then, like a musical adept,
To blow his pipe his lips he wrinkled,
Like a candle flame where salt is sprinkled;
And ere three shrill notes the pipe had uttered,
You heard as if an army muttered;
And the muttering grew to a grumbling;
And the grumbling grew to a mighty rumbling;
And out of the house the rats came tumbling!
Great rats, small rats, lean rats, brawny rats,
Brown rats, black rats, gray rats, tawny rats,
Grave old plodders, gay young friskers,
Fathers, mothers, uncles, cousins,

Cocking tails and pricking whiskers,
Families by tens and dozens,
Brothers, sisters, husbands, wives—
Followed the Piper for their lives ...[6]

Eye Contact

According to eye movement studies, it is possible for most adults to read between four and five words in a hundredth of a second. This means that the actual time required to see the words making up a sentence is very, very small—no more than half a second at outside. In actual practice, of course, those numbers don't work out quite so nicely. There's the glancing away from the page, and the search for one's place, and the voice change while one adjusts pitch and rate to suit the story.

But still, these studies demonstrate that it's possible to read aloud without burying one's nose in the book, as did Sartre's mother. When reading aloud, hold the book so that eye contact with the audience can be maintained. Practice—and familiarity with the story—make it possible to glance down, scoop up a sentence, and read it while looking not at the book but at those to whom one is reading. With the following sentences, try this: look down, read a phrase, look up and speak it, then glance down for the next phrase and read it. Practice until you can do this smoothly.

Once upon a time there ruled a king.

A fierce warrior was he, yet kindly toward his people.

And yet, wise though he was, and kindly, a sorrow lay, like a stone, in his heart ...

Sharing Picture Books

Picture books pose special challenges and opportunities. As a general rule, don't show the pictures if the audience can't see them. Try various ways of showing pictures; after reading the story, or after reading the page, or while you're reading the page, or with the book held to one side, or in front of you while reading from the text which is upside down for you. There's really no wrong way to share picture books, except for Rule One: *Don't show the pictures if the audience can't see them!*

Pre-Reading. And, speaking of rules, if I were to lay down one cardinal rule, it would be that one should never, never read a story aloud to an audience unless she has first practiced reading it aloud to herself. I am sure that there are occasional excellent extemporaneous performances, but the chances are pretty good that if you break that rule you will find yourself in one or more unenviable predicaments: there will be words in the reading you either don't know or don't know how to pronounce; or the story will run far too long or too short, and you won't be able to do the editing necessary to fit it to the needs of the audience; or the different characters—Papa Bear and Baby Bear and Goldilocks all sound alike, or you'll realize that the story takes you into territory you hadn't intended to inhabit.

I would not speak so surely of these pitfalls if I had not experienced them myself. You may wish to do the same. Go ahead. Make these mistakes, and then, having experienced that sinking feeling that goes with knowing—from a glance ahead—that there's a word halfway down the page you can't for the life of you remember how to pronounce, and that you've been reading now for fifteen minutes and there are still nine pages to go, and that the little girl on the left side of the rug is kicking her neighbor because she's lost interest in the story, and that the last time you read Pooh's lines you sounded exactly like Piglet—go ahead, and after you've made those mistakes, try pre-reading.

Selecting Literature. The oral interpreter has three duties. The first is to the author; and here the duty is to do more than simply read the words without mumbling. The reader must be faithful to the intent of the literature, knowing it and making a commitment to it, so that he understands what the author is saying and conveys that thought in his reading. The second duty is to the audience, and for them the reader provides not only entertainment but also understanding and excitement—a sense of the meaning of the selection in their lives. Finally, the reader must be faithful to himself. He must choose literature that has relevance to his own experience. He finds in books those ideas that interest him. He rejoices in the emotions that mirror his moods. He creates, in his reading, a bond between himself, the audience, and the author.

One cannot select stories for another person to read, or if one does, he must hope that eventually that person will begin choosing his own stories—choose them because they convey attitudes, ideas, and feelings that challenge him or because there is some peculiar grace or wit about the writing itself that draws him. These stories do not seem sentimental or over-written. Often they are stories that are better read than told.

These better-read-than-told stories are to be found at every level of literature, from the most elementary of books through those intended for adults.

Beatrix Potter's *Tale of Peter Rabbit* is such a story. The economy of words, the crisp writing—"round the end of a cucumber frame"—and the lack of sentimentalizing make this a classic read-aloud. We are charmed by the delightful interplay of whimsy and precise detail, by the dry humor and irony. When Mrs. Rabbit warns the children of the perils of Mr. McGregor's garden, she says, "Your father had an accident there; he was put in a pie by Mrs. McGregor." Even in the excitement of Peter's escape from Mr. McGregor, Miss Potter pauses briefly in the narrative to comment on Peter's jacket: "It was a blue jacket with brass buttons, quite new ..."

By all means, should you choose to share this book with a group, read from the original, so that you and your audience may relish the delicate and jewel-like illustrations. And be sure the group is a small one—so the pictures may be seen clearly by all.

If *Peter Rabbit* is a book which can be enjoyed by the youngest child, Robert Louis Stevenson's *Treasure Island* is one with broad appeal for both older children and adults. Indeed, it's one of the many books I've read to the youngest daughter in our nightly bedtime reading sessions. What follows is a portion of Chapter Two, "Black Dog Appears and Disappears."

With its lively adventures and youthful narrator, *Treasure Island,* like Mark Twain's *Adventures of Huckleberry Finn,* has found its primary audience among children. But it's not the light-hearted adventure it at first appears. Rather, it is a confrontation between two views of the world: the dark, dissolute predatory one of the pirates, and the cheery, disciplined one of Dr. Livesey and Squire Trelawney. And then, of course, there's Long John Silver—surely one of the most complex and appealing villains in all of literature.

Before this reading, one would want to summarize as briefly as possible what had gone before: that the story begins in the Admiral Benbow Inn, sometime in the early part of the 1700s; that Jim Hawkins, the teen-age son of the inn keeper and his wife, is the narrator; that a rough old sea captain had taken lodging with them, and pays Jim a small amount each week to keep his "weather eye open for a seafaring man with one leg." I'd suggest that you read only the left-hand column first, consider how you might present it to an audience, and then, after you've thought through your own plan for presenting the work, turn to the second column.

Chapter Two
Black Dog Appears and Disappears

It was not very long after this that there occurred the first of the mysterious events that rid us at last of the captain, though not, as you will see, of his affairs. It was a bitter cold winter, with long, hard frosts and heavy gales; and it was plain from the first that my poor father was little likely to see the spring. He sank daily, and my mother and I had all the inn upon our hands, and were kept busy enough without paying much regard to our unpleasant guest.

It was one January morning, very

This first paragraph might well be omitted if one is reading aloud only the selection as given here; the illness of Jim's father and the fact that this is one of several mysterious events may serve to distract the listener. A decision to omit material, incidentally, when reading aloud, is one which cannot be adequately made unless the material has been studied in advance

Here's a good starting point; setting the stage for action ...

early—a pinching, frosty morning—the cove all grey with hoar-frost, the ripple lapping softly on the stones, the sun still low and only touching the hilltops and shining far to seaward. The captain had risen earlier than usual and set out down the beach, his cutlass swinging under the broad skirts of the old blue coat, his brass telescope under his arm, his hat tilted back upon his head. I remember his breath hanging like smoke in his wake as he strode off, and the last sound I heard of him as he turned the big rock was a loud snort of indignation, as though his mind was still running upon Dr. Livesey.

Well, mother was upstairs with father and I was laying the breakfast table against the captain's return when the parlor door opened and a man stepped in on whom I had never set my eyes before. He was a pale, tallowy crea-ture, wanting two fingers of the left hand, and though he wore a cutlass, he did not look much like a fighter. I had always my eye open for seafaring men, with one leg or two, and I remember this one puzzled me. He was not sailorly, and yet he had a smack of the sea about him too.

I asked him what was for his ser-vice, and he said he would take rum; but as I was going out of the room to fetch it, he sat down upon a table and motioned me to draw near. I paused where I was, with my napkin in my hand.

"Come here, sonny," says he. "Come nearer here."

I took a step nearer.

"Is this here table for my mate Bill?" he asked with a kind of leer. I told him I did not know his mate Bill, and this was for a person who stayed in our house

---

What's "hoar-frost"? If you don't know, look it up before reading aloud. That goes for other words which might be either unfamiliar or used in a different context ...

"... as he strode off ..." is a good place to end this paragraph. The business about "loud snort of indignation" and Dr. Livesey relates to content which will be unfamiliar to the lis-tener, as it refers back to Chapter One.

And, of course, a pause here, as the listener imagines the captain heading off for his morning walk, and then is asked to turn his attention to events unfolding within the inn itself ...

and we meet this "pale, tallowy creature ..."

The narrator is a young, clever, decent boy. How will you pitch your own voice to suggest that?

"... what was for his service ..."—an archaic phrase, but one which should not be altered, as should none of the other language ...

And now, for the first time, we hear Black Dog speak ...

I imagine his voice as whining ... How do you hear him?

whom we called the captain.

"Well," said he, "my mate Bill would be called the captain as like as not. He has a cut on one cheek and a mighty pleasant way with him, particularly in drink, has my mate Bill. We'll put it, for argument like, that your captain has a cut on one cheek—and we'll put it, if you like, that that cheek's the right one. Ah, well! I told you. Now, is my mate Bill in this here house?"

I told him he was out walking.

"Which way, sonny? Which way is he gone?"

And when I had pointed out the rock and told him how the captain was likely to return, and answered a few other questions, "Ah," said he, "this'll be as good as drink to my mate Bill."

The expression of his face as he said these words was not at all pleasant, and I had my own reasons for thinking that the stranger was mistaken, even supposing he meant what he said. But it was no affair of mine, I thought; and besides, it was difficult to know what to do.

The stranger kept hanging about just inside the inn door, peering round the corner like a cat waiting for a mouse. Once I stepped out myself into the road, but he immediately called me back, and as I did not obey quick enough for his fancy, a most horrible change came over his tallowy face, and he ordered me back in with an oath that made me jump. As soon as I was back again he returned to his former manner, half fawning, half sneering, patted me on the shoulder, told me I was a good boy and he had taken quite a fancy to me.

"I have a son of my own," said he, "as like you as two blocks, and he's all

"... a mighty pleasant way with him, particularly in drink ..." loses some of its import without the first chapter, which describes the captain's drunken behavior at some length ...

This speech builds in a sinister way ... concluding with "Ah, well! I told you" ...

Jim's responses are always indirect with the exception of one brief speech toward the end of the reading ...
A hurriedly put question ... showing, perhaps, some anxiety on the part of Black Dog ...

And, of course, the listener suspects that that's hardly going to be the case ...

As does Jim ...

Stress "what" in the phrase, "difficult to know what to do."

Can your voice suggest the "horrible change ..." that came over Black Dog's face, and Jim's hasty response to it?

And a nice little lecture from Black Dog, which we recognize as pure blarney ...

the pride of my 'art. But the great thing for boys is discipline—sonny—discipline. Now if you had sailed along of Bill, you wouldn't have stood there to be spoke to twice—not you. That was never Bill's way, nor the way of sich as sailed with him.

And here, sure enough, is my mate Bill, with a spy-glass under his arm, bless his old 'art, to be sure. You and me'll just go back into the parlor, sonny, and get behind the door, and we'll give Bill a little surprise—bless his 'art, I say again."

So saying, the stranger backed along with me into the parlor and put me behind him in the corner so that we were both hidden by the open door. I was very uneasy and alarmed, as you may fancy, and it rather added to my fears to observe that the stranger was certainly frightened himself. He cleared the hilt of his cutlass and loosened the blade in the sheath; and all the time we were waiting there he kept swallowing as if he felt what we used to call a lump in the throat.

At last in strode the captain, slammed the door behind him, without looking to the right or left, and marched straight across the room to where his breakfast awaited him.

"Bill," said the stranger in a voice that I thought he had tried to make bold and big.

The captain spun round on his heel and fronted us; all the brown had gone out of his face, and even his nose was blue; he had the look of a man who sees a ghost, or the evil one, or something worse, if anything can be; and upon my word, I felt sorry to see him all in a moment turn so old and sick.

"Come, Bill, you know me; you

"... 'art." One must be careful here to put sufficient h at the front of this word so as not to confuse the listener ...

... and Black Dog continues his monologue, building tension all the while ...

Pause before "And here, sure enough ..." to suggest a change of pace. A good place, incidentally, for you, as reader, to mime briefly Black Dog's glance off in the distance to see the captain's approach ... Followed by another pause before "You and me'll just go into the parlor, sonny," spoken confidentially, as if to an accomplice ...

And cut back to Jim, and pick up the young boy's voice again, suggesting anxiety and fear ...

And an aside to the listener, drawing him in privately to the uneasiness Jim is feeling ...

As well as Jim's observations with regard to Black Dog's behavior ...

The action picks up again ...

Here's a challenge; a quick change of voice, from Black Dog's back to Jim's.

The pace quickens ...

We see Jim's inherent decency; his pity for the captain, suddenly so shrunken in spirit ...

know an old shipmate, Bill, surely," said the stranger.

The captain made a sort of gasp. "Black Dog!" said he.

"And who else?" returned the other, getting more at his ease. "Black Dog as ever was, come for to see his old shipmate Billy, at the Admiral Benbow Inn. Ah, Bill, Bill, we have seen a sight of times, us two, since I lost them two talons," holding up his mutilated hand.

"Now look here," said the captain; "you've run me down; here I am; well, then, speak up; what is it?"

"That's you, Bill," returned Black Dog, "you're in the right of it, Billy, I'll have a glass of rum from this dear child here, as I've took such a liking to; and we'll sit down, if you please, and talk square, like old shipmates."

When I returned with the rum, they were already seated on either side of the captain's breakfast-table—Black Dog next to the door and sitting sideways so as to have one eye on his old shipmate and one, as I thought, on his retreat.

He bade me go and leave the door wide open. "None of your keyholes for me, sonny," he said; and I left them together and retired into the bar.

For a long time, though I certainly did my best to listen, I could hear nothing but a low gabbling; but at last the voices began to grow higher, and I could pick up a word or two, mostly oaths, from the captain.

"No, no, no, no; and an end to it!" he cried once. And again, "If it comes to swinging, swing all, say I."

Then all of a sudden there was a tremendous explosion of oaths and other noises—the chair and table went over in

---

How will you represent Black Dog's mean, sly speech ...

Can your reading of that line suggest the gasp itself?
And the captain's voice ... how will it differ from Black Dog's?

Black Dog's voice grows more confident as he speaks ...

"Talons" ... a vivid choice of words to describe fingers ... If you haven't done so, look it up ... the various meanings will interest you ...
The captain, blustering now ...

A slight pause ...

And another pause ...

The captain speaks ... How will he sound here?

Pick up the rate here to build tension ...

a lump, a clash of steel followed, and then a cry of pain, and the next instant I saw Black Dog in full flight, and the captain hotly pursuing, both with drawn cutlasses, the former streaming blood from the left shoulder. Just at the door the captain aimed at the fugitive one last tremendous cut, which would certainly have split him to the chine had it not been intercepted by our big signboard of Admiral Benbow. You may see the notch on the lower side of the frame to this day.

"... a clash of steel"—all these good hard consonant sounds need to be spoken clearly

"... split him to the chine ..." Another interesting word, with various meanings ...

A comment to the audience, interrupting the narrative flow ...
And a pause before continuing...

That blow was the last of the battle. Once out upon the road, Black Dog, in spite of his wound, showed a wonderful clean pair of heels and disappeared over the edge of the hill in half a minute.

The captain, for his part, stood staring at the signboard like a bewildered man. Then he passed his hand over his eyes several times and at last turned back into the house.

"Jim," said he, "rum"; and as he spoke, he reeled a little, and caught himself with one hand against the wall.

"Are you hurt?" cried I.

"Rum," he repeated. "I must get away from here. Rum! Rum!"[7]

How will the captain's voice differ from the last time we heard it?

Here's Jim's first and only speech, followed by "cried I ..." an archaic verbal construction. Don't modernize it.
And the captain again ... and a good place to end the reading, although not the end of the chapter..

And If You Are a Teacher ...

I remember, as a boy, coming in from lunch recess at Springdale School and listening to my teacher read to us from Mark Twain's *Adventures of Tom Sawyer*. Under the spell of those words, stained plaster walls and a blackened wooden floor changed and grew into a deep forest, with the broad Mississippi flowing by.

I remember, as a young teacher, fresh out of college, weeping, along with my fifth graders, as I read to them from Marjorie Kinnon Rawling's *The Yearling*.

And I remember, years later, one of those same students—now a young mother—telling me about reading to her baby: "He sits so quietly I'm sure he's listening." I'm sure, too, and it's more than the story he's hearing. He's hearing the magic stream of a mother's speech. He's awakening to the sense that something marvelous waits on every page; something only his mother can breathe into life.

There's no question that books, carefully chosen, shared throughout the years, create worlds in the classroom that would otherwise be impossible to reach. Those of us who have had teachers share books with us know the inner distances we can travel when caught in a tale's web: ancient Greece or Lincoln's Illinois; a darkened garret or an endless rabbit hole, a windswept island, a dazzling city—these become ours when read to.

So, read aloud. Read to your children for a half-hour each day. Read only the finest, for you send a signal with what you read. Read poems. Read long, difficult books—books they'd not read themselves. Read portions of books—"book bait"—to hook potential readers. And after you've finished reading, leave the book in the classroom where it can be read again. And again.

Happy reading!

NOTES

1. Lee Wilson Dodd, "On Learning to Read," *Atlantic Monthly*, 150 (July 1932), p. 105.

2. Jean-Paul Sartre, *The Words*, transl. Bernard Frechtman (New York: George Braziller, 1964), p. 46.

3. From X.J. and Dorothy M. Kennedy. *Knock at a Star*, ill. Karen Ann Weinhaus (Boston: Little, Brown and Company, 1982), p. 14. "What has Happened to Lulu" was originally published by Charles Causley, *Collected Poems* (Boston: David R. Godine, 1975). Reprinted by permission of David. R. Godine.

4. *Op Cit*. p. 90.

5. Matthew Arnold, *Poems* (New York: Macmillan, 1893), p.153.

6. Robert Browning, *The Pied Piper of Hamelin* (London: Routledge, 1888).

7. R.L. Stevenson, *Treasure Island* (New York: Charles Scribner's Sons, 1925), pp. 10–14.

Other books referred in the chapter in the order of their appearance include:

Bemelmans, Ludwig. *Madeline and the Gypsies*. New York: Viking Press, 1959.

Ward, Lynd. *The Biggest Bear*. New York: Houghton Mifflin, 1952.

Hendershot, Judith, and Thomas B. Allen. *In Coal Country*. New York: Alfred A. Knopf. 1987.

Hepworth, Cathi. *Antics*. New York: G.P. Putnam, 1992.

Morris, Linda Lowe and David DeRan. *Morning Milking*. Saxonville, Massachusetts: Picture Book Studio, 1991.

Sendak, Maurice. *Where the Wild Things Are*. New York: Harper & Row, 1963.

Caldecott, Randolph. *Hey Diddle Diddle and Baby Bunting*. London: Frederick Warne & Co., 1882.

Rawlings, Marjorie Kinnan. *The Yearling*. Illustrated by N. C. Wyeth. New York: Scribner's, 1944.

Twain, Mark. *The Adventures of Tom Sawyer*. Illustrated by Donald McKay. New York: Grossett and Dunlap, 1876, 1946.

Three sources for current "best books" for reading aloud are:

Liggett, Twila C. and Cynthia Meyer Benfield. *Reading Rainbow Guide to Children's Books*. New York: Citadel Press, Carroll Publishing Group, 1994.

Lipson, Eden Ross. *Parent's Guide to the Best Books for Children*. New York: New York Times Books, 1991.

Trelease, Jim. *The Read Aloud Handbook*. New York: Penguin, 1995.

ACTIVITIES

1. Read a story to a group of friends. Tell the same story to a similar group. Which technique is more satisfactory for you? To your audience?

2. There are at present many recordings of talented artists reading aloud. Two which my own family have particularly enjoyed are Patricia MacLachlan's *Sarah, Plain and Tall* as performed by Glenn Close (New York, Caedmon #1793, 1986), and Rudyard Kipling's "The Elephant's Child," from *Just So Stories,* performed by Jack Nicholson, with music composed and performed by Bobby McFerrin, Stanford, CA. Windham Hill Productions, 1987.

3. Find someone—or more than one—to whom you can read a chapter a day.

Index